Karl Marx,
Historian of Social Times and Spaces

Historical Materialism Book Series

The Historical Materialism Book Series is a major publishing initiative of the radical left. The capitalist crisis of the twenty-first century has been met by a resurgence of interest in critical Marxist theory. At the same time, the publishing institutions committed to Marxism have contracted markedly since the high point of the 1970s. The Historical Materialism Book Series is dedicated to addressing this situation by making available important works of Marxist theory. The aim of the series is to publish important theoretical contributions as the basis for vigorous intellectual debate and exchange on the left.

The peer-reviewed series publishes original monographs, translated texts, and reprints of classics across the bounds of academic disciplinary agendas and across the divisions of the left. The series is particularly concerned to encourage the internationalization of Marxist debate and aims to translate significant studies from beyond the English-speaking world.

For a full list of titles in the Historical Materialism Book Series
available in paperback from Haymarket Books, visit:
https://www.haymarketbooks.org/series_collections/1-historical-materialism

Karl Marx, Historian of Social Times and Spaces

George García-Quesada

Haymarket Books
Chicago, IL

First published in 2021 by Brill Academic Publishers, The Netherlands
© 2021 Koninklijke Brill NV, Leiden, The Netherlands

Published in paperback in 2022 by
Haymarket Books
P.O. Box 180165
Chicago, IL 60618
773-583-7884
www.haymarketbooks.org

ISBN: 978-1-64259-784-4

Distributed to the trade in the US through Consortium Book Sales and
Distribution (www.cbsd.com) and internationally through Ingram
Publisher Services International (www.ingramcontent.com).

This book was published with the generous support of Lannan
Foundation and Wallace Action Fund.

Special discounts are available for bulk purchases by organizations and
institutions. Please call 773-583-7884 or email info@haymarketbooks.org
for more information.

Cover art and design by David Mabb. Cover art is a detail of *A pattern of
life 14*, plan of Letchworth Garden City on Morris & Co. design, limited
edition of 19 linocut prints on fabric (2019).

Printed in the United States.

10 9 8 7 6 5 4 3 2 1

Library of Congress Cataloging-in-Publication data is available.

In memory of my friend and mentor,
Elizabeth Muñoz Barquero

∴

Contents

Acknowledgements

My deepest gratitude goes to Peter Osborne, whose careful readings and observations always led to substantial improvements to previous versions of this writing. Useful suggestions and challenging questions about this work were formulated at different moments by Peter Hallward, Howard Caygill and Étienne Balibar. Héctor Hernández, Maria Chehonadskih, George Tomlinson, Eric-John Russell, Rebecca Carson and Francisco Víctor gently read one or more chapters, and their comments have made this a better book. The anonymous reviewers of the original manuscript have also contributed decisively to this version. I am also indebted to Pablo Quirós Solís and Danny Hayward for their help with this edition. The limitations of this work are nonetheless my exclusive responsibility.

I would also like to thank my mother Ingrid Quesada and her husband, Richard Doud (R.I.P.), for their decisive support before and during my research. I also extend thanks to Saray Córdoba as well as Sammy, Fabio and Yessika, for their valuable time and resources in helping me with diverse errands in Costa Rica, and to Eilyn Baltodano and her family for their hospitality during my first weeks in the United Kingdom. My friends and colleagues Minor Calderón, Giselle Marín, Alexánder Jiménez, Pablo Hernández and Mario Salas honoured me with their time and trust in dealing with other requirements. Last but not least, I want to express my gratitude to my partner Amanda Alfaro for her support at every level during the writing of this book.

The investigation leading to this book has been possible thanks to the partial sponsorship of the University of Costa Rica.

Figures and Tables

Figures

Table

For a Multilinear Science of History

Critics and interpreters have endlessly cited, to the point of boredom, the fact that Marx, 'by mere accident', had again picked up Hegel's *Science of Logic*. They want to find correspondences and analogies. But they have not investigated the other side, namely, how history – of the conditions of the workers and their struggles – entered into Marx's conceptual elaboration; how the structure of *Capital* is not deducible beginning from a presumed *Ausgangskategorie*, but has, rather, the discontinuity of strata in tension with each other; how the historical material is assembled in the text and enters into tension, but in the same constellation, with conceptual exposition. A report on a workers' struggle is not, for Marx, only a fact of journalistic sensation that can be cited as an example, but the point of condensation in which the entire theoretical exposition is concentrated and exploded.[1]

∴

This investigation seeks to establish a dialogue between Marx's conception of history and some current problems in the philosophy of history, through the analysis of the categories of social space and social time. Along these lines, I interpret and systematise Marx's conception of history in its various levels in order to clarify his explicit positions, but equally to explore possibilities that he did not always thoroughly develop. This helps us address and reformulate problems of historical theory and historiography. Although the reading presented here seeks to understand Marx's corpus rigorously in its philosophical, historical and philological aspects, my aim is not to present an 'original Marx' – an attempt that has proved impossible after more than a century and a half of conflicting interpretations[2] – but to highlight the possibilities of a 'best Marx'

---

1 Tomba 2013a, p. 158.
2 'We cannot maintain the naïve pretention of reading Sophocles's Oedipus Rex or Shakespeare's Hamlet as if Freud had not existed. When interpretations are effective, they do not

in terms of the capacity of his theory and historical research to account for complex, unevenly developing social totalisations.[3]

As the first chapter argues, Marx's formulations in the direction of a multilinear conception of history – based on social forms rather than on stages – first appear in his 1856–7 *Grundrisse*, and assume a perspective that enables the integration of diverse social space-times without reducing them to a single social principle. In this conception, knowledge about actual historical processes requires both empirical and theoretical grounding, and thus the study of Marx's conception of history implies not just the revision of his more abstract analyses of modes of production – with capitalism as the mode of production *par excellence* – but also, necessarily, an engagement with his analyses of actual historical cases.

In this manner, the epigraph by Massimiliano Tomba appropriately describes the importance of Marx's case studies and contingency in his conception of history. The historically particular is a 'point of condensation' inasmuch as it is comprised by multiple social relations and practices. Therefore, when properly done, historical explanation accounts for the complexity of phenomena by presenting the social totalisation through its contradictory relations. Historical knowledge is produced in the tension between the abstract and the concrete: Marx's concept of a 'mode of production' is essential for historical analysis, but particular socio-historical contexts are equally important to his theory of history. This is the argument of the second chapter.

This consideration is important in order to not exaggerate the distance between Marx's writings on political economy and those that deal with particular historical events. David Harvey's idea of 'two Marxisms' – one deterministic, the other voluntaristic – is complicit in this kind of exaggeration, by maintaining that there is 'a seemingly unbridgeable divide between the fluid, accidental and voluntaristic tone of the historical and political writings, on the one hand, and the rigorously scientific and lawlike political economy on the other.'[4] If Harvey's position were correct, Marx's writings about conjunctural processes would be completely devoid of theoretical content.

To be sure, these writings were produced under quite different circumstances and have different value in terms of their contribution to Marx's theory of history. As we will note in the third chapter, the conditions for the production of the different texts had a decisive influence on their contents. For instance,

---

simply translate a text rich with uncertainties into an intelligible code, but they are *incorporated* into the work and their context of reception'. Grüner 1995, p. 11.

3   Johnson 1982, pp. 153–201.

4   Harvey 2013, p. 15.

his entries for the American Encyclopedia were written merely for the sake of earning income, and have a distant relation – if none at all – with his theory of history, while *The Civil War in France* was written as a political communication from the International Workingmen's Association, and centred its analysis on aspects of the development of the French state. On the other hand, his articles on the Civil War in the United States, written for audiences unfamiliar with social conditions in that country, contextualise with historical materialist rigour the economic and political contradictions that led to this military confrontation.

In this sense, Kevin Anderson's praise of Marx's post-1856 writings about particular cases needs nuance: some of them contain, as he argues, significant theoretical analyses of specific historical societies – especially non-Western societies – with greater detail and depth than his writings on political economy,[5] while others, in contrast, possess a significantly more limited scope. In particular, I will be addressing Marx's analyses about the origins of capitalism in Volume One of *Capital*, on the Commune in *The Civil War in France*, and his and Engels's articles about the Civil War in the United States. These texts explain processes of varying spatial and temporal scales, and deal with different aspects of the development of capitalism, like dispossession of the means of the working people, modern slave labour, and the relations between classes and the state.[6]

In these analyses Marx concretely approaches each of the particular processes, and in order to do so he elaborates narratives for their explanation – even in the case of the articles about the US Civil War, which, in spite of their fragmentary condition, amount to a coherent narrative. Indeed, as I will argue, this narrative component is not opposed to structural explanation but is wholly necessary for the explanation of historical processes. This opens the theme of the literary dimension of historiography but, far from leading to an aesthetic formalism that downplays the epistemological value of historiography, a Marxian approach to narrative – which Marx himself does not develop – highlights the role of political positions in historical knowledge. This is a central concern of the fourth chapter.

---

5   Anderson 2010, pp. 5–7.

6   In spite of the analytical subtlety of texts like the *18th Brumaire* and *Class Struggles in France*, the dismissive remarks in them about the peasantry, for example, indicate that during this period Marx's conception was still indebted to the unilinearity of the predominant Enlightenment conception of history. Also, while these texts follow a rigorous conception of class struggle, they still lack a theory of capitalism through which to articulate politics and economy – a perspective that was especially advanced by the *Grundrisse*.

Because some of these cases – e.g. the two mentioned civil wars – took place while or shortly before Marx was writing about them, the consideration of these analyses in a work about the philosophy of history also requires a preliminary indication of Marx's conception of history. For reasons that will soon become clear, the title of this work should not be understood as an endorsement of history as the discipline that traditionally has had the past as its object of study: the categories of space and time at the core of Marx's concept of history radically differ from those of the most influential nineteenth-century historians. In contemporary terms, Marx comprehended the science of history as a transdisciplinary, totalising approach in the social sciences. Thus the title of this book, in deliberate reference to Eduardo Grüner's profound and suggestive preface to *Class Struggles in France*,[7] alludes to Marx as a social researcher at philosophical, theoretical and empirical levels. Underlying this dialectical unity is a conception of history as an object that can be grasped through appropriate categories, while at the same time the research of actual historical formations helps to advance historical theory.

Having said this, while Marx's conception of history is broader than that of traditional disciplinary historical studies, the problems in the latter are nonetheless closely related to those which the materialist conception deals with, especially due to the inescapable temporal dimension of historical research, which other disciplines in the social sciences traditionally ignored. However, the importance of the problems of the philosophy of history was downplayed in much of Marxist theory during the twentieth century, wherein, as Peter Osborne indicates, the concern for history

> was replaced by an interest in anthropological and sociological theories which tend to abstract from the problem of historical time altogether. Thus was the ground laid for the various syncretic combinations of Marxism and sociology that have since become the mainstream of a philosophically ambiguous 'social theory'. In the meantime, the pursuit of a better understanding of the idea of history was continued in non-Marxist debates about the methodology of historiography, the essentially transcendental form of which registers their continuity with the project of Dilthey's critique of historical reason.[8]

---

7   Grüner 2005. In a line close to the work of this and other Latin American authors – such as Enrique Dussel, Ludovico Silva and Bolívar Echeverría – the present investigation seeks to address Marxian and Marxist categories as means for the explanation of global capitalism and its peripheral formations in particular.

8   Osborne 2010, p. 32. See also Fracchia 2004, pp. 125–46.

Whereas the philosophy of history in the last few decades has been dominated by perspectives according to which historical knowledge is limited to the linguistic, and in particular to the literary, mechanisms of historiography,[9] one of the major non-Marxist contributions in this field has come from Paul Ricoeur's hermeneutical approach to history. This author considers that history has its roots in memory, but is also autonomous from it, and argues that it is both a scientific and literary discipline. Hence, he analyses the construction of historical knowledge as a multifaceted process whose account entails different moments. In his *Memory, History, Forgetting*, Ricoeur differentiates three indispensable epistemological phases, which are not meant to be considered as distinct successive chronological stages, but as equally important 'methodological moments, interwoven with one another.'[10]

He characterises these phases as follows:

> I shall call the 'documentary phase' the one that runs from the declarations of eyewitnesses to the constituting of archives, which takes as its epistemological program the establishing of documentary proof. Next I shall call the explanation/understanding [*explicative/compréhensive*] phase the one that has to do with the multiple uses of the connective 'because' responding to the question 'why?': Why did things happen like that and not otherwise? The double term 'explanation/understanding' is indicative of my refusing the opposition between explanation and understanding that all too often has prevented grasping the treatment of the historical 'because' in its full amplitude and complexity. Finally, I shall call the 'representative phase' the putting into literary or written form of discourse offered to the readers of history. If the major epistemological crux occurs in the explanation/understanding phase, it does not exhaust itself there inasmuch as it is the phase of writing that plainly states the historian's intention, which is to represent the past just as it happened – whatever meaning may be assigned to this 'just as'.[11]

It is arguable that an exaggeration of one of these phases – with the consequent obfuscation of the rest – leads to approaches that undermine the explicative possibilities of historiography. While a fetishism of the documentary phase lies at the heart of the late nineteenth-century allegedly non-interpretive history based on 'bare facts', an exaggerated emphasis on the explanation/under-

---

9   On the 'linguistic turn' in historiography, see in particular Ankersmit 2001, pp. 29–74.
10   Ricoeur 2004, p. 137.
11   Ricoeur 2004, p. 136. The English translator has bracketed the French terms in this quote.

standing phase led to schematic formulations with no awareness of the actual conditions of the specific social processes – theoreticism, where conceptual speculation substitutes empirical analysis.[12] In turn, the currently predominant philosophy of history, by considering that historical discourse is prefigured decisively by narrative forms and linguistic tropes independently of methodological and source conditions, tends to fetishise the third phase.[13]

Ricoeur's philosophy of history has the merit of actually being elaborated through the analysis of historiography and its methodological problems: his philosophical considerations abound on works from historians like Labrousse, Ginzburg, De Certeau, Braudel and Foucault. This effort of building bridges between the philosophy of history and historical research has been especially opportune in times when the former lost all relevance for the latter – if it ever had any – and philosophers of history seemed to consider historiography only as a source of examples for their already formulated positions. In addition to this, Ricoeur's interlocution with structuralism, poststructuralism and analytic philosophy makes his hermeneutical approach to the different aspects and phases of historical thinking a particularly productive point of departure for the systematisation of a materialist philosophy of history.[14]

In our dialogue between Ricoeur and Marx, however, not only the contents but also the order of the moments is changed: while the former, in a phenomenological manner, seeks to abstract from the 'things themselves' and thus arrive at their essences, Marx's dialectics start from abstractions and arrive at concrete objects of thought by adding determinations to them. Consequently, Ricoeur's philosophy of history analyses the epistemological phases before discussing their ontological implications; inversely, the Marxian approach considers that the abstract ontological categories should be the base upon which the theory of history – dealing especially with the construction of modes of production – is articulated. Thus, in this movement from the abstract to the concrete, the phase of theory functions as the mediation between the more general categories and the empirical analyses. Since reality does not directly appear to the human subject but has to be explained through scientific theories, this phase is fundamental to Marx's conception of history.

---

12   For a critique of theoreticism see Banaji 2011, p. 8. Also see below, Chapter 2.

13   Against such reduction, Ricoeur maintains that 'a gap remains between narrative explanation and historical explanation, a gap that is enquiry as well. This gap prevents us from taking history, as Gallie does, as a species of the genus "story"'. Ricoeur 1984a, p. 179. See below, Chapter 5.

14   In this sense, see Jameson's assessment on this philosopher: Jameson 2010, p. 486.

Because of the central function of this phase, the present work differs from Ricoeur's perspective in another significant way: while the French philosopher tends to maintain a descriptive attitude towards the different possibilities of explanation/understanding – as his very wording of this phase indicates – and thus his methodological considerations are vague, Marx's interest in the development of a *theory of history* leads to a normative methodology which seeks not only to describe the basic conditions of any historiography, but those conditions necessary for an epistemologically adequate historical explanation. In this sense, my reading of Marx is indebted to the critical realism of authors like Roy Bhaskar, Andrew Sayer and others who have contributed to a Marx-influenced philosophy of science.

This critical realist approach clarifies the production of historical knowledge, and in our case the Marxian conception of this. From this perspective, Tomba's call in the epigraph for the consideration of the relations between the 'historical material' and the conceptual exposition in Marx's work leads to the interplay between different levels of abstraction that produces historical knowledge. While the abstract concepts guide the research of particular cases, the analysis of the latter can also lead to new concepts of varying levels of abstraction. Even the higher levels of abstraction are subject to their reformulation under new circumstances or through the better understanding of the objects to which they refer.

The Marxian approach to history thus differs in another decisive way from Ricoeur's philosophy of history: while Ricoeur makes no explicit reference to the relations between the 'historical condition' and its historical conditions of possibility – he makes no reference to capitalism, or history in general beyond the realm of the conceptual – Marx's conception necessarily considers its own historicity. This thematisation of the material conditions of the ontology of history points not only to the temporal dimension of the latter but to its social space as well; space is an inescapable problem for a materialist conception of history, which has to account for social formations in different historical trajectories in terms of their spaces as much as their times. As the first chapter argues, social space and social time are forms – products of human praxis – that organise social processes, and their analysis therefore helps to clarify those processes and render the social agents within them visible.

The consideration of both social space and social time is thus a fundamental aspect of explaining history as a multilinear process of human production. By not reducing complex historical trajectories to a single principle, a properly spatio-temporalised approach both distinguishes and relates those processes in their uneven development. While the conceptual separation of time from space and space from time can be productive in order to clarify the diverse mechanisms at work, this should be approached as a result of space and time becoming relatively independent forms through specific historical mechanisms, as in the cases of the commodified space of land rent and of the alienated time of abstract labour, whose explanation requires knowledge about the capitalist mode of production.

The examination of the relation between space and time as forms within historical totalities avoids the overlaps and gaps that result from perspectives that overstate the scope of one or the other. For instance, Lefebvre and Agamben assign space and time, respectively, the fundamental role for social organisation and have consequently claimed in almost identical terms the priority of each of these social forms for revolutionary transformation.[15] It can be argued that this convergence results from a heavily temporalised concept of space in Lefebvre's theory and from a heavily spatialised concept of time in Agamben's work. The analysis of these categories as part of a wider conception of history can thus help to clarify them and their relations while showing their importance for historical explanation.

This work thus presents a transversal analysis, interpretation and discussion of the roles of social space and social time in Marx's philosophy of history. Since the 'best Marx' cannot be a museum piece, I develop my reading of his work in dialogue with recent authors and trends in social theory and philosophy, thus exploring the possibilities opened by his conceptual and his analytical works.[16] In this manner, I will argue for the relevance of Marx's work to the explanation of contemporary problems of historical research, both theoretical and empirical.

In this sense, the growing awareness in the social sciences in the last three decades about the active role of space and time in society – albeit usually treated separately, as in the so-called *spatial turn* – has led different Marxist and post-Marxist authors to formulate conceptual problems that call for clarifications at the level of ontology. Henri Lefebvre's *Production of Space* has been crucial for authors such as Harvey, Jameson and Soja, who develop their considerations on the culture and political economy of cities through the ontology outlined by the French Marxist philosopher. As to the concept of social time, Martineau has shown the historical development of the alienation of time in capitalism; Lefebvre himself develops the problematics of social time through his theory of a rhythmanalysis; and Pierre Bourdieu – whose general social

---

15   Lefebvre 1997, p. 190; Agamben 1993, p. 91.
16   In this brief account I do not deal with monographic works about space and time in Marx, which nonetheless form part of the discussions in later chapters of this book.

theory is not properly Marxist – maintains a theory of social practice where time is socially produced.[17]

As regards social space, while Soja, at a theoretical and methodological level, proposes the refoundation of Marxist theory as 'historical-geographical materialism' – to which I refer below – based on a spatialised ontology, Harvey applies Lefebvre's theory of the social production of space through the perspective of the political economy of the city, and Jameson explores the cultural implications of space in late capitalism. For the purposes of this book, the concepts of *space-time compression* and of *cognitive mapping* in Harvey and Jameson are particularly important for the conceptualisation of social time and space. The former argues that in capitalism there is a tendency for the necessity to accelerate the turnover time of commodities in order to maximise capitalist accumulation to generate an acceleration of social life and culture. The concept of cognitive mapping, on the other hand, plays a central role in Jameson's conception of politics in contemporary global society. This concept does not refer to a 'realist' representation of objective space, but to the 'practical reconquest of a sense of place and the construction or reconstruction of an articulated ensemble which can be retained in memory and which the individual subject can map and remap along the moments of mobile, alternative trajectories'.[18]

For Jameson, cognitive mapping thus serves the function that class consciousness used to play in previous stages of capitalism. But the postmodern city, he argues, makes cognitive mapping impossible by creating a perception of simultaneous and fragmentary spaces that suspends the subject's ability to situate him- or herself in a coherent temporal experience. In such a context, the alienation of space is manifested by the incapacity of people to map in their own minds their positions in the urban totality in which they find themselves. Jameson exemplifies this dislocation with the Westin Bonaventure hotel in Los Angeles and Frank Gehry's famous house in Santa Monica. In this sense, he interprets the latter's combination of interior spaces with seemingly incompatible perspectives – that is, perspectives that defy the expectations of spatial

---

17   Bourdieu affirms that social theory should reconstruct 'the point of view of the acting agent, of practice as "temporalisation", therefore revealing that practice is not *in* time but *makes* time (human time, as opposed to biological or astronomical time)'. Bourdieu 2000, p. 206. For a description and critique of the emergence of space and time in the social sciences, see Merryman 2012, pp. 13–27. On the concept and history of the 'spatial turn': Massey 2005 and Tally Jr. 2013, pp. 11–43. Harvey 1991; Jameson 1991; Soja 1989; Martineau 2016; Lefebvre 2004.

18   Jameson 1991, p. 51. On space-time compression, Harvey, *The Condition of Postmodernity*.

perception in the building – as a spatialised way of thinking the contradictions between the perception of unrepresentable abstract spaces and our everyday representations of space and place.[19]

As for social time, both Bourdieu's theory of practice and Lefebvre's rhythmanalysis focus on the more immediate and corporeal aspects of social time. In these authors, the *locus* of the creating activity is the socialised body, through an *intelligence of the body* (Lefebvre) or an *habitus* (Bourdieu). Likewise, there is a plurality of times derived from the variety of praxes, which Bourdieu frames within a total social field, comprehended as a multidimensional array of different kinds of social wealth (this is what he calls capital).[20] These are productive approaches in terms of the relations between subject and structure; however, by conceptualising temporality from the outlook of the individual body, they ignore the transgenerational problems of time – the problem of properly *historical time*.

Martineau's book puts the accent on the *socially produced temporal relations* and their relation to natural processes and cycles. This analysis assumes that different modes of production produce different social temporal relations, which in capitalism become alienated with the emergence of abstract time as expressed by clock-time. Capitalism apparently unites the diversity of temporal relations under this abstraction, but history as such is concrete time, which – as the author indicates – can be also understood as *many* concrete times, and this leads to the crucial question of why totalisation is necessary. While Martineau argues this in a historicist manner – by considering that the unity of history is produced by the totalising character of capitalism – which I consider correct, I maintain that, besides this path, the concept of praxis already presupposes a relation with historical totalisation.

Although these works deal with specific cases or formulate concepts and methods in order to analyse empirical problems, their theoretical frameworks imply more abstract problems about what society and history are, as well as their relations to the human being and nature – ontological problems. These theories encompass the different aspects of space and time in late capitalism: their objective or subjective (cultural) tendencies and the epistemological problems that correspond to the most recent social conditions. Perhaps one of the most evident problems is the very separation of space and time in most of this literature: even when time-space is treated as a unit (as Sassen and

---

19   On cognitive mapping, Jameson 1997, pp. 415–18, 160–1; about Gehry's house and the
      Westin Bonaventure, Jameson 1997, pp. 40–54, 108–129.
20   Bourdieu 1998, p. 7.

occasionally Harvey treat it) the reason for doing this is not argued. This is particularly a problem in Soja's book, whose argument for a historical-geographical materialism at moments assumes a dualism where space is exclusively geographical and time is exclusively historical – a position that is not compatible with Marx's totalising conception of history.

In contrast, the first chapter maintains that this importance of space *and* time in social theory has an ontological foundation that can be accounted for, precisely, through the concept of totalisation (especially as elaborated by Sartre), which not only clarifies the problems raised by these recent authors, but also enhances Lefebvre's theory of the production of space – which should also account for the production of social time. The spatial dimension of totalisation, in turn, has to be made explicit: both Sartre and Lefebvre are necessary to develop Marx's concept of praxis in the most productive manner. This should lead to an ontology capable of explaining uneven spatial and temporal development as part of a complex historical totalisation, while also helping to clarify the relations between history (with its praxical, objective and subjective moments) and our knowledge of it.

The second chapter, in turn, maintains a dialogue with the spatio-temporal conceptions of social researchers that have made scale a central element of their theories. Fernand Braudel's theory of large scale history is here a fundamental reference.[21] He not only argues convincingly for the advantages of studying geographically and temporally large social units, but also incorporates the consideration of spatial configuration or arrangement, as he calls it, and of differential temporalities (multiple temporalities developing with different rhythms): the first with the core-periphery model developed originally by the dependence theories, the latter especially through his use of secular cycles for the analysis of capitalist development. Hence, scale, spatial configuration and rhythm emerge as central determinations for historical research, helping to shape the analysis of uneven and combined development.

Theorists of globalisation such as Wallerstein, Castells and Sassen follow Braudel in their large-scale approaches but, while the former adds a third intermediate element – the semiperiphery – to the core-periphery model, the other two explore the more dynamic aspects of recent global capitalism, elaborating more nuanced concepts for the analysis of globalisation.[22] Hence, instead of the core-periphery model, Castells's theory shifts from a logic of the *space of places* in non-informational societies to one based on a *space of flows* (of cap-

---

21   Braudel 1984; Braudel 1982.
22   Wallerstein 1974; Castells 2010.

ital, organisational interactions, images, technology, symbols and, of course, information) in current globalisation. These flows are organised through a global network consisting of nodes and hubs of different densities and intensities, where a hub can become a centre or retreat into the periphery depending on the amount of flows it puts into motion. Sassen, on the other hand, analyses this global order as the coexistence and imbrication between the established national spatio-temporal order constituted by bureaucratisation, with a founding myth that lies in the past, and the emerging new order, which 'brings the experience of an instantaneously transnational time-space hinged on velocity and the future'.[23] The space-time of the national is hence centripetal, while that of the global is centrifugal. She treats this configuration of global spatio-temporal discontinuities and contradictions as an *assemblage* from which an *in-between* order emerges.

But, while the temporal and spatial large-scale approach explains the impersonal dynamics of the world-system, the experiences of individual lives and communities remain invisible to them. This path has been explored thoroughly by microhistory, in a much closer methodological relation to cultural anthropology than to sociology, and maintains that the reduction of the scale of observation, through an intensive study of the documentary material, may be applied to any object independently of its dimensions. Its treatment – in contrast with the large-scale approaches – is openly narrative, but this does not entail a concession to the old histories of events. It is an alternative (or a complement) to the quantitative and serial methods of approaching subordinate classes, one that allows social research to reconstruct not only indistinct masses, but also individual personalities, in a way such that dealing with the uniqueness of the particular case does not imply ignoring the more general historical trends. Hence, while agency resides in the individual characters of the narrative, the aim of microhistory tends towards the use of these characters as personifications of social situations. In this sense, class struggle is the totalising criterion within the narratives of authors such as Ginzburg and Levi.[24]

How, under the light of these contemporary concepts and problems on space and time, do Marx's analyses explain specific historical processes and help to develop explanatory models? In order to observe how Marx's theory and explanations deal with the determinations of scale, spatial configuration and rhythm, this question requires a clarification of the relations between the Marxian concepts of the mode of production, the social formation and the

---

23   Sassen 2008, p. 378.
24   Levi 1991; Ginzburg 1980.

conjuncture – and of their very ontological and epistemological differences. Also, as regards to the dialectic of macro- and microhistory, although large-scale is the main approach for the analysis of the historical development of the modes of production, Marx's case studies also allow us to examine the interplay between different scales of time and space, and to analyse in consequence the themes of structure and agency in history.

The third chapter deals with the problems emerging with the so-called *archival turn* which, as Ann Stoler has affirmed, elevated the archive to a new theoretical status, thereby shifting the perspective from archive-as-source to archive-as-subject.[25] The conditions and criteria by which certain documents are produced and gathered not only indicate a great deal about the voices in the archive shaping potential historical narratives, but also about its implicit exclusions. Source criticism should thus be complemented by an account of which archive the source was taken from: although each primary source is singular, the historiographical operation is not atomised because the conservation of sources is a socially practical – and often institutionalised – process. In historical investigation, therefore, there is not only a need to offer a critique of the sources, but a critique of the archive.

The recognition of the social determinations of sources and archives is then a central element of historical research in the documentary phase, and such a critical approach can be enhanced by considering their spatio-temporal characters. The transition from memory to historiography depends upon the archival act,[26] and it is hence imperative to problematise the institutional and sociopolitical underpinnings of the archive, as well as the historiographies resulting from them. Researchers like Foucault and Ginzburg have insisted on the necessity of making subaltern cultures visible by using sources in which the subaltern subjects left their mark almost accidentally. In such cases, the scarcity of sources condemns historians to fragmentary reconstructions and obliges them to read sources 'against the grain' – in manners different from the intentions of the archivers – in order to shed light on some aspects of the repressed popular cultures.[27]

Similarly, subaltern and post-colonial studies make a substantial contribution to the critique of the archive, by indicating its geopolitical criteria and its relation to historiography and empire. Authors such as Richards, Guha and Mbembe have explained different aspects of this matter: While the former

---

25   Stoler 2002, p. 86.
26   Ricoeur 2004, pp. 148–9.
27   Ginzburg 1980; Foucault 1997; Foucault 1982.

demonstrates the state-centrist bias of the traditional archive, which in the late nineteenth-century was imagined by the imperial élites as a project of total knowledge and shaped the relation between knowledge and the state, Guha argues that this imperial project introduced history (and specifically so-called *World-History*) to India, and enumerates several examples of histories which would have been lost if we were to have relied exclusively on traditional state archives. Mbembe, in addition to this, argues that the archive sets the limits of the temporalities – as well as the spatialities, we should add – woven together by the historian in order to compose the possible historiographical narratives. This is particularly important because it indicates that the critique of the archive – not only the state-centrist kind – should consider the space-time of the contents of the archived documents as much as the space-times determining the activity of registering them.[28]

In this sense, the use of the traditional state-centrist archive is unavoidable, but should be properly thematised, and eventually complemented with other archives in order not to obfuscate subaltern agents. The analysis of Marx's archive is of particular importance because it shows the possibilities of formulating counter-hegemonic interpretations on the base of mostly hegemonic sources. Moreover, it allows the assessment of his philosophy of history, and more specifically of his theory of history, as regards to the spatio-temporal bias – Eurocentrism – of which he has been repeatedly accused. Also, by analysing how later investigations of the specific cases studied by Marx consider space and time when formulating their explanations, we can enhance our understanding of the reach and limitations of his archive – and his explanations – in contrast to the archive available to recent researchers.

Finally, the fourth chapter deals especially with Ricoeur's account of the relations between time and narrative, from the point of view of historiography. After this philosopher, authors following the dialectical tradition such as Jameson and Osborne conceive narrative as the fundamental means by which language allows the subject to grasp temporality.[29] But, while Ricoeur argues for a pluralism of temporalities and narratives, in which a totalising narrative which accounts for all the implied temporalities cannot emerge, for the latter authors totalisation is a fundamental issue in dealing with the problems of historiographical representation.[30] Moreover, they argue that it is imperative to relate

---

28   Richards 1993; Guha 2009; Mbembe 2002.
29   Ricoeur 1984a; Ricoeur 1984b; Ricoeur 1990; Osborne 2010; Jameson 2010, pp. 475–612.
30   In the phenomenological tradition the unity of multiple narratives is ultimately based in contingent intersubjective prejudices. Koselleck 2002, pp. 117–8. Also: Carr 1991. On the re-vindication of prejudice, see Gadamer 2004.

the structures of social reality and their representation: hence the theoretical criterion of social totalisation should also be the thread of the corresponding historical narratives.

In the works by Osborne and Jameson, time is a product of history – which is not immediately apparent – and hence a theory of history is necessary in order to account for the narratives that shape diverse existential temporalities. Totalisation would be the operation by which the gaps, contradictions and relations in general between temporalities are incorporated into a contradictory history; there is one history, but it is not constituted by homogeneous times. However, the development of the category of temporality leads both Jameson and Osborne to problems of spatiality: the former through globalisation, the latter through the materiality of the conditions of everyday praxis. Their efforts to make history emerge from time end up making space emerge as well, be it at the 'micro' or planetary level – arguably the widest scale of social life. A materialist approach always has an immanent spatial as well as temporal dimension; how to relate space and narrativity is, hence, a central issue for a materialist conception of representation.

In this sense, I propose a re-formulation of Bakhtin's concept of the chronotope and of Marx's concept of presentation (*Darstellung*) following a critical realist reading of Ricoeur, in order to address the problem of developing narratives capable of explaining social processes and their outcomes by better accounting for their spatio-temporal dynamics. The formulation of a specifically historiographical concept of the chronotope also throws light on the crucial matter of the political side-taking of historiography. This ultimately leads the chapter to deal with narrativist authors like Hayden White, who typically hypostatise language while they overlook the role of time and space for historiography – and the need to relate them to a *theory* of history.

Finally, a note on my approach to Marx's work in this book. Since my intention is to systematise Marx's conception of history on the base of the categories of social time and social space – which, as I argue, should be fundamental at every level of the social and historical analysis – I deal with Marx's biographical conditions only secondarily. I do however pay close attention to the conditions in which his texts were elaborated and to his original wording in order to clarify the meaning of several key fragments in the work. My interpretation of Marx's conception of space and time – especially since the *Grundrisse* – is then guided by the phases defined by Ricoeur's philosophy of history, albeit adapted in a realist and materialist direction, which help to clarify the problems of historical knowledge in current discussions. My approach is thus in part hermeneutical and in part properly philosophical and theoretical: what is at stake with this book is, indeed, the argument for a materialist and realist approach to history, one with a direct relation to historical research – a relation broken by the prevalence of positions in philosophy of history that deny the possibility of historical knowledge.

The concept of history as a complex spatio-temporal totalisation, on the other hand, helps us to avoid the theoretical simplification of social processes, and allows for a better understanding of problems such as those generated by globalisation. In my view, Marx's conception – more clearly after the first half of the 1850s – is not Eurocentric, and in the occasions when he holds positions of this kind this happens because he does not follow his own method. His decentred conception of history, on the contrary, opens the possibility for different historical subjects depending on where oppression takes place – as Marx observed, for example, during the rebellions in India, China and Ireland. The necessary spatio-temporalisation of Marx's conception should then highlight the de-provincialised character of his approach to history and politics.

As we will observe in the next chapters, some tensions arise between the possibilities opened by Marx's theories and some of his actual historiographical accounts; the discussion of such tensions in this investigation will help advance a version of the 'best Marx', one who offers the best philosophical, theoretical and methodological framework for the most concrete explanation and exposition of history as a complex social reality. This writing argues, in consequence, that this framework is capable of articulating structural necessity with actual contingency, and that space and time are fundamental categories that best apprehend the multilinear transformations of diverse historical processes, while taking into account – as regards the formation of our world-system – the totalising drive of capital.

CHAPTER 1

History with Social Ontology

> History is no entity advancing along a single line, in which capit-
> alism for instance, as the final stage, has resolved all the previous
> ones; but it is a *polyrhythmic and multi-spatial entity, with enough
> unmastered and as yet by no means revealed and resolved corners*.[1]

∵

Ontology has not had a good reputation in the recent philosophy of history.
The rejection of ontological issues in the reflection on history was initially
part of a reconfiguration in the mid twentieth-century of the philosophy of
history as a surrogate to epistemology in analytical philosophy, but was consolidated with the arrival of poststructuralism and the linguistic turn after Hayden
White's influential *Metahistory* in the 1970s. Underlying this rejection was the
directive that the philosophy of history was only possible as a philosophy of
historiography: analytical philosophy dictated that the conditions of historical
knowledge were the only appropriate object of the philosophy of history, and
with narrativism the analysis of textual mechanisms – be it literary tropes or
chains of signifiers – substituted the consideration of history as *res gestae*.[2] The
question of the *being of history* was for the narrativists an unreachable referent.

The more conceptually-minded historians, on the other hand, became ac-
customed to developing their methodological considerations on the basis of
assumptions having a strictly operational validity: there could be no universal
applicability beyond their immediate objects of study. Foucault's image of theory as a toolbox is probably the most famous formulation of this trend, which
usually conceals an ontology behind a set of epistemological and methodological assumptions which otherwise attempt to avoid more abstract philosophical discussions.[3] But even when such discussions take place, theories of
history often propose 'weak' ontologies that are interchangeable, depending

---

1 Bloch 2009, p. 62.
2 Walsh 1960; Danto 2007; White 2014; Paul 2015, pp. 1–16; Jenkins 1997, pp. 1–30.
3 'I would like my books to be a kind of tool-box which others can rummage through to find a
   tool which they can use however they wish in their own area ... I don't write for an audience,

on the paradigms 'chosen' for the specific research. *Pragmatism* is the anti-philosophical philosophy behind this stance, which became especially fashionable during the time of postmodern critiques of 'grand narratives'.[4]

Hence, historians and philosophers of history who dismiss ontology consider that getting to know totalising structures in history – or eventually *any* structuration at all – is *a priori* impossible. In any case, it is arguable that there is not only an implicit ontology in 'pragmatist' theories of history, but also in the analytical approaches derived from Popperian epistemology and Whitean narrativism. In particular, since theories of history deal basically with the relations between concepts and empirical data, and thus operate at lower levels of abstraction, they can function without explicit ontological foundations. However, they do not necessarily exclude the latter: in fact, Marx's conception of history encompasses these levels, by relating the epistemological and methodological with the ontological aspects of historical research.

When Marx and Engels propose their 'science of history', they have a specific conception of what the social (natural-historical) world is, and only thus can it be the subject of this science. However, because Marx does not render the philosophical system that underlies this theory of history explicit, the matter of whether it is possible (or consistent with his method) to find and develop a Marxian ontology – or even specifically an ontology of history – from his essential categories has led to controversies.[5] Nonetheless, his work is loaded with considerations about the most general structures of the world – especially concerning history and society – and this is particularly expressed by his arguments about method.

The systematisation of these indications about the most general and abstract structures of human agency, history and society constitute what this chapter considers to be Marx's ontology of history: what Anievas and Nişancioğlu characterise as 'a general, abstract set of determinants highlighting a

---

I write for users, not readers'. Michel Foucault, 'Prisons et asiles dans le mécanisme du pouvoir', quoted in O'Farrell 2005, p. 50; Paul 2015, p. 13; Fulbrook 2002, pp. 35–7.

4   Osborne explains this perspective with regards to post-Marxist cultural studies, but the same point is valid vis-à-vis the post-Marxist theory of history. Osborne 2000, pp. 1–19. On weak ontology, see Rovatti and Vattimo 2013.

5   Schmidt, for example, argues that it is not possible to speak of an ontology in Marx except in a negative sense, because Marx assigns no content to positive metaphysical principles such as nature. However, Schmidt's references to this term are related to his rejection of unmediated objectivism, which in turn relates to his criticism of Soviet *diamat* as a dehistoricised ontology. This position assumes that ontology cannot be historicised, which I argue against in this chapter. See Schmidt 2014, pp. 83–93 and pp. 138–9.

general condition confronted by all societies irrespective of historical context,'[6] whose categories underpin the possibility of the knowledge of any particular historical process. Along with this ontology's focus on objective socio-historical processes, the ontology of historical being deals with the specifically *conceived* dimension of history – a hermeneutical horizon that Marx approaches as the problem of historicisation.

From this dialectic, Marx's conception of history emerges as a spatio-temporally complex global process. The root of this complexity, as I will argue in the first section of this chapter, ultimately lies for Marx in human praxis, which totalises history in a spatio-temporally differentiated manner through different strata (productive, political, cultural, etc.) and spheres of social reality in a mode of production. The latter, as a social totalisation, is hence shown to be always mediated by the different space-times that dialectically compose it: in this sense, the Marxian ontology of history is not related to a conception of continuous and homogeneous time or space, nor does it conceive the collective human activity in a reductive manner.

The second section deals with the relation between modes of production as part of a common human history, which leads to the problem of their common structure while considering the inherent historicity of Marx's categories. The expansion of capitalism opens the possibility of conceiving history as the unity of all human experience, and in consequence introduces the question of how to apprehend the apparent multiplicity of social forms through a unitary theory of history. Rather than by an evolutionist conception, I will argue, this is best achieved in Marx's work by means of trans-historical abstractions that guide the concrete historical explanations through empirical research.

The third section, in turn, argues that Marx developed his materialist conception of history most consistently during and after his writing of the *Grundrisse*, opening the possibility of conceiving the unity of human experience without reducing it to a unilinear path, in opposition to the unilinear conception of history that prevailed in writings such as the *Manifesto*. In the case of capitalism, such spatio-temporal complexity, I argue, is best accounted for through the Marxian concept of subsumption.

---

6 Anievas and Nişancioğlu 2015, p. 58.

1.1   Praxis and Spatio-Temporal Totalisation

As in the case of other scientific approaches to reality since the eighteenth century, an ontology of historicity lies at the heart of Marx's conception of history. Modern cosmology, geology and evolutionary biology have arisen from and developed within this conception of permanent structuration and de-structuration, whose historical conditions of possibility will be addressed in the next section. In this line, Marx argues that the role of human activity is *the* creative force that produces a specifically human history; his concept of history thus emerges from the consideration of historicity at the most general level, beyond the human, and seeks to account for social transformation through human production. Hence, even his most abstract categories about social being are themselves historical.

The ontological foundations of Marx's conception of social being are set by his early critique of Hegelianism, in which his concept of praxis plays the central role.[7] Marx elaborates the more abstract concepts of his social ontology into the concrete concepts he later applies to particular social forms and contexts, as in the case of his early concept of alienation, which reappears with more determinations in the concept of commodity fetishism – the cornerstone of his analysis of capitalism, no less. Hence, his later theoretical trajectory can be interpreted as a process of making his abstract concepts more concrete, rather than as a break in respect to his early texts; several levels of abstraction and concreteness coexist and interact throughout Marx's *oeuvre*.[8]

In particular, the importance of the concept of production in Marx does not stem from bourgeois productivism, as Baudrillard maintains, but from a Romantic ideal of creative activity and its influence on German Idealism. As early as his *Theses on Feuerbach*, praxis is the point of departure for Marx's formulation of materialism; human beings produce their world in their inter-

---

7   'In human terms, the energy of creation is extended and made manifest in and through the Praxis, that is the total activity of mankind, action and thought, physical labour and know-ledge. ... The Praxis is where dialectical materialism both starts and finishes'. Lefebvre 2009, p. 100.

8   As for one of Marx's cardinal anthropological concepts, Heller indicates that 'the elaboration of the category of value "need" is the work of the young Marx. In his maturity this category is already a given point of departure: he does not consider it necessary to analyse it anew. Nevertheless, it frequently appears later on, in a direct and open form'. Heller 1976, p. 38. On the thesis of Marx's epistemological break, Althusser 2005. On Marx's trajectory as a dialectical construction, Lefebvre 1948.

actions between themselves and with nature.[9] In this conception, as Lefebvre explains,

> only the human being and their activity exist. And yet everything happens as though humans had to deal with external powers which oppress them from outside and drag them along. Human reality – what humans themselves have made – eludes not only their will but also their consciousness. They do not know that they are alone, and that the 'world' is their work. (Here we are using the word 'world' to signify the coherent, organised, humanised world, not pure, brute *nature*).[10]

Praxis is thus the foundation of Marx's general ontology[11] and, like concrete labour – which is regularly characterised by Marx as the expenditure of human brains, muscle, nerves and bones – is a material and singular process of transformation. The intertwining between diverse individual praxes, leading to unexpected effects ('they do this without being aware of it'),[12] produces history as a consequence. This is clear in the *18th Brumaire*, where Marx famously affirms that:

> humans make their own history, but they do not make it just as they please; they do not make it under circumstances chosen by themselves, but under circumstances directly encountered, given and transmitted from the past. The tradition of all the dead generations weighs like a nightmare on the brain of the living.[13]

In the introduction of this book we mentioned how Lefebvre and Bourdieu construct their respective theories on the production of social space and time

---

9   Marx 1976a, pp. 3–5. On Marx's productivism, Baudrillard 1975; on Marx's relation to Romanticism, Löwy and Sayre 2002, pp. 88–98.

10   Lefebvre 1991, p. 167. Here and below I have changed the words 'man' and 'men' for 'human being' and 'humans', a substitution that does not alter the conceptual content of this passage but eliminates an outdated sexist expression.

11   'The onto-formative process of human praxis is the basis for the possibility of ontology, i.e., for understanding being. The process of forming a (socio-human) reality is a prerequisite for disclosing and comprehending reality in general. Praxis as the process of forming human reality is also a process of uncovering the universe and reality in their being'. Kosík 1976, p. 139. On praxis as the cornerstone of Marx's philosophy, see Osborne 2006, pp. 23–32; Lefebvre 2000b, pp. 33–55; Echeverría 2011; Grüner 2005; Sánchez 2003, pp. 127–208.

12   Marx 1976b, pp. 166–67. On labour as bodily expenditure, Marx 1976b, pp. 134, 164, 274–5, 643, 717.

13   Marx 1979a, p. 103.

by developing these concepts already inherent in the Marxian ontology of praxis.[14] The former theorist, in particular, systematises the relation between production and praxis, explaining how human beings *produce* their spaces and times through their praxes in relation to their already existing spatio-temporal conditions. First, he stresses the doubled sense of Marx's concept of production: in the restricted sense it refers to the specific economic labour-process, while in its broader, ontological sense it encompasses the results of human activity.[15] Second, in the latter sense and referring specifically to the production of space, Lefebvre creates a three-moment dialectic, where spatial practices produce representations of space – mental conceptions – and representational spaces – the *lived* spaces. Hence, the process of production *produces* both subjects and objects,[16] and does so by producing space-times at both subjective and objective levels.

With Kant, it is convenient to recall that in their most abstract sense, space and time cannot have a concept as all their definitions are self-referencing. The Kantian differentiation between these *intuitions* as outer and inner sense,[17] however, is not acceptable from a dialectical perspective, because the process of their social production implies that both space and time each have objective and subjective dimensions. Social times and spaces are not only ideal (conceived) conditions of praxis, but actual forms of worldly organisation (both subjective and objectively).[18] They are objectifications, though not of the same kind as the objects that are usually thought to fill them. Social times and

---

14 Whereas, in the context of his philosophy of nature, Hegel indicated that 'space and time first attain actuality in motion', social time and space are produced by human praxis. Hegel 1970a, p. 239.

15 Lefebvre 1997, pp. 68–72. According to *The German Ideology*, for example, 'this mode of production must not be considered simply as being the reproduction of the individuals. Rather it is a definite form of activity of those individuals, a definite form of expressing their life, a definite *mode of life* on their part. As individuals express their life, so they are. What they are, therefore, coincides with their production, both with *what* they produce and with *how* they produce. Hence what individuals are depends on the material conditions of their production'. Marx and Engels 1976b, pp. 32–3.

16 'Praxis encompasses both material production and "spiritual" production, the production of means and the production of ends, of implements, of goods and of needs'. Lefebvre 1991, p. 237. About the triad systematised in Lefebvre's concept of the social production of space: Lefebvre 1997, pp. 38–9.

17 'Time can no more be intuited externally than space can be intuited as something in us'. Kant 1998, p. 174.

18 This organisation sets limits to praxis, with death being its ultimate negation. As indicated above about Bourdieu's studies on social times, this temporalisation is mediated by the social place of the subject: the existential time of an immigrant subproletarian and that of a salaried professional are quite different from one another.

spaces are both material and formal, concrete and abstract, real and imaginary (*réel-fictive*) and indeed, as Lefebvre maintains, they can be separated only through abstraction; in his words, 'time is distinguishable but not separable from space.'[19] Social space is always already temporalised, just as social time is always already spatialised, and only through an operation of abstraction can they be distinguished as two different axes of the organisation of the social world.

Since in experience times and spaces are plural, the problem of how to totalise them is the starting point for Marx's approach to history. Although some authors have held that this spatio-temporal plurality is insurmountable,[20] if we adhere to Marx's conception of human praxis we find that the production of spaces and times is always already social, and hence necessarily related to a historical totalisation.[21] At this point, it is useful to bring Sartre's concept of totalisation to our attention, in order to account for the spatio-temporalisation of history. Sartre notes that the structure of history is ultimately founded on that of individual praxis. In his words, '*the entire historical dialectic rests on individual* praxis *in so far as it is already dialectical,* that is to say, to the extent that action is itself the negating transcendence of contradiction, the determination of a present totalisation in the name of a future totality, and the real effective working of matter'.[22]

In this sense, individual and history are not external to each other; while praxis is historically determined, history is the combined product of collective praxes, which brings results that are different from the intentions of each indi-

---

19   Moreover, as he writes in the same passage, 'phenomena which an analytical intelligence associates solely with "temporality", such as growth, maturation and aging, cannot in fact be dissociated from "spatiality" (itself an abstraction)'. Lefebvre 1997, p. 175.

20   Braudel, like Ricoeur and Koselleck, holds this position: 'Our problem now is to imagine and locate the correlations between the rhythms of material life and the other diverse fluctuations of human existence. For there is no single conjuncture: we must visualise a series of overlapping histories, developing simultaneously. It would be too simple, too perfect, if this complex truth could be reduced to the rhythms of one dominant pattern. It is impossible to define even the economic conjuncture as a single movement given once and for all, complete with laws and consequences'. Braudel 1973, p. 892.

21   In the *Grundrisse*, for example, he affirms that 'all production is appropriation of nature on the part of an individual within and through a specific form of society', and the theorised social totalisation should thus substitute the ideological centrality of the individual in previous political economy. Throughout these drafts, Marx demonstrates once and again the historical character of the individual, against the assumption of bourgeois political economists of it as an immediate, atomistic entity. Marx 1973, p. 87. On this *ontology of relations*, see Balibar 2014, pp. 27–33.

22   Sartre 2004, p. 80.

vidual. Since praxis is not conceivable without its corresponding social spaces and times, the latter are conditions for production both in the social-historical and transcendental sense. Although Sartre insists on the temporal character of the totalisation produced by praxis, it is more accurate to conceive praxis in relation to both space and time, because human action is both conditioned by pre-existing actual space-times and projected upon an ideal spatio-temporal order. Sartre's concept of totalisation would thus not necessarily exclude space, but gains in depth by taking this dimension into account.

Hence, each individual praxis is already historically conditioned within a certain range of spatio-temporal possibilities, and it is through them that discontinuity or continuity, production or reproduction, is generated in respect to the established social structure – therefore eventually changing the very conditions which initially made them possible. These conditions determine the possible processes of spatio-temporal production, whose combination produces history:

> the social structure and the state are continually evolving out of the life-process of definite individuals, however, of these individuals, not as they may appear in their own or other people's imagination, but as they *actually* are, i.e., as they act, produce materially, and hence as they work under definite material limits, presuppositions and conditions independent of their will.[23]

This production is well exemplified in *Capital*, where Marx argues that the difference between the worst of architects and the best of bees lies in the former's capacity to conceive the results of the labour-process before having done it: human work is purposeful activity which requires an object upon which to act and the instruments to do it. This teleological feature implies that an ideal future is always present in labour, just as much as the past is, and this is the case both through the labour's objective conditions and through the references to such a future that exist in the mind of the labourer.[24] Thus, the mentally projected result of the work of the architect presupposes a temporal path, but also an image, and hence a *conceived* space – an operation of *cognitive mapping*, as we have noted previously with regards to Jameson.

---

23   Marx and Engels 1976b, pp. 35–36.
24   Marx 1976b, p. 284. Harootunian observes that 'Marx was ... the first to see and record the experience of the past as constantly intruding in the lived present, thus persuading him of the necessity of negotiating the multiple temporalities of non-contemporaneity individuals must always confront in their daily lives'. Harootunian 2015b, p. 24.

We should observe that the *conceived* space-times of praxis are mental projections from the point of view of a subject in a determinate social place in a concrete form of society;[25] human praxis produces the world, but does so as a part of the social-natural totality it modifies. Then, it is also convenient to note that once the process of construction has been undertaken, social space and time are transformed through *collective* action. During the construction process, besides obviously changing the physical space, the building modifies the distribution of social times within itself and the adjacent social spaces with which it interacts. Likewise, at a broader level, a social formation is a combination of social space-times whose structuring processes exceed the intentions of their producers.[26]

Thus, collective praxes produce the *practico-inert* as their objectification, which in turn becomes the condition for new praxes, in a movement of totalisation, detotalisation and retotalisation. This process of spatio-temporally producing a social totalisation is dialectical in the measure that the partial praxes constitute the latter as a whole, and in consequence dialectics is necessary in order to render such totalisation intelligible.[27] A proper explanation should then take into account all the general social conditions that make a specific praxis possible, the framework that allows for its emergence and development. Since knowledge is itself a conceived retotalisation of the real process of totalisation, a materialist analysis of history should thus explain social processes in such a manner that it shows their spatio-temporal organisation as part of the logic of their functioning.

This leads us to the concepts by which Marx accounts for the products of praxis. In his conception, individual praxes are processes that produce materially singular objectifications,[28] but the latter respond to other levels of social life as particulars through the *forms* of their respective objectifications. *Form* is a quite generic concept that encompasses objects (*Objekte*) of very different levels of complexity: Marx refers to forms, for example, as moments of the

---

25 'The mode of production of material life conditions the general process of social, political and intellectual life. It is not the consciousness of men that determines their existence, but their social existence that determines their consciousness'. Marx 1987a, p. 263. See also Heller 1984, p. 3.

26 Marx's metaphor of a social formation as social metabolism adequately portrays the spatio-temporal character of different forms of society, each with its rhythms of circulations, development and exchanges with its environment. Schmidt 2014, pp. 76–93.

27 Sartre 2004, p. 66 and pp. 90–4.

28 Heller distinguishes between *objectification* as the production of an object and *objectivation* as the re-creation of the praxical subject. Both aspects are indissolubly linked. Heller 1984, pp. 47–8.

value-form (simple, total, general and money form), as concepts corresponding to social appearances, and as whole societies.[29] A form can be a determination of other forms, therefore, and should never be substantialised.

Forms have an existence beyond that of the objectifications from which they emerge, but their contents change according to the changes in the totalisations where they take place. Hence, Marx affirms that under a new totalisation, forms from earlier social organisations can remain as 'stunted', 'travestied' or 'caricatured'. Slavery in the Americas is an example of the adaptation of an ancient social relation that acquires new characteristics under a new mode of production – in this case, capitalism. Likewise, emerging forms can impose themselves over older ones while maintaining the older contents, as registered by Marx's concept of subsumption: 'even economic categories appropriate to earlier modes of production [e.g., commercial and finance capital, GGQ] acquire a new and specific historical character under the impact of capitalist production'.[30]

But while the generality of the concept of *form* is useful because it is applicable to all historical contexts, further precisions need to be made in order to grasp the specific historical mediations between objectifications and the particular totalisations which condition them. Marx's criterion of totalisation lies in the specific processes of production as the condition of possibility for all human activity, because humans have to organise themselves socially in order to satisfy their needs and survive. As Sartre indicates, 'the essential discovery of Marxism is that labour, as a historical reality and as the utilisation of particular tools in an already determined social and material situation, is the real foundation of the organisation'.[31] The key totalising concept for Marx is hence the mode of production.

In his 1859 *Contribution*, Marx proposes that a mode of production has three fundamental levels: the economic structure (the totality of the relations of production), the legal and political 'superstructure' (*Überbau; édifice* in J. Roy's

---

29   Marx 1976b, pp. 138–62; p. 677 and p. 682; Marx 1973, pp. 471–514.

30   Marx 1976b, p. 950; Marx 1973, pp. 105–6. As for Marx's views on modern slavery, see below, 1.3.

31   Sartre 2004, 152. As opposed to the Robinsonades of political economy in his lifetime, Marx repeatedly argues for the necessity of departing from the social character of the human being, who is by nature not merely gregarious but political, i.e., a producer of specific social relations. See Marx 1973, p. 84, Sartre 2004, pp. 122–52, Basso 2012, pp. 142–50 and also Jameson 2002, pp. 85–88. Moreover, Marx states that the standpoint of the isolated individual only became possible with the development of capitalist social relations in eighteenth-century Europe. Marx 1973, pp. 83–5.

Marx-approved translation in French),[32] and the forms of social consciousness arising from the latter – the legal, political, religious, artistic and philosophical forms 'in which people become conscious of this conflict [between material productive forces and property relations] and fight it out'.[33]

In order to avoid interpretations that substantialise these levels – like, most notably, that which comes out of so-called 'orthodox Marxism' – it is useful to understand them, as Collier suggests, as *strata* with different causal hierarchies in the same totalisation. Following critical realism, a *stratum* is an objective system of *generative mechanisms*, i.e., ways-of-acting of objects and relations which, given certain conditions – usually other mechanisms – generate determinate events. Specific social generative mechanisms not only play their role in regards to the contradictions in their social totalisations, but can themselves generate contradictions, as in the case of the commodity form.[34] Each stratum relies on lower strata, but has its own rules; for instance, the biological stratum emerges from the stratum studied by chemistry, which in turn emerges from that explained by physics. The lower strata enable the functioning of the higher ones, but also, as Collier argues, 'each emergent stratum will effect alterations in the entities governed by the stratum from which it emerged, which would not have been effected had the new stratum not emerged.'[35]

From a broad perspective, each society as a *social metabolism*[36] develops from definite biological conditions which in turn presuppose definite geographical conditions. However, this is not a geographical determinism, because

---

32 See Silva 2009, pp. 101–2. Silva argues that Marx's scarce use of the terms *Basis*, *Überbau* and *Superstruktur* – as opposed to his constant appeal to a concept like *ökonomische Struktur* – suggests that they are strictly illustrative metaphors that should not substitute for properly explanatory concepts. Silva 2009, pp. 99–101.

33 Marx 1987a, p. 263. Marx's characterisation of these forms of consciousness as 'ideological' is problematic, since it suggests either a functional (non-dialectical) approach or a wide concept of ideology, different from his use of this concept as false consciousness. These *forms of consciousness* are also explained as *forms of appearance* in Marx 1976b, pp. 675–82.

34 'Each category in *Capital* defines a determination of a social form, and each determination specifies a real mechanism at work in the capitalist mode of production'. Smith 1997, p. 190. On the theory of strata, see Sayer 1992, pp. 104–5; Collier 1998. On the critique of 'orthodox Marxism' see, among others, Jameson 2002, pp. 17–25.

35 Collier 1998, pp. 263–64. As Sayer affirms, 'while we don't have to go back to the level of biology or chemistry to explain social phenomena, this does not mean the former has no effect on society. Nor does it mean we can ignore the way in which we react back on other strata, for example through contraception, medicine, agriculture and pollution'. Sayer 2000, p. 13.

36 Besides Schmidt 2014, see Foster 2000, pp. 141–77. On the natural-historical character of the human being and society, see also Osborne 2006, pp. 33–44. Marx's studies on chem-

human adaptations to the same natural environment, albeit limited by the conditions of the latter, are open to different possible kinds of organisation.[37] It is
also important to note that the theory of social stratification suggests that the
higher strata emerge from the pre-existing lower strata, and hence the times
of the former are always longer than those of the latter, and their spatial range
is also wider.[38] In this sense, Braudel's consideration of geography as a structure developing at a very *longue durée* may be understood as a complement to
Marx's multi-layered conception of society: under the stratum where the contradiction between the forces and relations of production exists, is the stratum
of geographical conditions.[39]

Interpreting Marx from this stratified conception, the economic structure
would be the condition of possibility for the stratum of the legal and the political (in their widest sense), and the forms of social consciousness constitute a
higher stratum. Every praxis contributes to the production of different strata at
the same time, since mechanisms are composed by *aspects* of praxes and not by
types of praxes,[40] and since the mechanisms in each stratum have their respective space-times, a single praxis produces several space-times, corresponding
to the different strata it produces through its objectifications. Consequently, a
single geographical-chronological unit has several different overlapping social
space-times. Thus albeit mediately related to one another in a process of totalisation, economic, political and cultural spaces and times in the same particular society are distinct and respond to different mechanisms.[41]

---

istry, recently analysed in the light of their coming publication in the second edition of
the *Marx-Engels Gesamtausgabe* (MEGA2), further demonstrate his efforts to think the
relation between nature and society. Saito 2014.

37   Bhaskar illustrates this non-reductive position with the example of the writing of a pen:
while this operation does not violate any of the laws of physics, they don't directly define
what is written, and therefore cannot explain it *qua* writing. Bhaskar 2008, p. 105.

38   Although the rules for the combination of atoms are universally valid, life only emerges
under certain conditions, i.e., in particular space-times. See Sayer 1992, pp. 118–21; Bhaskar
2008, pp. 168–70.

39   When developing his theory of social space based on Marx, Lefebvre distinguishes three
kinds of spaces, corresponding to three different ontological levels: physical, social and
mental spaces. This division – which does not exclude further internal divisions – can
be addressed as consisting of three different *strata* of reality. Lefebvre 1997, pp. 11–14. On
geographical conditions as a *longue-durée* stratum, see Braudel 1982, pp. 25–54.

40   See Collier 1998, pp. 266–7. In this sense, it would not be accurate to speak of merely *economic praxes*, but of praxes that have economic implications among others. The commodity, for example, is not merely an economic form, but also exists as a legal and ideological
form.

41   As Osborne indicates, 'different objects of study, within the same empirical space, will
require different primary levels of socio-spatial totalisation (locale, province, nation, fed-

As an example of this, a school lecture takes place in a classroom and under a schedule, and is expected to enhance the students' abilities through the cultural and ideological activity of education. But this implies a differentiated legal status between students and teacher, where each have distinct rights and responsibilities, and is also an economic activity where the teacher gets paid and the students can attend the class because they do not have to engage in labour themselves – at least not during the school time. The same collective activity thus has effects at the same time on different strata of social life, with each stratum having a different spatio-temporality. The space-time of the lecture in terms of education is produced in the classroom and refers to a regional, national or transnational culture – to which it also contributes. The juridical space-time of the lecture depends under most Western-based educational systems on the state- and national legal framework, while its economical space-time is ultimately the world market – albeit through the mediation of a national currency and market.

But Marx's famous paragraph in the *Contribution* also suggests a 'horizontal' coexistence of systemic forms in a stratum: they do not directly condition each other, but develop independently because each one responds to different rules. In a particular society, for example, art and religion may not follow the same mechanisms, but are conditioned by the same strata under them.[42] Such complexes of forms – which are themselves forms – correspond with what Lukács refers to as *spheres* of objectification (e.g., economy, law and art), whose heterogeneity in relation to each other in Marx's ontology, the author of the *Ontology of Social Being* argues, is given by the relation between their respective teleological projects and materialities.[43] However, his interpretation completely overlooks the spatio-temporal aspects of the uneven development of such spheres – aspects that, I have argued, are inherent both in the project and in the materiality of the objectification.

The stratum of economic production conditions the emergence of all social objectifications, but the forms in the latter can adapt to transformations in the conditions of the lower strata. Indeed, the observable plurality of social space-times has to do with the heterogeneity of forms as mechanisms with differentiated rules and histories; the uneven spatio-temporal development of a

---

eration, region, space of flows) which will subsequently require mediation at other levels. Hence the potential structural disjunctions between, for example, the economic, political and cultural histories of any particular territoriality. Totalisation is a re-territorialising as well as a re-temporalising process'. Osborne 2000, p. 17.

42   On 'vertical' and 'horizontal' explanation, see Collier 1994, pp. 42–51.

43   Lukács 1978, pp. 124–7.

particular form of society is the necessary corollary of the different means and modalities of the praxical transformation of the world.[44] The example in the *Grundrisse* about the uneven development of ancient forms of art and law in respect to modern material production is therefore better comprehended as a case of differential times of particular forms in western Europe. Marx already approaches other cases of this kind of uneven spatio-temporal development in his early writings, when he compared the situation of politics and philosophy in England, France and Germany, as well as the disparities between corresponding spheres – such as the intellectual and the productive – in other nations.[45]

Forms are determined partially by their place in respect to the social totalisation, but their space-times do not necessarily correspond directly with those of the modes of production where they develop; the history of a form is defined through the interaction between its internal and external determinations – the classic dialectical relation between part and whole.[46] The forms in a society, hence, are possible due to the conditions of economic production, but they are 'vertically' and 'horizontally' mediated by their situation in the three strata of society. Hence, in capitalist societies philosophy and agriculture, e.g., have quite different functions and respond to mechanisms differently from one another; their spatio-temporal differences are also easily observable.

Overall, the interactions of diverse praxes ultimately lead to uneven social totalisations.[47] Since each mechanism has its own spatio-temporal tendencies (e.g., the current conflict between global scale economy and national scale politics, and their respective space-times, as conceptualised by Sassen), a concrete society functions as the organisation of multiple social spaces and times; social totalisation is mediated by the spatio-temporal production of spheres and their relations with one another. Such development is, therefore, uneven not only between spheres, but also within each sphere: a social mechanism, given that it is based on unequal relations, produces contradictory outcomes

---

44   See Heller 1984, pp. 47–113. See also Heller 1990, pp. 48–60.

45   Marx 1973, pp. 109–11; Marx 1975, pp. 175–87; Marx and Engels 1976b, pp. 74–5 and pp. 81–3.

46   See Kosík 1976, pp. 17–32.

47   'Praxis also reveals itself as a totality. We would maintain that the idea of totality derives from praxis. However, this totality never appears to be other than fragmentary, contradictory, and composed of levels, of contradictions on differing levels, and of partial totalities. How do we reach totality, i.e., society itself from within? Precisely, via these partial totalities and levels which cross-refer to each other, and via these fragments which presuppose a whole and which necessitate the concept of a whole of which they are the evidence and the elements, but not the entirety. Fragmented in one sense but already total in another, every act of thought or social effectiveness refers to the totality via the other levels. It reveals a total praxis, and points the way towards it'. Lefebvre 2002, p. 237.

in space and time in a single moment. In this sense, as Marx argues, the most simple formulation of the production of capital consists of the double process of C-M-C (the point of view of the labour force) and M-C-M' (the point of view of capital). These formulae entail the unequal distribution of the outcomes of the process, as well as the unequal spaces and times of its sides.[48]

Finally, I think a clarification about the relation between praxis and labour – concepts often conflated in the Marxist tradition – should be made, especially since Marx elaborates his mentioned example of the architect's activity in order to specifically conceptualise labour. Petrović indicates that Marx repeatedly opposes praxis – or *self-activity*, as he calls it from *The German Ideology* onwards – to labour, having characterised the latter in his 1844 *Manuscripts*, specifically, as 'the act of alienation of practical human activity'.[49] Hence this opposition, as the Yugoslavian philosopher stresses, implies that praxis is the non-alienated form of human activity, but overall, his account of the concept of praxis suggests that Marx did not fully develop this concept.

However, other passages in Marx's early work conceptualise praxis as the generic form of human activity. Thus, in his 8th Thesis on Feuerbach Marx affirms that 'all social life is essentially *practical*. All mysteries which lead theory to mysticism find their rational solution in human practice and in the comprehension of this practice'.[50] Since Marx considers class societies, and particularly capitalism, as early as 1844, as inherently alienating, in this formulation praxis encompasses alienated as well as non-alienated activities. Moreover, Marx's central claim that the organisation of production fundamentally structures society would not be possible in this 8th Thesis if Marx's concept of human practice did not include labour.

The relation between praxis and labour would not then be one of opposition, but rather that between genus and species, and the passages where they appear as opposed would refer strictly to alienated labour, not because the latter is a different and independent category to praxis, but because it is a specific case of praxis transformed into a limitation of the possibilities of its agents.[51] Accordingly, labour – whether alienated or not – would be a specific, although fundamental, modality of praxis. Due to his consideration of economic production as the totalising criterion of social relations, Marx gave priority in his work to the dialectical development of the concept of labour. His purpose was not

---

48   Harvey's theory of capitalist space is based on the consequences of this fundamental
       Marxian formulation. See Harvey 2009.
49   Petrović 1991, p. 437.
50   Marx 1976a, p. 5.
51   On alienation as a negation of praxical possibilities, see Lefebvre 2001, pp. 160–1.

primarily to formulate a social theory *tout court*, but a theory of the capitalist mode of production, whose explanation implied other, more general categories of social being and history. This movement from the abstract concept of praxis to the more concrete concept of labour, nonetheless, did not mean the elimination of the former or of other specific kinds of praxes.[52]

Hence Lukács considers that labour is for Marx the most basic form of social practice and its model because it 'is the underlying and hence the simplest and most elementary form of those complexes whose dynamic interaction is what constitutes the specificity of social practice', albeit, for this very reason, 'it is necessary time and again to point out that the specific features of labour should not be transposed directly to the more complicated forms of social practice'.[53] According to Lukács, although the structure of every social practice would have the structure of labour at its core, the former cannot be reduced to the latter. The Hungarian philosopher dovetails with Engels's *The Role of Labour in the Transition from Ape to Man* about the historico-genetic pre-eminence of labour in the process of humanisation, but argues that teleology – labour's key ontological category, that through which the human agent posits a new objectivity – is the fundamental feature which labour transposes onto every social practice.[54]

It should be noted, against Habermas's claim that Marx's concept of praxis is framed within the limits of instrumental reason, that the teleological character of praxis does not imply the calculation, constant search for efficiency and inversion of means and ends that characterises instrumental reason in Horkheimer's classic account.[55] Lefebvre, on the other hand, has argued that for Marx human production encompasses both the domination of nature and the appropriation by the human being of their own conditions of existence, thus separating praxis from *poiêsis*,[56] but this distinction, albeit useful, was not developed by Marx. In his concept of praxis, both of these components form a dialectical unity which – as part of Marx's Romantic heritage – prevents it from being just a productivist or utilitarian category.

In any case, the model character of labour should not be highlighted at the expense of that of praxis, as is done, for example, in Carol Gould's classic study on Marxian anthropology and social ontology. This author maintains that, for Marx, it is labour that creates time, quoting the famous *Grundrisse* pas-

---

52   Agnes Heller develops a systematic account of social praxes, from the point of view of their objectifications, in Heller 1984.

53   Lukács 1980, p. 59.

54   Lukács 1980, p. 3.

55   Habermas 1987, pp. 25–42; Horkheimer 2013, pp. 1–40.

56   Lefebvre 2002a, p. 26.

sage stating that 'labour is the living, form-giving fire; it is the transitoriness of things, their temporality, as their formation by living time'.[57] However, it would seem to us here that Gould unjustifiably generalises this assertion at the most abstract level of social being, when it is actually located within a paragraph that deals specifically with the objectifications of labour, and not with all social products.[58]

For Marx, each society has to organise its time – or, more precisely, its available praxical *times* – 'in order to achieve a production adequate to its overall needs'.[59] Yet while the temporal organisation of production (in the narrow economic sense) is fundamental to this organisation, it cannot be deduced from this that the time of every social practice is reducible to the time of labour. The latter has a social priority over other kinds of praxes because it is the means by which human beings overcome necessity in order to survive, but the other praxes also temporalise (and spatialise) the social world.

1.2   Historical Being, Historicity and Categories

The differentiality of spaces and times in a form of society becomes even more complex when considered in relation to the transformations (or apparent staticity) that it undergoes, and how the people in it think and act in relation to them, in spite of not having, as individuals, a direct experience of them. Accordingly, the negation of praxis – the Marxian foundation of social being, as argued in the previous section – marks the transition from *social being* to *historical being*: while the expectancy of death spatio-temporalises praxis and shapes social being, the *actuality* of death is the condition of possibility for the idea of history. In *The German Ideology*, before introducing his more abstract conceptualisation and methodology for the study of societies, Marx affirms that history can be described as 'nothing but the succession of the separate generations, each of which uses the materials, the capital funds, the productive forces handed down to it by all preceding generations'.[60] The problematic relation of

---

57   Marx 1973, p. 361. Gould 1980, pp. 56–68.
58   See Gould 1980, pp. 59–64. Again, *labour is a condition of possibility for other praxes*, but not their essence; the preeminence of labour in the human struggle against necessity should not obfuscate the plurality of praxes in every social organisation. Furthermore, the conflation of labour and praxis can unnecessarily lead to politically productivist and theoretically economistic implications.
59   Marx 1973, p. 173.
60   Marx and Engels 1976b, p. 50. Likewise, for Hegel, death marks the transition from the singular to genus, from natural being to spirit. See Hegel 1970b, pp. 210–13.

the living with the dead is a recurring topic in Marx's writings throughout his life, be it as a burden for political imagination or as the alienating force of dead versus living labour, to mention two famous examples.[61]

In this sense, history constructs the spatio-temporal unity broken by death by presenting collective agents as its protagonists, usually defined by geographic criteria. As Osborne argues, the transcendental horizon of history lies in the transgenerational unity of the human – a feature that shows the inherent utopianism of the concept of history.[62] This unity implies not only how to think *about* history, but also how to act *in* history since, as Lukács points out, 'social practice always unfolds in a mental environment of ontological conceptions'.[63] The construction of this unity, however, takes different paths – as we will see especially in the cases of World-History and Marx's mature concept of history in the last section of this chapter – through different spatio-temporal configurations.

Ricoeur deals with the construction of this unity by drawing especially from Koselleck's theory of historical temporalities, which according to the German author are based on the relations between the past as a *space of experience* and the future as a *horizon of expectation*: one of his most important contributions has been the demonstration of the divergence between the temporality of the *Ancien Régime* – where the future was expected not to differ from the past – and the one emerging in the last decades of the eighteenth century in western Europe – which, initially from the standpoint of *progress*, thought the future as distinct from the past. This temporalisation, Ricoeur argues, belongs to the fundamental level of the ontology of historical existence (what he calls the *historical condition*), an 'unsurpassable mode of being'.[64] Therefore, temporal

---

61   Marx 1979a, pp. 99–197; Marx 1976b. As Tomlinson argues, following Sartre, Heideggerian being-for-death provides a philosophically fruitful temporalisation for the teleological dimension of Marxian praxis. Tomlinson 2015, pp. 78–96. Along with this temporalisation, however, there is the spatialisation of the body, with its growing, ageing and exchanges with its environment, without whose consideration we run the risk of reducing the human subject to an abstract conscience. See Lefebvre 1997, pp. 169–76.

62   Osborne 2013, pp. 193–94. In the same vein, Bloch indicates that 'precisely the generations pass away; in endless sedimentations they lie above one another everywhere, shrunken together, and ... the functional problem persists: who or what lives life as a whole life, *as the broad, historical life granted to humanity as a whole*?' Bloch 2000, pp. 256–7. The emphasis is from the original.

63   Lukács 1980, p. 59.

64   Ricoeur 2004, p. 343. On the historical emergence of historicity, Koselleck 2004, pp. 255–75. Hartog calls these relations between past, present and future *regimes of historicity*. Hartog 2012.

configurations underpin historical thinking and all phases of historical investigation; the ontology of history should thus be seen as part of an ontological
hermeneutics.

However, and as will be explained in the next chapter, while I consider that
this differentiation of the levels of knowledge (albeit incomplete) is valid, Ricoeur's disavowal of the possibility of historical knowledge reflecting upon itself
and its conditions of validity seems formalistic and de-historicised, and ultimately inconsistent with the very bases of the modern historical condition.[65]
The categories of *space of experience* and *horizon of expectation* – and their
modern disassociation – are constructed by Koselleck at the level of historiography, by recourse to the comparison between two different historical temporal configurations – a comparison that has only became possible from the
vantage point of the historical condition of the *Neuzeit*. Given this characteristic of Koselleck's argument, it is quite odd for Ricoeur to claim that historical
investigation is incapable of contributing to the ontology of historical existence: on the contrary, the latter would require a dialectical approach between
the levels of historical knowledge. In line with this critique, the main problem
in Ricoeur's formulation is its neglect of the material conditions underlying
this specific ontology – an aspect that is closely related to the de-spatialised
character of his philosophy of history.[66]

Indeed, the unity of human experience – its existence as a collective singular – has only become a regulative idea of historical thinking with the world-
wide expansion of capitalism; the historical condition analysed by Ricoeur is
founded on specifically capitalist social relations.[67] Koselleck himself demonstrates that the separation of space from history is a product of the late eighteenth century, and Lefebvre argues that the detachment of space from time – a
central feature of abstract space – has only been able to fully develop under
capitalist conditions.[68] This separation conceals the necessary relations between temporal and spatial categories; it is possible to think of a social process

---

65   Ricoeur 2004, p. 333. Osborne finds this problem in Koselleck's formulation of this cat-
      egorical opposition – the source from where Ricoeur draws the bases of his ontology of
      historical existence. Below I will revisit his critique of this conception of historical time.
      See Osborne 2013, pp. 190–211; and also, Osborne 2013, pp. 69–70.
66   This limitation in Ricoeur's philosophy of history has been examined and criticised in
      detail by Dussel. Dussel 1996, pp. 214–30.
67   This neglect of space by Ricoeur and Koselleck goes in hand with the deterritorialising
      tendencies to which Marx referred with his image of the 'annihilation of space by time'.
      Marx 1973, pp. 107, 524, 539.
68   Koselleck 2001, pp. 93–111; Lefebvre 1997, p. 175.

in exclusively temporal terms, but only on the condition of implicitly presupposing a space with constant characteristics. Likewise, merely spatial accounts always assume a certain type of social time.

The supposedly de-spatialised approach in the phenomenological tradition is therefore unable to historicise its ontology of history. In contrast, one of the foundations of Marx's method is the thesis that the modern concept of history – 'history as world history [is] a result'[69] – emerges with the expansion of capital, which

> drives beyond national barriers and prejudices as much as beyond nature worship, as well as traditional, confined, complacent, encrusted satisfactions of present needs, and reproductions of old ways of life. It is destructive towards all of this, and constantly revolutionises it, tearing down the barriers which hem in the development of the forces of production, the expansion of needs, the all-sided development of production, and the exploitation and exchange of natural and mental forces. But from the fact that capital posits every such limit as a barrier and hence gets *ideally* beyond it, it does not by any means follow that it has *really* overcome it.[70]

This passage highlights the historical conditions that gave rise to both world-history and to the ideal spatiality of capitalism – the space of the world market. As for the latter aspect, it implies that the relation between experience and expectation is temporal, but also in the same measure historically and conceptually spatial – as the metaphors of these Koselleckian concepts suggest. Just as the accumulation of capital functions on the base of an ideally infinite and continuous temporality, it assumes a tendentially global and commodified spatiality (an *abstract space*, as conceptualised by Lefebvre):[71] when considered historically, the apparently formal relation between the *space* of experience

---

69   Marx 1973, p. 109. As Harootunian indicates, 'it was capital's logic that made possible history, as we know it, and defined the relationship between itself and the past. It occurred at the point when capitalism's abstract logic entered a received history and began altering and directing it on a new course, which produced uneven temporalities along every step of the way but sought to conceal it by implanting homogeneous time as the measure of capital's progressive vocation'. Harootunian 2015b, p. 26. See also Tomlinson 2015, pp. 134–82.

70   Marx 1973, p. 410. The italics are from the original.

71   For capitalism, the world market would be 'the conclusion, in which production is posited as a totality together with all its moments, but within which, at the same time, all contradictions come into play. The world market then, again, forms the presupposition of the whole as well as its substratum'. Marx 1973, pp. 227–8. Lefebvre 1997, pp. 229–91.

and the *horizon* of expectation is revealed as driven by the spatial expansion of capitalist social relations.

Marx's ontology of history and its particular categories are themselves openly historical, and their historical condition of possibility is the accumulation of capital, which has given form to the configuration of space-times upon which the modern historical condition relies (both objectively and subjectively).[72] Historicity thus not only refers to a context defined by a singular geographical space and chronological time, but to the social-natural relations that produce and are themselves produced by concrete social times and social spaces responding to definite generative mechanisms; and since it is an operation that seeks to apprehend the concrete, historicisation cannot separate time from space.

For Marx, the relation between the unity of human experience and the plurality of singular space-times is mediated by the mode of production – the proper historical totalisation. The mode of production is hence the basic discontinuity in history, organising the diverse forms of society according to the interactions between human praxes and their material conditions, rather than to a predetermined pattern of evolution. In this sense, as Jameson argues, the approach to temporally, culturally – or, we can add, spatially – distant social artifacts consists, first of all, not in a relationship between a personal reading and an individual text (or, more generally, a source), but in 'the confrontation of two distinct social forms or modes of production'.[73]

In this regard, Marx states that

> even the most abstract categories, despite their validity – precisely because of their abstractness – for all epochs, are nevertheless, in the specific character of this abstraction, themselves likewise a product of historical relations, and possess their full validity only for and within these relations.[74]

---

72   Along these lines, Osborne indicates that 'today, the contemporary (the fictive relational unity of the spatially distributed historical present) is transnational because our modernity is that of a tendentially global capital. Transnationality is the putative socio-spatial form of the current temporal unity of historical experience'. Osborne 2013, p. 83. In a similar line, see Martineau, 2016, and on the historical character of ontology in Marx, see Lukács 1980, pp. 62–3.

73   Jameson 2008a, p. 478. While I agree with this essay about the necessary character of this mediation, it is not sufficient for a concrete (properly historicised) analysis: the critique of a historical source demands – once its legitimacy is verified – the consideration of the specific social conditions of the production of the source: the classic Marxian ideological critique. See Chapter 3, below.

74   Marx 1973, p. 105. Adorno has correctly pointed out that, 'in Marx, who, of course, came

Thus, the historicity of the categories means for Marx, on the one hand, on the side of the object, that the forms to which these categories refer should be considered in the context of their corresponding form of society. Only then do they have explanatory validity: abstract categories like labour or population are not useful for the analysis of particular social processes unless they are conceptualised in relation to their respective form of society. On the other hand, this historicity implies that the *categories* through which a form of society is comprehended are themselves a product of objective social conditions, and hence the theoretical approach is always rooted in the society where it is formulated.[75]

An apparent paradox thus arises: Marx's hermeneutics relies on the discontinuity of the modes of production, each of which generates its own cultural forms in order to deal with their relations with their social space-times, but at the same time this formulation is a product of a particular mode of production: capitalism. Since Marx insists on the realist character of his method, this poses a difficulty that does not exist for non-realist philosophies of history, like those created by Nietzsche or Heidegger. Hence Marx accounts for the historicity of his own theory – and consequently, of its ability to explain other historical formations – in two manners, which we may call, in broad terms, evolutionist and abstractionist.

The first stance, sustained in the *Grundrisse* by an argument about the validity of the categories of capitalism for the explanation of the formations which led to that mode of production, using the famous image of the anatomy of the ape being comprehensible through the study of human anatomy,[76] is problematic for at least two reasons. First, given that this argument assumes *one* line of development among others (the one that led to nineteenth-century Western European capitalism), it excludes the possibility of explaining modes of production that do not belong to the pre-history of capitalism, and hence possess a radical alterity that disavows the unity of human experience that underpins

---

from Hegel, the categories used are not only so-called systematic categories developed from concepts, but are always also, and intentionally, historical categories'. Adorno 2000, p. 144.

75 As Schmidt affirms, for Marx human beings 'grasp the objectively existing laws of nature through, and by means of, the historical forms of their practice'. Schmidt 2014, p. 126. This does not mean, however, that categorical apparatuses can be reduced to their social context without mediations, as will be explained later in this chapter.

76 Marx 1973, p. 105. In spite of the problems indicated here about the evolutionist line of argumentation, it should be kept in mind that Marx criticised teleological illusions already since the time of *The German Ideology* and maintained that position until his final years, as can be observed in his correspondence with Vera Zasulich and the *narodniki*.

Marx's concept of history. Second, this reasoning is not capable of explaining properly pre-capitalist formations either, since the dialectical transition from one mode of production to another is not only a process of gaining new determinations, but also of losing others.[77]

Also against this evolutionist vein in the *Grundrisse*, Grüner argues that, although the introduction to this text claims that the study of bourgeois society provides key elements for the analysis of its previous formations, in these very drafts the development of the categories in non-capitalistic societies responds to particular conditions of their social totalisations – which cannot be directly deduced from capitalism. The primacy of use-values in pre-capitalist economies, for example, decisively transforms categories as basic as *labour*, and makes it impossible to understand these categories from the point of view of modern formations without major changes.[78]

The second explanation of the historicity of Marx's approach follows the path of abstraction, and is also present in the *Grundrisse*. As quoted above, Marx indicates that the most abstract categories are valid for all social formations, and in this same line, argues that

> all epochs of production have certain common traits, common characteristics. ... Some determinations belong to all epochs, others only to a few. {Some} determinations will be shared by the most modern epoch and the most ancient. ... There are characteristics which all stages of production have in common, and which are established as general ones by the mind; but the so-called *general preconditions* of all production are nothing more than these abstract moments with which no real historical stage of production can be grasped.[79]

Hence, instead of characterising less and more developed social forms in a historical continuum – an approach more appropriate to the World-history of the Enlightenment – historicisation can proceed by abstracting from the categories of the capitalist mode of production into the most general preconditions, valid for every mode of production. In this case, the analytical primacy of capital-

---

77 Hegel points out that *Aufheben* (to sublate) 'equally means to means "*to keep*", "to preserve", and "to cause to cease", "*to put an end to*". Even "to preserve" already includes a negative note, namely that something, in order to be retained, is removed from its immediacy and hence from an existence which is open to external influences'. Hegel 2010, pp. 81–2.

78 Grüner 2015. For a critique of this evolutionist line, see also Sayer 1987, pp. 126–30.

79 Marx 1973, pp. 85, 88. The braces in this citation are from Martin Nicolaus, the translator of this edition.

ism does not reside in being the most 'advanced' mode of production, but *in its condition of* being a mode of production based on abstraction.[80] This approach implies that abstract transhistorical categories guide a Marxian ontology of the modes of production, even as they must acquire concreteness – through empirical research, we can infer – in order to explain a social formation properly. Thus the most abstract categories provide the basic framework for the intelligibility of any social formation.[81]

The validity of trans- or meta-historical categories in Marxism is often a matter of controversy; recently, Postone in particular insists on the notion that Marx's conception of history is strictly limited to capitalism and thus lacks the categorical capacity for the analysis of non-capitalist societies. However, this position not only contradicts the existence of a rich tradition of Marxist historiography about non-capitalist formations,[82] but also ignores the numerous cases where Marx refers to such formations from the standpoint of his materialist conception of history. Joseph Fracchia correctly points out that, for Marx, transhistorical and abstract categories are 'the foundation for the construction of historically specific categories', and provide a standpoint for the critique of social forms.[83] The basic categories of this kind, he indicates, are concrete labour, use-value and material wealth, which are rooted in human corporeal-

---

80   'We can think abstractly about the world only to the degree to which the world itself has already become abstract'. Jameson 2002, p. 51.

81   In this line, Jameson affirms that 'the Marxian concept of a mode of production is essentially a *differential* one, in which the formulation of a single mode of production (as, for instance, Marx's own model of capital) at once structurally projects the space of other possible modes of production by way of Difference, that is, by a systematic variation in the features or semes of any given initial mode. This is the sense in which each mode of production structurally *implies* all the others'. Jameson 2008a, p. 477. The interpretation based on abstraction, however, does not think of the categories of the different modes of production as elements of a possible combination (as the Althusserians did), but as the most basic framework upon which each specific mode of production should be apprehended, both conceptually and empirically.

82   In words of Postone, 'the Marxian theory should be understood not as a universally applicable theory but as a critical theory specific to capitalist society. It analyses the historical specificity of capitalism and the possibility of its overcoming by means of categories that grasp its specific forms of labour, wealth and time'. Postone 2003, p. 5. Some of the discussions about relevant marxist historiography are reviewed and developed in texts that have been important to the present investigation: Banaji 2011; Anievas and Nişancioğlu 2015; Harootunian 2015b.

83   Fracchia 2004, p. 128. See also Sayer 1987, pp. 126–49. Echeverría has further developed the thesis of the *natural form* as normative criterion against the capitalist primacy of the value-form. See Echeverría 2014, pp. 24–38.

ity,[84] but which are abstracted from their concrete relations in capitalism.

It is initially through the transhistorical categories, those dealing with the most abstract social forms as *determinations belonging to all epochs*, that we can grasp the unity of human experience, however heterogeneous in its diverse spatio-temporal particular forms. Hence, the Marxian ontology of history functions at this level by thematising common traits in different modes of production, which we might think of as a sort of 'backbone' of all 'social metabolisms'. The abstraction which underpins this ontology of history has its historical conditions of possibility, as mentioned above, in the world-wide expansion of capitalism, but also in the development of abstraction within capitalist social relations. In this sense, the tension between the unity of human experience and the particularity of the different modes of production sets the conditions that make this transhistorical abstraction possible, in a similar manner to the concept of value which, as Marx indicated, 'is entirely peculiar to the most modern economy, since it is the most abstract expression of capital itself and of the production resting on it'.[85]

In this argument, the historically modern condition forms a dialectical unity with its underlying socio-historical processes (and the development of their space-times, both actual and tendential), hence making an opposition between a substantial and analytical philosophy of history useless. The philosophy of historical knowledge and the philosophy of history therefore necessarily imply each other; likewise, historical processes and historiography are not separated by an unbreachable chasm – as assumed by both neo-Kantian and Nietzschean philosophies of history. This unity does not imply an idealist closure for historical thought, since for Marx, dialectical methodology must be able to incorporate the determinations of reality as new categories.[86] This realist character of Marx's theory of history, as will be noted in the next chapter, involves know-

---

84 Fracchia 2004, pp. 127–8, 138. Such considerations – essential to his materialist conception of history – lead Marx to state, for instance, that 'the Middle Ages could not live on Catholicism, nor could the ancient world on politics. On the contrary, it is the manner in which they gained their livelihood which explains why in one case politics, and in other case Catholicism, played the chief part. For the rest, one needs no more than a slight acquaintance with, for example, the Roman Republic, to be aware that its secret history is the history of landed property'. Marx 1976b, p. 176.

85 Marx 1973, p. 776. Marx's explanation of Aristotle's inability to reach the concept of value is another illustrative example of his thesis of the historicity of the categories. Marx 1976b, pp. 151–2.

86 Osborne indicates that this approach, which he characterises as *immanent*, avoids the circularity of the transcendental method by relying on specific historiographical contents, and hence its validity is continually subject to historical contingency. Osborne 2010, pp. 35–6.

ledge of relations between diverse generative mechanisms, in order to explain particular historical cases. But it is necessary to first clarify how Marx conceives the spatio-temporal development of social forms at the largest scale.

1.3   From World-History to Spatio-Temporal Complexity

Marx's overall vision of human development – following the *unity of the human experience* posed by the modern concept of history – needed to account for the global and regional diversity of social forms, and in this sense it went through two phases, with the 1856–7 *Grundrisse* marking a turning point between them. Although Marx's basic ontology of social being did not go through major transformations after the mid-1840s, the *Grundrisse* is where Marx establishes the ground for his spatially and temporally complex conception of history. As for his earlier conception, there is indeed an implicit unilinearity that underpins his formulations about history, in texts like *The German Ideology*, the *Communist Manifesto* and his articles on India for the *Daily Tribune*, which is indebted to the *world-history* (*Weltgeschichte*) of the Enlightenment.

As Koselleck demonstrates, German philosophers elaborated their Enlightenment conception of world-history in the late eighteenth century, in order to replace the existing universal history (*Universalhistorie*) which they deemed to be a simple aggregate of a few historical facts serving as an auxiliary science for theology and philology. Against this, Schlösser affirmed in 1785 that the study of world-history leads one 'to think the main transformations (*HauptVeränderungen*) of the human genus (*MenschenGeschlecht*) and its environment in order to get to know the reasons for their present state'.[87] World-history would therefore be a general, totalising history, that would bring the multiplicity of particular histories together into a collective singular.[88]

The diverse versions of world-history in the eighteenth and nineteenth centuries, however, did not live up to their claims of thinking the generality of human development. Due to a barely concealed Eurocentrism, these narratives justified Western Europe's dominance over the rest of the globe by conceiving the history of the world as a unilinear path led by their allegedly more advanced civilisation. The emergence of the conception of world-history went

---

87   Cited in Koselleck 2010, p. 100. This edition is a partial translation of the entry 'Geschichte' in volume 2 of the *Geschichtliche Grundbegriffe*.

88   Koselleck 2010, pp. 101–4; also Ricoeur 2004, pp. 298–305. Besides the economic process of capitalist expansion, the elaboration of world-history was made possible by the centralisation of information in imperial archives, as Chapter 3 of this book describes.

hand in hand with the notion of historical *progress*, especially in texts from the French Enlightenment philosophers Turgot, Condillac and Condorcet, but also in some of Kant's most famous political essays. These authors share the vision of Europe as the driving force of 'progress', and thereby condone colonialism.[89]

In line with this conception, a division of history into successive stages became widespread within European intellectual circles. In the second half of the eighteenth century the French physiocrat Turgot, and Scottish moral philosophers like Adam Ferguson, Adam Smith and John Millar, proposed a succession of four stages, from nomadism to the urban societies of their days, defining trade as the most important factor in the development to the last, more complex kind of society.[90] This series of transformations, which is presented as an analysis of history, implies a hierarchy where the last stage – 'modern Western European civilisation' – is the standard from which the others are to be judged, and to which they are to be subjected. In this sense, Guha criticises Hegel's version of successive stages in history, according to which the higher principle prevails over the lower, the West over the East.[91]

Leaving aside the political implications of world-history as an apology for colonialism, this conception contributed little to historical knowledge. Its methodology of inferring wide spatio-temporal conclusions from a quite limited number of – often unjustifiably – selected sources eventually came into contradiction with the development of its critical method, which called for a growing specialisation. The vagueness of world-history had little to offer to the explanation of specific historical processes; it is, as Guha argues, 'a view of history that allows all the concreteness to be drained out of the phenomena which constitute the world and its historicality'.[92] World-history is indeed the reference *par excellence* of what analytical philosophers call *speculative philosophy of history* – a mode of interpreting history through *a priori* criteria, with no empirical rigour at all.[93]

This tradition of world-history is the context from which Marx and Engels begin their theoretical work on history. For them, the bourgeois world was on the verge of creating a fully integrated system, in which the development of the most advanced historical epoch – capitalism – would destroy the isolation of

89   Iggers, Wang and Mukherjee 2008, p. 31.
90   Meek 1977, pp. 18–32; Iggers, Wang and Mukherjee 2008. See also Berry 2013, pp. 32–65.
91   Guha 2002, p. 43.
92   Guha 2002, p. 2. On the specialisation of the historical discipline, see Koselleck 2010, p. 105.
93   Walsh 1960, pp. 9–28.

separate nationalities, turning history into world-history by integrating them 'by intercourse and by the natural division of labour arising as a result'.[94] Consequently, the *Manifesto* argues that

> the need of a constantly expanding market for its products chases the bourgeoisie over the whole surface of the globe. It must nestle everywhere, settle everywhere, establish connections everywhere. ... The bourgeoisie, by the rapid improvement of all instruments of production, by the immensely facilitated means of communication, draws all, even the most barbarian, nations into civilisation. The cheap prices of its commodities are the heavy artillery with which it batters down all Chinese walls, with which it forces the barbarians' intensely obstinate hatred of foreigners to capitulate. It compels all nations, on pain of extinction, to adopt the bourgeois mode of production; it compels them to introduce what it calls civilisation into their midst, i.e., to become bourgeois themselves. In one word, it creates a world after its own image.[95]

The world market not only gives production and consumption in every country a cosmopolitan character, but produces a global culture beyond old local and national limits: a world literature. The underlying assumption in the early Marxian version of world-history is that the expansion of capitalism (as the most advanced stage) imposes a single spatio-temporal totalisation upon the multiple space-times of its coeval societies with less productive modes of production. Insofar as this conception considers that the world is already homogenised by the expansion of capitalism, there is only one social class that can fully realise the emancipatory potentialities of capitalism: hence, as the *Manifesto* famously affirms, 'the proletarians have nothing to lose but their chains. They have a world to win'.[96]

Since the development of capitalism on the world-scale is here a condition for the communist revolution, colonialism was justified as a necessary stage on the way towards a classless society, thus appearing as a necessary evil.[97] This is

---

94   Marx and Engels 1976b, p. 51. About *The German Ideology*, see Carver and Blank 2014.

95   Marx and Engels 1976a, pp. 487–8.

96   Marx and Engels 1976a, pp. 488, 490, 519. In *The German Ideology*, 'the proletariat can only thus exist *world-historically*, just as communism, its activity, can only have a "world-historical" existence.' Marx and Engels, 1976b, p. 49.

97   See Osborne 2006, pp. 110–21. Post- and de-colonial authors have written abundantly about texts from this phase in Marx's production, to which they often imply that his whole *oeuvre* is reducible. Said 2003; Lander 2006, pp. 209–43. Some replies from Marxist authors include: Parry 2004; Bartolovich and Lazarus 2002.

exemplified by Marx's writings in the early 1850s about India, in which he celebrated the destructive effects of railroads and industry on ancient institutions like the caste system, which from his point of view fettered the potentialities of the Indian people, but also by Engels's 1849 remarks about the annexation of previously Mexican territories by the United States.[98]

The early Marxian view of the development of history is a socialist (and certainly more complex) version of the four-staged world-history of the Scottish Enlightenment and the French physiocrats, which, as Meek observes, was a materialist conception of history as well.[99] John Millar's formulation is representative of this conception, according to which

> development should be regarded as proceeding through four normally consecutive socio-economic stages, each based on a particular 'mode of subsistence', namely, hunting, pasturage, agriculture, and commerce. To each stage there corresponded different ideas and institutions relating to both property and government, and in relation to each, general statements could be made about the state of manners and morals, the social surplus, the legal system, the division of labour, and so on.[100]

Althusser's well known criticism of *expressive totality* (disregarding its validity as a criticism of Hegel) is aimed at this stagist conception of history of which texts like *The German Ideology* and the *Manifesto* partake – although the French

---

98   Marx 1979b, p. 221. Regarding Marx's writings about India, see: Habib 2002; Ahmad 1994, Chapter 6. At that time Engels asked the question: 'Is it perhaps unfortunate that splendid California has been taken away from the lazy Mexicans, who could not do anything with it? That the energetic Yankees by rapid exploitation of the Californian gold mines will increase the means of circulation, in a few years will concentrate a dense population and extensive trade at the most suitable places on the coast of the Pacific Ocean, create large cities, open up communications by steamship, construct a railway from New York to San Francisco, for the first time really open the Pacific Ocean to civilisation, and for the third time in history give world trade a new direction? The "independence" of a few Spanish Californians and Texans may suffer because of it, in some places "justice" and other moral principles may be violated; but what does that matter compared to such facts of world-historic significance?' Engels 1977, pp. 365–6.

99   See Meek 1967, pp. 34–50.

100   Meek 1977, p. 19. Scholars like Robert Brenner and Ellen Meiksins Wood – probably the best known proponents of the school currently known as *Political Marxism* – have insisted on Marx's debt to this conception of history in his pre-*Grundrisse* writings, specifically emphasising the influence of the Smithian model of development. This influence can be observed especially in the predominance that these texts assign to urban development in the transition from feudalism to capitalism: they affirm that the larger towns were the sites

Marxist does not address them in his critique. The stagist view of history supposes that any moment in history can be intellectually abstracted as a whole from the rest – through an *essential section* – and the relations between all its elements will express their internal essence by this operation. When an essential section is taken out of a totality, each of its parts expresses the social totality: they are *contemporary*. In Marx's early conception of history, this contemporaneity is defined by the contradiction between forces of production and forms of intercourse.[101]

Thus the stagist vision of history presupposes homogeneity *within* a determined stage, but it also presupposes homogeneity *between* the stages: a *continuum*. Although it would be exaggerated to reduce Marx's early conception of space-time to a formalised, quantitative vision – as in Althusser's other aspect of his criticism of expressive totality – his conception of modes of production ultimately does hold that levels of productivity are a transhistorical criteria on the world-historical scale. As a result of this, stagism makes it impossible to grasp historicity, and instead obfuscates the plurality of social forms in a mode of production, along with their contradictions and agents.[102]

For all its epistemological and political limitations, it is important to indicate that this conception, as Marx reiterated, is not deterministic in a narrow sense: even in the case of his famous article on India, he affirms that the Indians will only benefit from the innovations introduced by the British when the proletariat emerges in Great Britain as the ruling class, *or when the Indians themselves overthrow English domination*. The *Manifesto* – ultimately a political document in the imminence of the Revolutions of 1848 – predicted the triumph of the proletariat, but also insisted on the need for the workers to organise themselves into a revolutionary party. Even if the conditions were favourable for the working class, the outcome of the class struggle depended on their political praxis.[103]

However, the *Grundrisse* signal Marx's rejection of the world-historical conception and outlines his more definitive conception of history. As previously

---

of nascent capitalism and of the first elements of the bourgeoisie. Marx and Engels 1976b, pp. 69–70; Marx and Engels, 1976a, p. 485. Wood 2010, pp. 86–7; Brenner 1977, pp. 25–7.

101   Althusser and Balibar 2009, p. 105. Jameson argues that in Althusser's critique 'Hegel' is a codename for Stalinism. Jameson 2002, pp. 13–21. Marx and Engels 1976b, pp. 74–5.

102   Harootunian argues that an implicit stagism is persistent even in strong recent readings of Marx, such as in Negri, Backhaus and Postone. Harootunian 2015b, pp. 68–9.

103   Marx and Engels 1976b, 50; Marx 1979b, p. 221. While the diagnosis of bourgeois society begins the argument in the *Manifesto*, the discussion of the most effective socialist political organisation and the argument in favor of communism constitute its conclusions.

indicated, while there are still some problematic evolutionist assertions in these pages (particularly those related to his analogy of ape and human), the decisive moment of transition towards a science of multi-spatial and multi-temporal totalisations occurs in these drafts. Kevin Anderson, for his part, argues that with the introduction of the Asiatic mode of production in the *Grundrisse*, Marx abandons the unilinearity of his earlier texts – a change of perspective that coincides with a more hostile attitude from Marx towards capitalism, and a more nuanced assessment of non-capitalistic forms.[104] Bensaïd also highlights the *Grundrisse* as the introduction of a *new way of writing history*, breaking from the speculative notion of a universal History, towards the notion of *uneven development* between spheres of social activity. This entails a critique of progress and a deepening of the relationship between chance and necessity in history. Although Marx does point to some kinds of uneven development in his earlier writings, it is only from the *Grundrisse* on that he explores its implications for history in a systematic manner, introducing the notion of non-timeliness.[105]

In the *Grundrisse*, for example, Marx affirms that

> when an industrial people producing on the foundation of capital, such as the English, e.g., exchange with the Chinese, and absorb value in the form of money and commodity out of their production process, or rather absorb value by drawing the latter within the sphere of circulation of their capital, then one sees right away that the Chinese do not therefore need to produce as capitalists. Within a single society, such as the English, the mode of production of capital develops in one branch of industry, while in another, e.g. agriculture, modes of production which more or less antedate capital.[106]

Thus a more 'productive' mode of production does not necessarily eliminate others coexisting with it; Marx's new conception allows us to understand com-

---

104   Anderson 2010, pp. 154–63. Dussel arrives at a similar conclusion about the *Grundrisse* in the 1980s: he argues that these drafts mark the moment in which Marx articulates his definitive discourse, useful for the analysis of the peripheral Latin American formations. Dussel 1985, pp. 12–13.

105   Bensaïd stresses Marx's 1843 treatment of the non-contemporaneity of economic, political and philosophical development in England, France and Germany. Bensaïd 2002, pp. 20–4. On the discussion about the terms and concepts of *contemporaneity*, *synchronicity* and *timeliness*, see Osborne 2015, pp. 39–48.

106   Marx 1973, p. 729.

binations under a dominant form. The complexity of the concrete social formations should be totalised by first determining the specific kind of production which predominates over the rest and 'whose relations thus assign rank and influence to the others', but then also has to deal with the subordinated forms that it turns into 'stunted' or 'travestied' forms.[107]

In the section in the *Grundrisse* about precapitalist formations, also known as the *Formen*, Marx deals with modes of production from their point of view as forms of appropriation.[108] These forms are not mere analytical constructs, but abstractions from actually existing historical societies. Moreover, they are not chronologically successive stages, but have coexisted side by side; in this new conception of history, *forms* replace *stages*, making it impossible to conceive a single linear course of world-history. In this respect, the difference with the famous sequential treatment of the four modes of production in the 1859 *Contribution*[109] stands in contrast to the more theoretical interest of the *Grundrisse*, rendering this sequence a statement on the particular historical process of Western Europe alone.[110]

The *Grundrisse* propose three kinds of precapitalist forms of appropriation: the communitarian (of which there are two varieties: the primitive and the 'oriental despotic', encompassing more specific cases such as the Asian, Mexican, Peruvian, Slavonic, etc.), the ancient Greco-Roman and the Germanic form – each one of them producing its particular space-times, as we will learn in the next chapter. These forms, according to Marx, share the characteristic of the production of use-values, an example being that the ancient Greeks and

---

107   Marx 1973, pp. 107 and 105–6. On the prevalence of production as a criterion of totalisation, see Basso 2013, pp. 434–5; Musto 2010, pp. 10–15.

108   Each form of appropriation is determined by a different mode of production, the latter being the proper criterion of totalisation. Marx points out that 'the original unit between a particular form of community (clan) and the corresponding property in nature ... has its living reality in a specific *mode of production* itself, a mode which appears both as a relation between the individuals, and their specific active relation to inorganic nature, a specific mode of working (which is family labour, often communal labour)'. Marx 1973, p. 495.

109   'In broad outline, the Asiatic, ancient, feudal and modern bourgeois modes of production may be designated as epochs marking progress in the economic development of society'. Marx 1987a, p. 263. Although translated as 'epochs marking progress', *progressive Epochen* can simply mean 'successive epochs' (in the sense of *Progression*), which would be consistent with Marx's reiterated critique of the ideology of 'progress' (for which Marx uses the term *Fortschritt*). It is also convenient to observe that there is quite a difference between an 'epoch' and a 'stage', as it is frequently interpreted. Marx 1961, p. 9.

110   This position is maintained, among others, by Hobsbawm and Basso. Hobsbawm 1965, p. 38. Basso 2013, pp. 332–4.

Romans did not care about which kind of property creates greater wealth, but about which creates the best citizens.[111]

As Wood notes, Marx's portrayal of these forms is based on principles immanent to each one,

> and not by some impersonal transhistorical law of technological improvement or commercial expansion … One way of characterising what Marx has done, already in the *Grundrisse*, is to say that he has replaced teleology with history – not history as mere contingency, nor history as a mechanical succession of predetermined stages or a sequence of static structures, but history as a process with its own causalities, constituted by human agency in a context of social relations and social practices which impose their own demands on those engaged in them.[112]

Harootunian maintains that Marx consolidated this conception of history in the mid-1860s through the concept of *formal subsumption*, which allowed him to theoretically 'grasp the refractions of specific forms' by which (absolute) surplus value is generated for capitalism from production relations that are not immediately capitalist.[113] Marx uses this concept to explain the means by which capitalism takes over an available, already existing labour process and modifies it by making work more intensive, extending its duration, making it more continuous, or subjecting it to the direction of a capitalist: under formal subsumption, technological changes are not introduced to the labour process, and valorisation is produced by the exaction of absolute surplus value.[114]

Harootunian's characterisation of the role of the Marxian concept of *real subsumption*, however, has been criticised for its conflation of this concept with a 'completion' of capitalism and hence to deny this form for the analysis of non-European societies.[115] Since Harootunian's own analyses draw upon the

---

111 Marx 1973, p. 487. Against this thesis, Banaji has argued that even in Marx's times, sources on Roman history preclude the characterisation of pre-capitalist modes of production as natural economies. Banaji 2011, pp. 7–8.

112 Wood 2010, pp. 88, 90. Lawrence Krader highlights Marx's arguments against unilinearism as well, in his introduction, Krader 1974, pp. 1–85.

113 Harootunian 2015b, p. 8. Dussel indicates that the chapter where the concept of subsumption was developed was written in 1864. Dussel 2001, p. xxxii.

114 Marx 1976b, p. 1021. Tomba identifies a third kind of subsumption in Marx, besides formal and real: the intermediate or hybrid forms of subsumption, which are forms of surplus-labour extorted by means of direct coercion. Tomba 2013a, pp. 148–50.

115 See Osborne 2016, p. 50. Also, against the Negrian conception of real subsumption underlying Harootunian, see Sáenz de Sicilia 2016, pp. 199–200.

concept of *hybrid subsumption* in order to complement its *formal* counter-part,[116] it is indeed arguable that the consideration of capitalism as a structur-ally heterogeneous totalisation does not preclude other forms of subsumption, but on the contrary calls for a more nuanced analysis of the modalities that labour relations actually assume.

This conceptual discourse about subsumption coincides with the first years of the International Workingmen's Association – founded in 1864 – which Scaron defines as the experience that decisively helped Marx to get rid of polit-ical and theoretical elements inconsistent with his own internationalism.[117] The development of his concept of abstract labour in the first volume of *Cap-ital* (1867), on the other hand, allowed him to 'synchronise' the diversity of the global without turning it into an abstract universality. This anti-Eurocentric approach only deepened in the period before Marx's death. In this manner, his exchanges with the Russian populists during the 1870s and early 1880s, as well as his readings about India, allowed him to gain solid knowledge about the Rus-sian rural commune and other peasant forms.[118]

Indeed, García Linera, referring to Marx's notebooks on Kovalevsky, says that this interpretation is useful for understanding the history of the Bolivian peasantry not only as a result of the colonisation and oppression of its local communities by other nations, but also and especially by other forms of pro-duction:

> in his annotations he demonstrates, as he had previously done (in the *Grundrisse*), that the subjugators can let the ancient mode of produc-tion survive, subjecting it to tributes and promoting certain changes in its relations of distribution and control of surpluses, as did the Romans, Turks and Englishmen in their colonies and, as I think, happened in the communities in our Andean high plateau, at least in some cases until the selloff of community lands in the 1880s, and in general until the 1952 Revolution.[119]

---

116   He does so in his presentation of Lenin's *The Development of Capitalism in Russia*. Har-ootunian 2015b, pp. 79–93.

117   Scaron 1972, pp. 7–9.

118   See Tomba 2013a, pp. 144–50. On the resulting contemporaneity as a *living disjunctive unity of multiple times* through abstract labour, see Osborne 2013, pp. 79–84. On the late Marx, Shanin 1983, pp. 3–39.

119   García Linera 2015, pp. 114–15. Marx's dramatic change in his political stance on European colonisation in his articles of 1853 can be observed in different fragments of *Capital*, e.g., in Marx 1979b, p. 473 and Marx 1981, p. 451.

As a result of these theoretical developments, history cannot be conceived anymore as a confluence of the multiplicity of social space-times into a single (relatively) homogeneous organising principle. Marx's conception of the capitalist mode of production is, unto itself, not simple: spatio-temporal contradictions, overlaps and gaps are constitutive of this social organisation. But when we pass from the *logical* consideration of the capitalist mode of production to the *historical* analysis of capitalism, history is revealed as an even more complex topography of social forms, producing times and spaces in tension with capital's ideal conditions of accumulation – what Tomba, following Bloch, calls a *multiversum* and Quijano characterises as the historical-structural heterogeneity of capital.[120]

Consequently, Banaji has called for a more complex conception of the modes of production, one that assumes different possibilities in which a mode of production can be historically configured, albeit dismissing the concept of a social formation.[121] While coinciding with this exhortation to think about modes of production in a way which would be impossible from a stagist perspective, this position nevertheless runs the risk of conflating the logical and the historical aspects of this concept – a distinction to be expanded in the next chapter. If we must in any case differentiate between a genus (e.g., capitalism) and its variations (e.g., peasant-labour or slave-labour capitalism), why should we keep the same term for both levels of analysis?

In a social formation, this process of spatio-temporal production is best grasped by the concept of uneven and combined development – a concept famously developed by Trotsky[122] – where unevenness is inherent to the mode of production (e.g., generating wealth and poverty in the same movement), and combination is produced by the subsumption of specific labour processes and industries under a dominant mode of production from which they have not emerged. The concrete analysis of a social formation should account for how the multiplicity of times and spaces set up a field of contradictions: different kinds of oppression and exploitation are made visible by this conception, as are its victims and its beneficiaries.

The conception of uneven and combined development, as Anievas and Nişancioğlu indicate,[123] subverts and transcends the stagist conception of history,

---

120 As regards to the capitalist mode of production at the logical level, this has been developed with detail in Tombazos, *Time in Marx*. On world-scale synchronisation, see Tomba 2013a. For a discussion of this approach, see Osborne 2015, pp. 39–48. Quijano 2014, pp. 285–327.

121 Banaji 2011, pp. 22–3.

122 Trotsky 1959. See Joel Wainwright 2013, pp. 371–91.

123 Anievas and Nişancioğlu 2015, pp. 54–5.

rejecting the notion that Western European history is a normative criterion from which other regional or local historical trajectories are to be judged. With the *Grundrisse* Marx opens the possibility – later theoretically developed in the 1860s – of conceiving history as *a spatio-temporally complex totalisation of social forms*; and with this conception of history the last traces of linearity and Eurocentrism give way to the materiality of human activity, which, with its determinations and contingencies, thus claims its central role.

Epilogue

When, in their early work, Marx and Engels claim that they knew only the science of history, their concept of history was far from the disciplinary limits then established in the intellectual division of labour. In line with this concept, Marx is a historian in a very particular manner: his conception is profoundly historical in the same measure as his vision of historical knowledge is profoundly conceptual.[124] The historical science, as he conceives it, is thus not external to the historical processes, just as the empirical and the conceptual are not external to each other.

Consequently, space and time are not external to Marx's dialectic, but inherent (both as a condition and a consequence) to the totalising character of the human praxis. Ernst Bloch's words at the beginning of this chapter – whatever the limitations of his philosophy of time[125] – capture the spatio-temporal complexity of Marx's concept of history, especially in regards to his theoretical developments since 1857. This conception broke away from the prevailing perspective of historical unilinearity by considering societies as forms rather than stages, and by insisting that social totalisations are products of human agents in specific social conditions. For Marx, a form of society, no matter how abstractly considered, is constituted by simpler forms (whose dynamics can be accounted for by generative mechanisms, in the terms of critical realism) that have their own space-times and are totalised by the conflictual relations between forces and relations of production.

Hence, in this conception, the science of history is not confined to the study of past deeds, but thematises the coexistence of different social space-times (with different scales and ways of functioning) in a single physical context. Social times and spaces are produced in history as a consequence of collective social praxes, which means that each social form – as a totalisation – is consti-

---

124   See Grüner 2005.
125   See Osborne 2015, pp. 42–7.

tuted by its own configurations of space-time, rather than a simple sequence of past, present and future on a homogeneous topography. Thus, Bensaïd has indicated that in Marx's concept of history,

> construed as 'backwardness' in relation to an imaginary temporal norm, anachronism ends up imposing itself not as a residual anomaly, but as an essential attribute of the present. Non-contemporaneity is not reducible to the immaterial unevenness of its moments. It is also their combined development in a novel historical space-time.[126]

Subsumption, under its various modalities, is the mechanism that integrates non-capitalist relations of production into the spatio-temporal network of global capitalism, totalising the socio-historical heterogeneity through abstract labour. By grasping this process as a geopolitical (spatio-temporalised) totalisation, Marx's conception of history avoids the trap of an abstract pluralism while at the same time arguing for the ultimate unity of human history – itself forged by the expansion of capitalism. In this sense, the consideration of space and time, ultimately derived from the spatio-temporalising character of the human praxis, are fundamental for the understanding of the uneven development of societies, since these categories help to make visible the unequal organisation and distribution of their praxes and products.

Following Marx, each form of society has a hierarchy of strata, with its own generative mechanisms, causalities and contradictions, which account for the diverse spaces and times in a social totalisation. Consequently, a historical conjuncture cannot be *reduced* to a single principle: in the Marxian method, each stratum is enabled by the lower ones, but its rules are not directly defined by them. Totality cannot function as a dialectical category unless it acknowledges mediations.

Far from speculative philosophies of history, Marx's social ontology has productive implications for historical knowledge. It opens the possibility for the explanation of particular social processes and phenomena through the decisive concept of *mode of production* – the foundation of his theory of history. Since Marx's method looks for real social forms in order to organise the categories, space and time are indispensable for his epistemology of history, and thus provide criteria for the next phases of historical research: theory, archive and presentation. But each of these phases has its own specificities, while at the same time, as argued above, maintaining a dialectical relationship with the level of ontology.

---

126   Bensaïd 2002, p. 24.

Theory, Models and Explanation

... one of those fascinating combinations of continuity of the discontinuous, of simultaneity of the nonsimultaneous, of recognition of the unknown – that challenge the historian's interpretive abilities ...[1]

• • •

What is perhaps even more important for the Marxist theory of history is the question of uneven development.[2]

• •
•

The phase of theory addresses the problems of the concepts and categories used in order to later organise the documentary data into causal explanations. The existence of this phase in Marx's approach to history, as Cohen indicates, marks the crucial difference in respect to Hegel's: while a *philosophy* of history provides an interpretation of a social phenomenon, a *theory* of history (which is based on the former) explains its inner dynamics.[3] The function of a theory is to provide an explanation of the object it studies.

In turn, the nature of explanation, according to Ricoeur, resides in answering the question 'why?', through a variety of uses of the connector 'because', and hence this operation has a direct relation with the problems of causation. Causal explanation is inherent to historical research, however unconscious a historian may be about this: historians are not simply narrators – although they necessarily are – because they also have to justify why they consider that the factors that sustain their explanations are better than others. They have to argue for the 'causal skeletons' that hold together their explanations.[4]

---

1   Echeverría 2010, pp. 125–6.
2   Lukács 1978, p. 118.
3   Cohen 1978, p. 27.
4   Ricoeur 2004, pp. 181–2. Ricoeur 1984a, p. 186.

In this sense, Mary Fulbrook indicates that a theoretical framework for historical explanation – or what she calls, following Kuhn, a paradigm – encompasses elements such as:

- a framework of given questions and *puzzles*
- presuppositions about what to *look at*: the constitution of the 'subject' of enquiry; a set of analytical concepts for 'describing' the character of past worlds
- presuppositions about what to *look for* (clues, also known as 'sources'): and an associated set of methodological tools and concepts through which to capture and analyse the 'evidence'
- a notion of what will serve *to answer* the question
- a notion of the *principal purpose(s)* of historical reconstructions, and hence of appropriate *forms of representation* for different types of audience.[5]

As this chapter argues, whereas some of these elements are more typical of other moments of historical knowledge, theory has an undeniable role in determining them. In specific regards to Marx's theory, Eric Hobsbawm stresses the importance of his conceptualisation of societies as systems of relations between human beings, where the relations of production and reproduction are decisive. In his words, Marxism

> insists, first, on a hierarchy of social phenomena (such as 'basis' and 'superstructure'), and second, on the existence within any society of internal tensions ('contradictions') which counteract the tendency of the system to maintain itself as a going concern. The importance of these peculiarities in Marxism is in the field of history, for it is they which allow to explain – unlike other structural-functional models of society – why and how societies change and transform themselves: in other words, the facts of social evolution.[6]

Although Hobsbawm's appreciation of the importance of the relation between basis and superstructure may be exaggerated in respect to Marx's theory,[7] his overall exposition rightly emphasises the idea that the fundamental aim of this theory is the explanation of historical transformation through the analysis of systems of social relations.

---

5   Fulbrook 2002, p. 34.
6   Hobsbawm 1998, 196.
7   In contrast Lefebvre, for example, argues in favour of an investigation primarily based on the category of *social formation*, which allows one to grasp the complexity of social activity better

In this chapter, following a critical realist epistemological approach, I examine the role which spatio-temporal elements play in Marx's historical explanations, and their utility in establishing a methodological framework such as that described by Fulbrook. To this end, the first section addresses abstraction as the foundation of Marx's methodology, and the implications this has for historical theory. The distinction between levels of abstraction allows for the distinction between the mode of production and the social formation, which is necessary for historical explanations. In consequence, the second section analyses the place Marx gives to spatio-temporal categories in his treatment of modes of production, and the final section analyses the role of spatio-temporal elements in some of Marx's particular case studies.

2.1 Abstraction and Method

Since history is a product of the combination of the collective praxes into a totalisation, dialectical explanation primarily refers to how the conditions of the internal relations of such totalisation – with its tendencies and counter-tendencies – make a particular phenomenon possible and give sense to it. The very intelligibility of history, as argued in the previous chapter, depends on properly apprehending this dialectic. The Marxian approach to historical explanation can thus be broadly described through what Tilly calls *system explanations*, which 'consist of specifying the place of some event, structure, or process within a larger self-maintaining set of interdependent elements, showing how the event, structure, or process in question serves and/or results from interactions among the larger set of elements'.[8]

Totalisation is thus the cornerstone of Marx's theory of history and its corresponding methodology. Given the ontological priority of production in social life, the mode of production is the criterion of such socio-historical totalisation,[9] and abstraction plays the fundamental methodological role in apprehending this basic structure of a society. This can be observed in Figure 1 below, where Dussel summarises the path proposed in the *Grundrisse* from immediacy to abstraction. In Hegelian fashion, the introduction to the *Grundrisse* argues that it is necessary to depart from the apparent immediacy of social phenomena by abstracting their basic determinations, in order to arrive at

---

than the basis-superstructure model, particularly since the latter frequently leads to mechanistic interpretations. Lefebvre 1991, p. 52.

8   Tilly 2006, p. 569.

9   Marx 1973, pp. 89–90.

more concrete concepts which can theoretically recreate the dynamics of the social totalisation. Abstracting the basic determinations of a particular form of society, Marx indicates, leads 'towards a reproduction of the concrete by way of thought'.[10] He emphasises that these abstractions are not just mental constructs, but that they correspond to the structures of the reality inquired into; the task of science is thus to grasp real relations and not just 'balance' concepts dialectically. In Marx's words, 'what is at issue here is not a set of definitions under which things are to be subsumed. It is rather *definite functions that are expressed in specific categories*'.[11] Thus abstraction should not lead to a realm of heuristic fictions, as proposed by Neo-Kantian methodologists – most notably Max Weber.[12]

Looking at Figure 1, after the process of abstraction between a. and c., the concrete totality 'in general' – moment 4 – totalises the abstracted concepts into a mode of production, and establishes its necessary relations with its own fundamental spatio-temporal determinations. This totality is concrete – 'concreteness is, first of all, precisely *the universal objective interconnection and interdependence of a mass of individual phenomena, unity in diversity, the unity of the distinct and the mutually opposed* rather than an abstract unity'[13] – but it needs to 'return' to particularity through the corresponding categories, in order to explain what Dussel calls the 'historical concrete totality' (moment 6), or the level of the social formation. Drawing from *Capital*, Dussel states that the relation between moments 4 and 6 is exemplified by how the concept of 'capital in general' explains bourgeois society.[14]

In terms of Bhaskar's critical realism, this method outlined by Dussel starts with the *empirical*, observable social phenomena and, by abstracting from

---

10   Marx 1973, p. 101.

11   Marx 1978, p. 303. The emphasis is mine. See also Marx 1973, p. 90.

12   See Weber 1949. As I maintain below, this feature of Marx's epistemology has important consequences for his use of theoretical models.

13   Ilyenkov 2008, p. 88.

14   Dussel 1985, p. 54. Dussel's figure is also useful insofar as it relates theoretical with non-theoretical activity, and thus raises the question of the historicity and politics of theory. In class societies, social theories and their methods are themselves part of an epistemic struggle and as such imply class positions, which in Marx's case is openly done from the position of the dispossessed classes. Hence, as Marx indicated, 'in the theoretical method, too, the subject, society, must always be kept in mind as the presupposition'. Marx 1973, p. 102. For the sake of clarity, this book deals with this political aspect of historical knowledge in the fourth chapter. For the rest of this chapter I will treat the theoretical-methodological aspects of Marx's approach to history without overt reference to their politics.

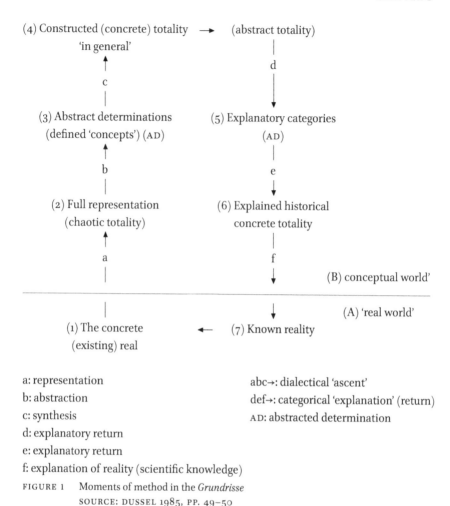

a: representation
b: abstraction
c: synthesis
d: explanatory return
e: explanatory return
f: explanation of reality (scientific knowledge)

abc→: dialectical 'ascent'
def→: categorical 'explanation' (return)
AD: abstracted determination

FIGURE 1   Moments of method in the *Grundrisse*
           SOURCE: DUSSEL 1985, PP. 49–50

them, constructs the mode of production as a *real* structure that serves as the foundation for the explanation of the *actual* social formations and conjunctures. Actuality is hence not the same as reality: the real is the domain of the possible, which is only actualised under certain conditions. This conception of knowledge is summarised in Table 1.[15] The generative mechanisms – which, as argued in the previous chapter, are forms in action – constitute the domain of the real, which is not directly observable, nor is it reducible to the actual

---

15   Bhaskar 2008, pp. 56–7. On the relations between reality, possibility and actuality, also see
      Lefebvre 2002, pp. 193–206.

TABLE 1   Domains of reality

	Domain of real	Domain of actual	Domain of empirical
Mechanisms	✓		
Events	✓	✓	
Experiences	✓	✓	✓

SOURCE: BHASKAR 2008, P. 56

events that such mechanisms generate. Or as Marx puts it, 'all science would be superfluous if the form of appearance of things directly coincided with their essence'.[16]

Since the empirical is the realm *par excellence* of the pseudo-concrete (which does not mean that it totally obfuscates reality),[17] abstraction is necessary so as to determine how the forms, *qua* mechanisms, operate behind particular processes. This operation determines their functioning under a limited number of necessary interrelated categories, and excludes conditions considered as contingencies, which are not a part of the mechanisms analysed, but of other mechanisms.[18] From this abstract totality, necessary relations – which were previously not apparent – give way to categories accounting for them (moment d in Figure 1). In this sense, the process of abstraction described in the *Grundrisse* intends to determine the mode of production as a *closed system*, from which necessary consequences can be deduced – such as the *general law of capitalist accumulation* in *Capital*.[19] These laws register inner tendencies within a mode of production and should not be mistaken for laws beyond modes of production, as Marx repeatedly emphasises (particularly in his well-known letter to the Russian populists).[20]

---

16   Marx 1981, p. 956.

17   The path of abstraction is the process of breaking with the pseudo-concreteness of everyday perceptions, as described by Kosík 1976, pp. 1–32.

18   For example, when explaining the composition of capital, Marx indicates that 'in a general analysis of the present kind, it is assumed throughout that the actual conditions correspond to their concept, or, and this amounts to the same thing, actual conditions are depicted only in so far as they express their own general type'. Marx 1981, p. 242.

19   Marx 1976b, pp. 794–802. Broadly, Bhaskar considers a closed system as one 'in which a constant conjunction of events obtains; i.e., in which an event of type a is invariably accompanied by an event of type b'. Bhaskar 2008, p. 70.

20   See Marx 1989b, vol. 24, pp. 196–201.

Indeed, the fundamental aim of the Marxian method is to determine the laws within the abstract level of the particular modes of production.[21] Hence, as Harootunian argues, methodological necessity obliges Marx to start from the presumption of capitalism as a closed system, and to deal with other forms only after establishing its basic structure. The society portrayed in *Capital*, comprised of only capital and labour, is a *real* mechanism (specifically a mechanism of mechanisms: a form composed from other, more elementary, forms), and thus helps as a means of understanding more complex *actual* historical forms by considering formal subsumption besides real subsumption.[22]

The examination of modes of production as closed systems can thus lead to the formulation of abstract spatio-temporal models – whose most basic characteristics would be the determinations of scale, configuration and rhythm – that help to explain the actual development of concrete social formations. From a realist perspective, the possibility of constructing models relies on the distinction between the real and the actual. Max Weber and Neo-Kantianism correctly conceived models as conceptual constructions that cannot be found empirically, but whereas the epistemology of transcendental idealism supposes that the necessity of a generative mechanism is imposed on the pattern of events by the researcher and hence considers models as ideas belonging strictly to the subjective realm, Marxian critical realism maintains that mechanisms exist independently of actual events, and hence that causal relations cannot be inferred directly nor refuted by observation alone. Therefore, the fact that models are imagined does not mean that they are imaginary, just that they are abstractions from actual conditions.[23]

Models are useful for social research because they allow it to approach new cases on the basis of already established knowledge. It is not necessary to go through the entire process of abstraction and synthesis of the mode of produc-

---

21   See Marx's 'Postface to the Second Edition', in Marx 1976b, pp. 100–2.

22   Harootunian 2015b, pp. 67–8; see also the criticism of Harootunian's privileging of formal subsumption, above, in 1.3. However, against Harootunian's tendency to comprehend modes of production as 'ideal types', we should recall that modes of production are real mechanisms and *not* heuristic fictions; Haldon appropriately argues that a mode of production is not 'an a prioristic construct within a series of such constructs generated in the abstract and against which historical data can be measured, but on the contrary a set of relations generated and generalised out of actual historical examples'. Haldon 1993, p. 41.

23   See Bhaskar 2008, pp. 45–7 and pp. 145–6. In this conception, as Sayer notes, 'scientific "laws" are therefore not understood as well-corroborated, universal empirical regularities in patterns of events, but as statements about *mechanisms*'. Sayer 1998, p. 124. Under the Neo-Kantian conception, on the other hand, models in historical explanation are a product of scientific imagination, which carries the historian's mind into the range of the possible. Ricoeur 2004, p. 182. See also Rose 2009.

tion in order to explain a social formation with characteristics that suggest that an already known mode of production underpins its social dynamics. Marxist social scientists – Marx himself included – have always used models in order to seize new social forms and, as we will see below, in Marx's theory not only modes of production function as models,[24] but so do other simpler social forms and processes of social transformation. Naturally, the researcher should be cautious about assuming too much from a model and not being sufficiently aware of the particular conditions of the formation – which eventually could show the model to be inappropriate for the newly-approached case.

Whatever their complexity, models are derived from closed systems, and spatio-temporal models in particular are constructed on the basis of the laws of the modes of production. A mode of production thus produces (equally abstract, but also real) space-times that can be theoretically apprehended through their corresponding models. As for their application, since the laws inferred from the mode of production assume a closed system, they do not necessarily lead to the same expected results when applied to an open system, with other mechanisms at work. Because of this, Collier argues that

> for a law to be true, it must hold when the mechanism it designates works unimpeded – i.e. in a closed system. And for a law to be useful, it must contribute to explaining events in open systems in which that mechanism is operating alongside others.[25]

The study of an open system then consists of relating different mechanisms at work in an *actual* situation. Hence after establishing how the mode of production works at the abstract level, Marx's method demands what Dussel (in the path from 5 to 6 in Figure 1) calls the *explanatory return*, which refers to the creation of the social formation for the explanation of a particular, concrete material society. These levels correspond to the distinction that Bhaskar establishes between the two basic moments of science:

> the moment of *theory*, in which closed systems are artificially established as a means of access to the enduring and continually active causal struc-

---

24 Witold Kula's model of the Polish economy between the sixteenth and eighteenth centuries as a particular case of feudalism is one of the best examples of a model approach in the Marxist theory of social formations. See: Kula 1976.

25 Collier 1994, p. 43.

tures of the world; and the moment of its open-systemic *applications*,
where the results of theory are used to explain, predict, construct and dia-
gnose the phenomena of the world.[26]

This differentiation between closed and open systems is hence the basis for the
distinction between modes of production and social formations and, as both
kinds of systems are real, their difference depends on their respective levels of
abstraction. We can observe the levels of abstraction in the Marxian conception of history in Figure 2 below – a modified version of Sayer's interpretation
of the Marxian levels of abstraction.[27] The first two levels serve as the matrix
making historical knowledge conceptually possible, and refer to Marx's ontology of history, analysed in the previous chapter.

The higher levels of abstraction contain more general concepts, with fewer
determinations. The higher the level, the broader the scope of phenomena it
accounts for, and the less it can account for their specificities. Hence Level 1, the
most abstract in historical knowledge, encompasses the foundations of historical materialism: categories of social being, praxis, nature, etc. Level 2, on the
other hand, deals with the most basic conditions and relations necessary for
every form of social organisation.[28] Sayer characterises it as the realm of transhistorical claims (e.g. teleology of labour, social relations of production) and,
although he dismisses the importance of the concept of *mode of production*,[29] it
is at this level where the theory of this fundamental Marxian concept belongs.

Levels 3 and 4 refer to a particular mode of production (e.g. capitalist, feudal)
and deal, respectively, with categories abstracted from empirical data and from
other theories, and with the mechanisms inferred from them (e.g. law of value,
general law of capitalist accumulation). Since production is the criterion for the
totalisation of the form of society for Marx, it is wrong to consider the mode of
production only in the terms of its economic foundation; the mode of production is the totality of both foundation and 'superstructure'.[30] Following another

---

26   Bhaskar 2008, p. 118.

27   Sayer 1998, p. 129.

28   See McLennan 1982, pp. 45–65.

29   Following Banaji, Sayer concludes that the modes of production 'are not limited in terms of
      possible forms of interlocking combinations of relations and forces of production as was
      originally thought', and hence 'the concept of a mode of production can be inadequate
      both as an abstract or a concrete concept'. Sayer 1998, p. 126. Nonetheless, Marx's method
      does call for totalisation on the base of production, and Banaji himself does not abandon
      this concept, but indicates paths in order to make it more complex, while warning against
      formalistic uses of it. See Banaji 2011, pp. 45–101.

30   For example, Lange affirms that a mode of production – defined as an ensemble of the

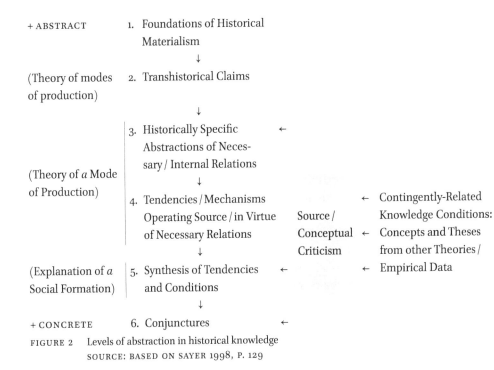

FIGURE 2   Levels of abstraction in historical knowledge
SOURCE: BASED ON SAYER 1998, P. 129

metaphor, the economic foundation is the skeleton, but not the whole organism; the forms of political organisation and ideology are as much a part of the mode of production as the forces and relations of production – albeit referring to different strata of causality. Marx's planned project of conceptualising the state, foreign trade and world market beyond his analysis of *Capital* would have also belonged to these levels of abstraction.[31]

The tendencies and conditions in the mode of production are synthesised in Level 5, with new sources that are incorporated on top of the framework of mechanisms from the previous level – it is the explanatory return once the mode of production has been constructed. This step marks the transition from a closed to an open system. This synthesis forms concrete concepts (e.g. Marx's

---

relations and forces of production – becomes a social formation when we consider it in relation to its corresponding superstructure. According to our reasoning in the previous chapter, this position conflates strata of causality and levels of abstraction. Lange 1963, pp. 15–45.

31   See Rosdolsky 1989, pp. 10–56. Matters of gender – insofar as they refer to the conditions of social reproduction – are also a part of this level and hence internal to the modes of production. See Vogel 2013, pp. 133–82.

concept of *Bonapartism* from his *18th Brumaire*, stemming from the particularities of the development of the French state) that help to explain an actual social formation, though these concepts can eventually become useful as models to explain other formations as well.

The social formation is then the most concrete form of society, understood through the mode of production prevailing in it, but also in relation to other social forms and relations that do not emerge from it. At the level of the social formation, social forms which were considered contingent at the level of the mode of production are understood in relation to it. Based on a methodological paragraph in *Capital* on the theme of ground-rent, the Venezuelan philosopher Ludovico Silva points out that while the scientific procedure leading to modes of production purifies social knowledge from what Marx calls 'adulterations and blurring admixtures', the concept of a social formation explains them as actual 'modes of existence' of the mode of production.[32]

The concept of a social formation, as argued in the previous chapter, introduces complexity in the theory of history through the combination of social forms that do not develop from the prevailing mode of production, but coexist or eventually adapt to it. Responding to the growing importance of imperialism in the first decades of the twentieth century, Luxemburg and Trotsky theorise about the necessity of capitalism to expand at the expense of non-capitalistic modes of production, whose inner development is therefore modified. Trotsky's *History of the Russian Revolution* systematises this idea through the law of uneven and combined development, which seeks to account for the unevennesses in the logic of development in a single mode of production, while also observing the effects of the combination of modes of production in each of them.[33]

This conception not only spatialises capitalism – at both the world- and local-scales of central and peripheral formations – but also implies a critical (non-homogeneous, multilinear) conception of historical time. Historicisation should hence account for this complex spatio-temporal topography and the social struggles that shape it. However, since the classics – by Marx, Lenin, Luxemburg, Trotsky – elaborate their theories in relation to the expansion of

---

32   Silva 2009, p. 137. Marx's observations on ground-rent appear in Marx 1981, p. 762.

33   Luxemburg 2003, pp. 328–9; Trotsky 1959, pp. 2–3. Although Trotsky uses evolutionary language when formulating this concept (by referring to 'advanced' and 'backwards' societies, especially), his work does not depend on a conception of unilinear development, and is most productive at explaining structural heterogeneity in capitalism. See Anievas and Nişancioğlu 2015, pp. 54–63. For Marx, as indicated in the previous chapter, this capacity of capitalism to profit from non-capitalist relations of production is realised through the different modalities of subsumption.

capitalism, there is controversy as to whether or not the concept of uneven and combined development is applicable to non-capitalist formations. In this regard, Anievas and Nişancioğlu argue for the use of this concept in order to explain the origins of capitalism by indicating that, more than a theory in itself, uneven and combined development is a methodological fix that allows social researchers to examine historical totalisations from different vantage points – just like Marx does with the different social forms of capital.[34] In any case, the *Grundrisse* repeatedly exemplify the heterogeneity of social forms in non-capitalist modes of production.[35]

Reservations also apply to the concept of social formation as a combination (or *articulation*, in the Althusserian formulation)[36] of modes of production. Although Banaji's criticism of the concept of social formation can lead to the conflation of the real and the actual,[37] his distinction between the idiom *mode of production* as a social and technical labour process and as an epoch of production helps to clarify this issue:[38] the notion that a social formation combines different modes of production under a dominant mode of production is then best understood as a process in which a totalising form of production (a mode of production in the second sense) subsumes labour processes (modes of production in the first sense) from previous modes of production (here again in the second sense). This interpretation is consistent with Marx's explicit conceptualisation of subsumption as a subordination of labour processes,[39] as well as with Banaji's own valuable contributions to the theory of modes of production.

Since his early writings Marx observes that older forms adapt to the prevailing totalisation process, which 'on the one hand, continues the traditional

---

34 Anievas and Nişancioğlu 2015, pp. 60–1. Indeed, Marx plays with historical forms taken from different contexts and subject to different conditions (e.g. his comparison of Japan's feudalism with that of the European Middle Ages), similar to how his economic writings compare the possible outcomes of forms when the related variables are changed (e.g. when he draws conclusions from the possible arithmetical relations between the times of the working period and of circulation in respect to prices), an approach that is quite common in the second volume of *Capital*. Marx 1978, pp. 334–68; Marx 1976b, pp. 876, 878.

35 Some social groups not only developed in the 'interstices' (or 'pores') of the prevailing modes of production – like the Jews in feudal formations – but so did some complete societies – like the Phoenicians and Carthaginians – thus forming a regional system of dependency of some formations on others. Marx 1973, p. 223.

36 Balibar 2009a, pp. 231–2; see also, Amin 1976.

37 Banaji 2011, pp. 22–3, 92. Also, see above, 1.3.

38 Banaji 2011, pp. 50–2.

39 Marx 1976b, pp. 1019–34.

activity in completely changed circumstances and, on the other, modifies the old circumstances with a completely changed activity'.[40] Marx demonstrates that social forms which transcend more than one mode of production – such as money – do so by adapting to the conditions of the different prevailing modes of production,[41] but he also refers to other forms not directly belonging to the stratum of production as cases of the uneven development of social spheres. His remarks on the validity of the antique Roman law and Greek art are perhaps his most famous examples of this non-contemporariness of social forms, but many other cases testify to Marx's spatio-temporally complex conception of history.[42]

The sixth level, that of the conjuncture, refers to the analysis of a specific social process from the point of view of the multiple social mechanisms that, relative to the main mode of production, determine its situation and development. It therefore focuses on a particular event or actor within a social formation. In this sense, the history of a form – e.g. of a city, an institution, class or a singular person – belongs to this conjunctural level, and its explanation is formulated from the perspective of the actual form, in relation to its corresponding social totalisation. The analysis of the conjuncture thus allows us to observe the movement of diverse mechanisms at work in a social formation in relation to a specific form. Bhaskar indicates that most events within an open system are conjunctures of at least two mechanisms whose combination produces effects that cannot be known *ex ante* and thus are not deductively predictable.[43] When applied to a present situation it can, however, be a means for a social agent (a party, labour union, etc.) to project possible outcomes in order to accomplish an effective political intervention.[44]

These levels maintain a relation with the empirical domain through their interactions with notions, concepts and theses from other theories, as well as with empirical data. Sayer's original figure includes among these *contingently-*

---

40   Marx and Engels 1976b, vol. 5, p. 50.

41   Besides the above referenced passages in *Capital* Volume III on the history of merchant's and usurer's capital, Marx explains in the *Grundrisse* the functional changes of money under guild conditions and under capitalism, relating those changes to the separation of working people and the means of production. Marx 1973, pp. 504–6. In these drafts, Marx also indicates that when relations from pre-capitalist forms of society are transposed to the bourgeois society, they become 'developed, or stunted or caricatured forms'. Marx 1973, p. 106.

42   Marx 1973, pp. 109–11. See also Lukács 1978, pp. 125–32. Bensaïd 2002, pp. 7–93.

43   Bhaskar 2008, p. 119.

44   Gallardo 1990. About the concept of conjuncture, see also Koivisto and Lahtinen 2012, pp. 267–77.

related conditions every kind of circumstance potentially affecting the process of socio-historical knowledge; in contrast, our modified figure limits those conditions to the specifically epistemological. Contingent conditions of a different kind (e.g., class and gender struggle, as he mentions, or ecological problems, we can add) not only affect Levels 3, 5 and 6, but also the most abstract levels;[45] yet this refers to conditions which affect the production of knowledge from without, and thus are not properly methodological conditions. By limiting the figure to internally epistemological criteria, such contingent conditions only encompass concepts from other theories, empirical data, and notions implicit in observation.[46]

Consequently, the contingency of these conditions in Figure 2 is logical but not methodological: the social researcher chooses sources and theoretical interlocutors according to the research problems to be addressed – and the problems are themselves oriented by theory. Additionally, an intermediate step of source/conceptual criticism has been added in the figure between the levels of abstraction and the contingently-related knowledge conditions, by which the empirical is called upon to enrich the theoretical components. This is crucial because, as Sayer indicates, the role of deduction in the movement between levels of the diagram is rather limited; aside from the movement from Levels 3 to 4, such movement requires the addition of historical – contingent – information.[47]

Hence, Marx's method consists in 'the unfolding, exposing and "complicating" of contradictions, the unfolding of the thing by way of contradictions',[48] rather than the reduction to an abstract principle or homogeneous field. This method of starting from the abstract and advancing to the more concrete is exemplified by *Capital*'s basic architecture: the commodity, as the basic unit of

---

45 This is the case of the transition in Marx from a unilinear to a multilinear conception of history: it is an issue of the ontology of history (Level 2 in Figure 2) that evolves from his own concepts and theoretical problems, but in relation to historical and political conditions such as anti-imperialistic struggles and the formation of the International Workingmen's Association, as indicated in Section 1.3. above.

46 Since observation is always loaded with concepts or notions, such conditions are both of an empirical and conceptual kind. Hence, albeit not explicit in the methodological remarks in the *Grundrisse*, Marx's method implies the critique of concepts and sources. It is hard to exaggerate the importance of this operation, since it is the necessary mediation that allows the abstract concepts to become concrete through the input of new empirical data, and hence to make them able to account for the specific social forms being analysed. The particularities of this archival phase belong to the next chapter.

47 Sayer 1998, p. 130.

48 Kosík 1976, p. 16.

the capitalist economy, starts out as a quite abstract form, but the deployment of its internal relations and the addition of new determinations render the concepts more concrete with the successive moments of the method. As a result of this, the concept of *commodity* is more complex in *Capital* Volume III than it is in the first chapter of Volume I; it also develops into different, more specific forms.

If we are to attend to the possibilities of Figure 2, instead of following only one line, as Sayer does for the sake of clarity, its shape looks more like a root: as the abstract forms become more concrete, different and new forms arise. Hence, the step from 2 to 3 potentially leads to several different modes of production (in 3 and 4), each of which – e.g., slavery, feudalism, capitalism – can develop into several different social formations in the steps from 4 to 5. Naturally, the real existence of such modes of production and social formations would depend on historical rather than merely logical conditions.

As regards the possibility of constructing models on the basis of the different levels of abstraction, we should note that beyond the modes of production – the historical scheme *par excellence*, according to Vilar[49] – concepts abstracted from social formations and conjunctures serve Marx's analyses of diverse contexts. For example, Marx's analysis of Bolívar is tainted by his concept of *Bonapartism*, which leads to his harsh criticism of South America's *Libertador*,[50] and he is not writing metaphorically when he compares the Roman plebs with the poor whites in the southern states during the U.S. Civil War: in both cases he observes common forms in different social formations.[51] But this is also true for *longue-durée* historical processes: in particular, as we will see, 'so-called primitive accumulation' has both a specific historical and general model character – although Marx does not consider the latter as a universally necessary path to capitalism.

In all of these cases, Marx finds certain mechanisms which could be used as models in contexts other than those of the social phenomena being analysed. In particular, spatial and temporal models – e.g. Lefebvre's abstract space and Sassen's medieval spatio-temporal assemblage[52] – help to clarify the tendencies that produce unevenness in the development of the diverse social organisations and the social relations and activities in them. In this light, Braudel's assessment of Marx as the first author 'to construct true social models, on the

49   Vilar 1999, p. 70.
50   Marx 1982b, vol. 18, 219–33. Also, see below, 3.2.
51   Marx 1984e, pp. 40–1.
52   Lefebvre 1997, pp. 229–91; Sassen 2008, pp. 31–73.

basis of a historical *longue durée*'[53] can be treated as an accurate description of the Marxian methodology.

Since space and time are transhistorical categories that acquire concreteness through successive levels of abstraction,[54] the heuristic use of spatio-temporal models should take the actual spatio-temporal conditions into account when applied to an open system – i.e., at the levels of the social formation and of the conjuncture. As Braudel argues, if the historian avoids the temptation to treat the kind of models elaborated by Marx as universally valid explanations, they would be indispensable as the basis for a more complex explanation of historical processes:

> if they were put back within the ever-changing stream of time, they would constantly reappear, but with changes of emphasis, sometimes overshadowed, sometimes thrown into relief by the presence of other structures which would themselves be susceptible to definition by other rules and thus by other models.[55]

Thus, when Braudel rightly indicates the need of 'putting back' these models into the stream of time, he is referring precisely to Marx's method of returning from the abstract to the concrete; it is the step from real mechanisms as models in a closed system to the explanation of an open, actual system. The models are to be contrasted with the particular conditions of the social formation; socio-historical knowledge is achieved by placing the mechanisms proposed by the models into tension with historical particularities – i.e. other mechanisms.

---

53   Braudel 1982b, p. 51. Braudel's concept of *model* is further clarified in this book, pp. 38–47; pp. 122–5 (in respect to Otto Brunner); pp. 141–9 (about Sauvy); and pp. 193–5 (about Toynbee). Also, in Braudel 1973, 418–61.

54   Social times and spaces are both objectivations and conditions of possibility of all other objectivations – and of all collective activity – and hence essential forms of the organisation of material social life. In a dialectical approach, different categories overlap without identifying with each other, revealing different aspects of a same object of study. *Capital* presents numerous examples of this: the *simple, relative, general* and *money* forms account for different moments of the value-form, while the transformations of capital – itself a form of value – are explained through categories such as *constant* and *variable, fixed* and *circulating, industrial, commercial* and *money-dealing* capital. Since social time and space are both material and formal, real and imaginary, it is important to keep in mind that these categories do not substitute for other transhistorical categories, but are necessary determinations of the organisation of a socio-historical totalisation. This consideration is important in order to avoid both economism and spatial or temporal fetishism. Marx 1976b, pp. 138–54; vols. II and III.

55   Braudel 1982b, p. 51.

Finally, it is important to recall that, although each social mechanism produces its own social space-time, it is analytically useful to separate space from time and vice versa in order to clarify different aspects of the social forms. Marx argues that the method of calculating necessary and surplus labour can be 'transferred from the spatial sphere, in which the different parts of the completed product lie side by side, to the temporal sphere, in which those parts are produced in succession'.[56] In this sense, abstraction can lead to models that emphasise either time or space in order to explain different aspects of the process of social totalisation.

2.2   Modes of Production and Spatio-Temporal Models

Braudel's argument for Marx's use of models leads to the question of how space and time specifically help to conceptualise modes of production. While in this section I concordantly argue for the importance of social theory for these categories and the use of spatio-temporal models, it is clarifying to start by addressing objections against their validity at this level of abstraction. Sayer voices such an objection, concluding that what can be said in advance about space – although his discussion is directed against theories of space such as those by Lefebvre, Harvey and Soja, the logic of his argument includes social time as well – is inevitably vague because most social processes have a degree of 'spatial flexibility'. He articulates this position with the following statement:

> for capital accumulation to occur, capital needs to be accessible to a labour force, and labour markets have spatial constraints created by the time and expense of linking up dispersed workers and jobs. Nevertheless, this doesn't say much about space, nor could it be expected to say much more, for the variety of spatial configurations which meet this constraint is considerable. Which spatial forms do eventuate will depend on a host of contingently-related processes.[57]

According to Sayer, social space (and time) are then only useful for the analysis of open systems, and of little use for the explanation of mechanisms in closed systems. Social space and time, we can therefore rephrase, are necessary at the level of social formations – and from the perspective of the conjuncture – but

---

56   Marx 1976b, p. 332.
57   Sayer 1992, p. 149. See also Sayer 2000, pp. 108–30.

not for the knowledge of the modes of production. Ironically,[58] this position does not take into account the characteristics of the levels of abstraction in the mode of production, instead judging the explanatory possibilities of space at the level of the mode of production by the standards of the more concrete level of the social formation. Since the 'modes of production are only a definite totality of historical laws of motion'[59] their spaces and times do not describe a social form in its actual historical-geographical concreteness, but are tendencies of such a complex mechanism. Between the contentless abstractions at the level of the transhistorical categories and the most concrete level of the actual social formations, the space-times of the modes of production are tendencies like any other in a mode of production.[60]

In order to argue for the pertinence of space and time in Marx's theory of the modes of production, I will now turn to the three basic spatio-temporal determinations mentioned in the introduction: scale, configuration and rhythm. The first has to do both with space and time, while the other two primarily refer, respectively, to space and to time. These determinations are the fundamental features of the spatio-temporal models in Marx's work; *Capital* and the *Grundrisse* provide key examples.

We can clearly observe Marx's use of predominantly spatial models in his pages on pre-capitalist forms of appropriation,[61] which he refers to through three conceptual constructs: the Asian or *oriental despotic* form (the most developed among the first communitarian forms), the ancient Greco-Roman, and the Germanic form. Characterised as fundamentally territorial, space appears as their central organising category, while in contrast to his treatment of capitalism, their temporal characteristics are not developed in detail. Each of these forms entails a different scale and configuration for its corresponding social space, which Marx especially defines through the relations between city and countryside:

---

58   Castree attributes Sayer's stance to the latter's 'failure to engage the question [of space] to dialectics in any sustained way'. Nonetheless, Sayer's own reflections on abstraction and method might have led him to a position that conceives of space in a way similar to Harvey's (which Sayer opposes). Castree 2002, p. 208.

59   Banaji 2011, p. 60.

60   On the concrete universality of the tendencies in a mode of production: Ilyenkov 2008, pp. 223–89.

61   Marx 1973, pp. 471–514. Marx's treatment in this passage coincides with Braudel's affirmation that 'spatial models are the chart upon which social reality is projected, and through which it may become at least partially clear; they are truly models for all the different movements of time (and specially for the *longue durée*), and for all the categories of social life'. Braudel 1982b, p. 52.

the Germanic commune is not concentrated on the town; by means of such concentration – the town as center of rural life, residence of the agricultural workers, likewise the center of warfare – the commune as such would have a merely outward existence, distinct from that of the individual. The history of classical antiquity is the history of cities, but on cities founded on landed property and agriculture; Asiatic history is a kind of indifferent unity of town and countryside (the really large cities must be regarded here merely as royal camps, as works of artifice erected ... over the economic construction proper); the Middle Ages (Germanic period) begin with the land as seat of history, whose further development then moves forward in the contradiction between town and countryside; the modern [age] is the urbanisation of the countryside, not ruralisation of the city as in antiquity.[62]

While the Asiatic and ancient forms are both spatially concentrated, their spatial configuration is quite different because of the lack of difference in the former between town and countryside – which leads to self-sustained villages – and the hierarchisation in the latter, where the city depends on the production of rural wealth. In contrast, the spatial fragmentation of the Germanic form leads to more egalitarian relations between households within it. Hence, only the ancient form would have a core-periphery configuration similar to that produced by capitalist uneven development, but it would not possess the predominance of an urban economy, as in capitalism. The spatial scale for each form is also determined by its respective economic totality: the ensemble of villages in the Asiatic form,[63] the city-countryside territory for the ancient forms,[64] and the household for the Germanic form. Capitalism, on the other hand, is the

---

62   Marx 1973, p. 479. In *Capital*, Marx also stresses the historical importance of these spatial conflicts: 'the foundation of every division of labour which has attained a certain degree of development, and has been brought about by the exchange of commodities, is the separation of town and country. One might say that the whole economic history of society is summed up in the movement of this antithesis'. Marx 1976b, p. 472.

63   Since in this form cities are not autonomous from villages and are insufficiently differentiated from each other, except in terms of size, it has no need for roads (it could be considered practically a 'nodeless space'), a feature that 'locks them into their closed-off isolation and thus forms an essential moment of their survival without alteration'. Marx 1973, p. 525; also pp. 472–4.

64   In this form, the city as a *centre* (with its officials) exists as an organism, independently of the houses that make it up; Marx, notably, overwrites the geometrical term (*Zentrum*) on top of 'seat' (*Sitz*). Marx 1973, p. 474. For a recent critique of this characterisation of Greek and Roman societies, see below, 3.2.

first mode of production that relies on indefinite expansion in order to exist.[65] Spatial scale and configuration are therefore generated by these forms as social mechanisms, and are not arbitrary elements introduced by the researcher.

Marx proposes different kinds of political organisation for each one of these pre-capitalist forms of appropriation, in relation to their respective spatio-temporal models: the Asiatic form, where self-sustained villages combine agriculture and manufacture, cities emerge only in advantageous places for external trade or where the head of state – as incarnation of the higher community, and responsible for war and religion as well as for the administration of the communal reserves and infrastructure – and his satraps exchange their surplus product for labour. The Asiatic, like the ancient form, implies warfare as an essential condition, in order to relate to other communities competing for the appropriation of soil. As for the latter form, another spatial element is central to the particular cases of Athens and Rome: the organisation of clans eventually leads from ancestry (whose extreme case is the caste systems) to locality as their founding principle. This eventually leads to a partition of the countryside into districts and villages, which do not depend on blood relations.[66]

Finally, since the Germanic form is composed of independent households separated in the forest by long distances, its existence is guaranteed by the bond with the other households with which they form a tribe; the commune exists only as the coming-together of the individual landed proprietors. The social space produced by this form of appropriation is more fragmented than those produced by Asiatic or ancient forms; since the Germanic households are self-sustaining, they can be studied in relative independence from their coming-together. The agriculturist is not a citizen, and the commune only exists because of the independent clans' need for war, religion and adjudication. Marx hence finds a necessary relation between the space produced by forms of appropriation and their respective political organisation, even if the latter is only indicated in the broadest terms. This relation is not contingent, but internal to the functioning of the mode of production, of which the political stratum is a part.[67]

---

65 'As the sole predominant forms of an epoch, the conditions for capital have to be developed not only locally but on a grand scale'. Marx 1973, pp. 505–6. See also Marx 1973, pp. 227–8; Pradella 2014.

66 Marx 1973, pp. 491, 478. The centralising feature of the Asiatic mode of production was later explored by the historian Karl Wittfogel through his concept of 'hydraulic societies'. Wittfogel 1963.

67 Marx 1973, pp. 483–4. As Anievas and Nişancioğlu affirm in their criticism of Haldon and Berktay, a mode of production cannot be considered without its 'superstructure': 'by defining a mode of production in terms of an economic basis distinct from a political

As for time,[68] although there is a plurality of spans in each mode of production,[69] their overriding temporal scale is for Marx the *longue-durée*: each of them evolves for several centuries before eventually facing a crisis or fading away.[70] The contradictions in the analysed forms are far outweighed by their inherent tendency towards stability: Tomba correctly notes that Marx tries to emphasise the element of invariance in them, in contrast with capitalism's dynamism.[71] Nonetheless, they have different rhythms of transformation and decline. The older modes of production are the most stable: the Asiatic form – with its supplementation of agriculture with manufactures – is especially durable, while the ancient is more dynamic and therefore more prone to crisis; the development of productive labour – through manufacture – and consequently of exchange, dissolves this mode of production and its corresponding communes. However, the preservation of the ancient commune, with its transformation of villages and landscapes, slowly leads to the destruction of its own conditions.[72] Since Marx argues that less independence of the individual in relation to the commune leads to more stability of the form of appropriation, the Germanic form, which later gives rise to feudalism, is the least durable form of commune.[73]

---

superstructure, ... they exclude the very social relations that make such exploitation an historical possibility, as conjuncture and contingent specificities that lie outside of the "mode of production"'. Anievas and Nişancioğlu 2015, p. 97.

68   Since the *Formen* deal with the specific problem of the conditions leading to the separation between the human subject and land, Marx does not refer to other times in these forms of appropriation, e.g. those of other spheres.

69   Marx exemplifies temporal differentials in capitalism with an analogy to the human physiology: 'in the human body, as with capital, the different elements are not exchanged at the same rate of reproduction, blood renews itself more rapidly than muscle, muscle than bone, which in this respect may be regarded as the fixed capital of the human body'. Marx 1973, p. 670.

70   Banaji 2011, pp. 87–92. The *longue durée* encompasses the apparently immutable elements of geology as well as other structures with much shorter time spans; its defining feature is its persistence over several generations. Among these structures, Braudel also mentions biological and mental frameworks. See Taylor 2012, pp. 35–64.

71   Tomba 2013a, p. 71. Through a quite different path, Koselleck agrees with Marx's vision of precapitalist temporalities: it is only since the eighteenth century when historical change became an everyday notion in Europe, displacing the until-then predominant idea of cyclical history as *magistra vitae*. Koselleck 2004.

72   Marx 1973, p. 474; pp. 493–5. Interestingly, this passage relates spatial change with subjective transformation: while changing their world, the producers develop new ideas, powers, needs, language, social relations, etc.

73   Marx 1973, pp. 486–7. Dussel highlights that in the *Grundrisse* slavery is a secondary form derived from the ancient form, as is feudalism in relation to the Germanic form. Dussel 1985, pp. 238–40. About the differences between the Germanic and the feudal modes

Hence the development of productive forces beyond the needs of human reproduction dissolves these communal forms. This is especially true regarding population: while capitalism requires its growth and spatial concentration (the need for surplus labour and the consumption of commodities), in these other modes of production such growth leads to systemic problems. Therefore, the emergence of slavery and serfdom – except in the Asiatic form – modifies the forms of appropriation and marks their decline.[74] In these cases, the growth in the importance of marginal forms leads to the negation of the main mode of production. This is the case with the ancient Romans, among whom

> the development of slavery, the concentration of land possession, exchange, the money system, conquest etc., although all these elements up to a certain point seemed compatible with the foundation, and in part appeared merely as innocent extensions of it, partly grew out of it as mere abuses.[75]

The *corruption* of these modes of production thus eventually leads to their exhaustion. Again referring to the ancient Romans, the *Grundrisse* argues that the massive explosion of money – acquired through the plundering of neighbours – in their social formation replaced the existing community, because money as the general form of wealth is *the* community itself, and does not tolerate competition.[76] The pre-capitalist modes of production analysed by Marx are organised and limited by the natural cycles; the barriers to production help to protect and stabilise them.[77] In this line, Lefebvre argues:

> societies built on a (relatively) stable but stagnant base are destined to be balanced in a static way. In this very stagnation they demonstrate an extraordinary ability to resist and to persist. The cohesion of primit-

---

of production, see Wood 2010, pp. 83–5; also, Tomba 2013b, pp. 396–7. Amin and Haldon include feudalism within the wider category of tribute-paying modes of production. Amin 1976; Haldon 1993.

74   Marx 1973, pp. 539–40; pp. 495–6; p. 493.

75   Marx 1973, p. 487. This is also the case in the search for wealth as an end in itself, which drove peoples like the Carthaginians, Phoenicians, Jews and Lombards in their interactions with ancient and medieval societies where exchange value did not determine production. Marx 1973, pp. 253, 858, 223.

76   Marx 1973, p. 223. The same occurs with manufacture, which also relies on the exchange of surplus products. Marx 1973, p. 494.

77   Marx 1973, p. 545.

ive communities removes them from the historicity which could shatter them from without, and from the 'incidental' history which would destroy them from within.[78]

The capitalist mode of production follows a very different dynamic in terms of space and time. If Marx's precapitalist modes of production are fundamentally conceptualised in spatial terms, with capitalism time returns with a vengeance: the dissolution of the former modes of production goes hand-in-hand with Marx's famous formulation of the *annihilation of space by time*. This process is made possible by the commodification of soil,[79] leading to the predominance of the urban, and a transition to a reterritorialised (Deleuze and Guattari), contradictory space (Lefebvre).[80]

While the *Manifesto* already indicates that modern industry established the world market, the *Grundrisse* expands upon the spatial contradictions involved in this process. The space of capitalism is world-scale because, given the national limits, capitalist production cannot exist without foreign trade, but the tearing down of national barriers is not an uncontested process. Firstly, because this expansion entails the conquest of the whole planet as the necessary realisation of capital's inherent tendencies; and secondly, because capital has to create the physical conditions of exchange – the means of communication and transport – without which massive commercial traffic is impossible. Capital requires its space not only to be world-wide, but interconnected.[81]

Capital totalises world space, but it does so in a structured manner, through historically produced articulations (or nodes, to use Castells's terms). Historically, this means that spatial routes have been built and controlled by certain states or companies with the means to do so, and this condition has led to the

---

78   Lefebvre 1991, p. 317. The non-accumulative character of these formations thus implies the prevalence in them of 'a time scale made up of intertwined cycles'. Lefebvre 1991, p. 319.

79   'Men have often made man himself into the primitive material of money, in the shape of the slave, but they have never done this with the land and soil. Such an idea could only arise in a bourgeois society, and one which was already well developed. It dates from the last third of the seventeenth century, and the first attempt to implement the idea on a national scale was made a century later, during the French bourgeois revolution'. Marx 1976b, p. 183.

80   Capital produces a stage 'in comparison to which all earlier ones appear as mere *local developments* of humanity and as *nature-idolatry*'. Marx 1973, p. 410. See also Deleuze and Guattari 1983, pp. 222–40; Lefebvre 1997, pp. 292–351. These theorisations were admittedly inspired by the *Grundrisse*.

81   Marx and Engels 1976a, pp. 485–6. Marx 1973, pp. 409–10, 280, 524–5. See also Marx 1978, p. 546.

development of some spaces at the expense of others. Marx demonstrates that different markets are spatially distributed both within and without national borders; for example, money in a country is concentrated in a single location, while the other regions develop product or raw material markets according to their place in the division of labour.[82] It should be highlighted that the patterns of unevenness are inherent to the development of capitalism at the local as well as the international level.

Space in capitalism is thus developed in an uneven and combined fashion: geographical unevenness due to the unequal distribution of the products of human labour is inherent to the capitalist mode of production, while the combination with other modes of production under expanded reproduction takes place through the various modalities of subsumption.[83] This sets the foundations for the development of the uneven configuration of the world-system: control over the conditions of spatial specialisation and the circulation of capital leads to the consolidation of the geographical relations of center-semiperiphery-periphery theorised by Wallerstein and revised by Castells.[84]

Castells's theorisation of the *network society* helps to shed light on Marx's conception of capitalist space-times by underlining the rhythms of transformation in the spatial configurations of capitalism. This mode of production produces a hierarchised space, but the neoliberal deregulation of capital markets, or 'globalisation', has shown that the socio-economic morphologies are currently more fluid than they used to be in previous stages of the capitalist world-economy, and hence has relativised the relations between centre, semiperiphery and periphery (which could be comprehended as *hubs* of different densities). The annihilation of space by time is a process of abstraction (in the sense of Lefebvre's *abstract space*), and thus makes pertinent the use of

---

82   Marx 1973, p. 280.

83   Marx demonstrates that there is discontinuity and eventual contradiction between the space-times of the national and the international economies. Marx 1973, pp. 410–11, 280. Sassen's spatio-temporal assemblages are constructed on this tension of the *inbetween* historical time-spaces; every analysis of space or time in a capitalist formation should have this contradiction as its point of departure. Sassen 2008, pp. 378–98.

84   Wallerstein 1974, pp. 349–50; Castells 2010, pp. 440–8. Dussel interprets the section on money in the *Grundrisse* as the moment when Marx introduces the problem of dependency (albeit not its concept) and the concrete world market into his theory of capitalism. Dussel also argues that, according to Marx, uneven development and dependence are inherent to value – a position he shares with Pradella's more recent account of Marx's theory of globalisation. Dussel 1985, pp. 104–5; Pradella, 2014.

highly formal concepts such as Castells's *nodes, hubs* and *flows*.[85] This fluidity of the spatial configuration of the world-system space is explained through Marxian concepts by Harvey, according to whom the contemporary prevalence of finance capital over the other moments in the metamorphoses of capital – production or merchant capital – promotes 'the sort of hypermobility and "flitting around" of capital that has characterised capitalism over the last few decades'.[86]

Until recently, the transformations in the spatial configuration of the world-system have been a matter for the *longue-durée* approach,[87] but newer conditions in the flows of capital have forced researchers to reconsider the timescale as not geographically fixed.[88] In this sense, the Wallersteinian model of centre-semiperiphery-periphery is useful to underline asymmetries of power and resources, but under the light of the current hypermobility[89] – and particularly now with the internet – it should be considered as a concrete historical spatio-temporal form of Castells's more abstract theorisation of nodes and hubs.

The Marxian theory of capitalism articulates multiple coexisting social times, a consequence of the multiple mechanisms that structure this mode of production. This is not only due to social forms from previous modes of production and other 'antediluvian' economic elements subsumed by capital, but is also, as Marx argues, due to very productive processes of capitalism expressing differences in respect to one another: '*the simultaneity of the different orbits of capital*, like that of its different aspects, becomes clear only after many capitals are presupposed. Likewise, the course of human life consists of passing through different ages. But at the same time all ages exist side by side, distributed among

---

85   Castells 2010, pp. 443–5.

86   Harvey 2013, p. 40.

87   Besides Wallerstein's aforementioned *The Modern World-System*, see also: Arrighi 2002; Braudel 1973.

88   This implies, as Sassen shows, that the material conditions for the circulation of the various kinds of flows should also be considered in order to explain the concrete spatio-temporal assemblages.

89   Referring to the concrete historical development of neoliberalism, Harvey indicates that since the 1970s the increasing geographical mobility of capital 'was in part facilitated by the mundane but critical fact of rapidly diminishing transport and communications costs. The gradual reduction in artificial barriers to movement of capital and of commodities, such as tariffs, exchange controls, or, even more simply, waiting times at borders (the abolition of which in Europe had dramatic effects) also played an important role. ... This greater openness to capital flow (primarily US, European, and Japanese) put pressures on all states to look to the quality of their business climate as a crucial condition for their competitive success'. Harvey 2007, p. 92.

different individuals'.[90] At a more specific level, even within a single process of production, there are several different times at stake, depending on their material qualities and the technologies with which they operate.[91]

However, the turnover cycles of capital are the driving force of all spatio-temporal processes in a capitalist formation. And just as national borders constitute barriers to the spatial expansion of capital, interruptions in the circuit of capital (time of production plus time of circulation) are barriers for capital's reproduction; the optimal space-time of capital is continuous and homogeneous.[92] Since the efficiency of capitalist accumulation is heightened by shortening turnover times, individual capitalists are driven to overcome every spatio-temporal obstacle; the contemporary social hypermobility of capital is an effect of this tendency.[93] Hence,

> while capital must on one side strive to tear down every spatial barrier to intercourse, i.e. to exchange, and to conquer the whole earth for its market, it strives on the other side to annihilate this space with time, i.e. to reduce to a minimum the time spent in motion from one place to another. The more developed the capital, therefore, the more extensive the market over which it circulates, which forms the spatial orbit of its circulation, the more does it strive simultaneously for an even greater extension of the market and for greater annihilation of space by time.[94]

---

90   Marx 1973, p. 639. On the 'antediluvian' elements: Marx 1973, pp. 105–6; Marx 1981, pp. 444–5.

91   'The various elements of fixed capital in a particular investment have differing lifespans, and hence also different turnover times. In a railway, for example, the rails, sleepers, earthworks, station buildings, bridges, tunnels, locomotives and carriages all function for different periods and have different reproduction times, and so the capital advanced in them has different turnover times'. Marx 1978, p. 248.

92   Thus, according to *Capital*, 'the circuit of capital proceeds normally only as long as its various phases pass into each other without delay. If capital comes to a standstill in the first phase, *M-C*, money capital forms into a hoard; if this happens in the production phase, the means of production cease to function, and labour-power remains unoccupied; if in the last phase, *C'-M'*, unsaleable stocks of commodities obstruct the flow of circulation'. Marx 1978, p. 133. See also, Marx 1978, pp. 183–4, 219. The relevance of finance capital is promoted by the temporal discontinuities inherent to the materiality of capitalist production. Commercial capital, on the other hand, seeks to deal with the problems of faster circulation. These are crucial sections in *Capital* dedicated to the metamorphoses of capital and its circuits. Marx 1978, pp. 109–229; Marx 1981, pp. 566–73.

93   See especially Marx 1973, pp. 533–5; also p. 634, pp. 543–5.

94   Marx 1973, p. 539. On the reach and limitations of this metaphor, see Massey 2005, pp. 90–99.

The gradual overcoming of these barriers produces what Harvey characterises as the processes of spatio-temporal compression, derived from the acceleration of turnover times.[95] The annihilation of space by time may thus better
be understood as a structural tendency in capitalism, rather than as a *fait
accompli*. Sassen's theorisation of the *inbetween* therefore encompasses the
contradictions specifically generated from the relations between national and
global markets – which Marx would have presumably explained in his treat-
ises on competition and the world market[96] – as well as the mechanisms of
subsumption necessary to incorporate non-capitalist production into the capitalist world market. The concept of the *inbetween* can thus be considered as
the dialectical counterpart to the annihilation of space by time: it highlights
the dynamics of historical spatio-temporal barriers, politically, technologically
and at the level of production relations, rather than their mere 'overcoming'.

Marx's considerations on social space and time are in this sense decisively
marked by the role of political organisation – and of the state specifically, in the
case of capitalism. This reinforces our previous indication about the necessity
to assume political forms as part of the mode of production. Harvey's reading of
Capital Volumes II and III shows how the functioning of capitalism, albeit ultimately depending on surplus value, also relies on the state's investment in basic
social conditions. Among the latter is the construction of infrastructure, the
enforcement of laws, funding for education and health care, etc.; these belong
to the secondary and tertiary circuits of capital, which traditionally depend on
the state.[97]

Because each mechanism generates its own spatio-temporal tendencies, a
mode of production, as a complex mechanism, produces different, hierarch-
ically totalised space-times. Marx's *Capital* discusses the production 'foundations' upon which the upper strata of the capitalist mode of production emerge,
as a totalisation that serves as the fundamental criterion of periodisation.
However, he also outlines some elements about the kinds of political organisation that emerge from this stratum: in particular, the state – which can assume

---

95   Marx 1973, pp. 516–23. On the spatio-temporal problems of circulation, see Dussel 1985,
       pp. 251–65.
96   According to Dussel, the concept of 'dependency' would have been elaborated by Marx
       in his treatises on competition between capitals, through the concept of 'total national
       capital'. Regarding the latter concept, Dussel indicates that 'the existence of the "national
       fact" in no way denies dependency, nor vice versa. Both exist: one as the partial substance
       (the nation), the other as the connection in competition (and therefore, explaining the
       transfer of surplus value from one "nation" to another, nothing more and nothing less)'.
       Dussel 2001, p. 262.
97   Harvey 1989, pp. 61–6.

many historical contents – is shown as a necessary product of capitalist rela-tions[98] that generates its own social spaces and times different from those of production, but related to them through diverse mediations and, eventually, through direct contradictions. The territorial spatio-temporal logic of the state thus comes into conflict with the transnational tendencies of capital – the world market being capital's immanent and predominant spatial tendency.

It is thus convenient to conclude, against Sayer's position, that the explan-ation of the development of a social form requires its spatio-temporalisation in respect to the mode of production. Under capitalism, in particular, such explanation locates the form within systemic cycles (the Kondratieff waves especially), and in relation to centre-semiperiphery-periphery configurations as well as the alternating scales of the world- and regional- (especially national) markets. These considerations are necessary in order to explain uneven and combined development in the capitalist mode of production, but are not necessarily valid for other modes of production, whose mechanisms call for other spatio-temporal models.[99]

2.3   Space-Time in Historical Explanation

A mode of production determines a set of laws, but their concrete functioning occurs in contexts where other mechanisms interfere with them, generating the processes and events that constitute actual history. In this sense, Marx's theory of capitalism as a mode of production, as Echeverría observes, estab-lishes the conditions of possibility of corresponding actual historical realities, and yet the explanation of particular cases in capitalist societies requires the consideration of other historical conditions.[100] Thus when analysing specific cases, the development of the specific states and their international economic relations are fundamental for Marx's explanation; his concept of a 'mode of

---

98   Jessop 1982, pp. 1–31.
99   Pierre Vilar mentions Juglar and Ancien Régime cycles as examples of non-capitalist sys-temic cycles. See Vilar 1999, pp. 98–105.
100   Echeverría 1995, p. 112. As Wacquant indicates, 'societies grow not as structural types but as social formations plunged in specific natural and sociohistorical environments. This requires that the analyst curtail the span of attention to definite geo-temporal ensembles; this is exactly what Marx does in his own historical studies'. Wacquant 1985, p. 35. In a similar manner, Wallerstein's characterisation of historical capitalism – as opposed to the abstract, theoretical explanation of capitalism – illustrates the difference between the levels of the mode of production and the social formation at the world-system scale. Wall-erstein 2011, pp. 18–19.

production' does not exhaust his theory of history, but is rather its necessary point of departure. His analyses of particular cases suggest elements that he might have included in his theory of history, had he seen his plan of the theorisation of the modern world to fruition.

In any event, like the scientific objects of meteorology, evolutionary biology and geology, actual history is an open system, and causality in it is more complex than in a closed system; its capacity to predict events is much more limited than in a closed system. This is not due to any flaw in this scientific approach, but to its very object: its mode of explanation is *a posteriori*, through the incorporation of other mechanisms, along with those that are central to the theory – that of a mode of production in Marx's case. Thus the analysis of social formations necessarily entails a degree of contingency which does not exist in the more abstract level of the mode of production.[101]

Marx argues, for example, that capitalist production developed earliest in Italy, but the revolution in the world market at the end of the eighteenth century destroyed the Italian commercial supremacy, reversing that process with an unprecedented impulse towards small-scale cultivation.[102] The case in *Capital* shows that the existence of capitalist relations based on a dispossessed labour force does not guarantee on its own the development of capitalism; here the emergence of a new world-system largely aborted northern Italy's ongoing path of production. This adequately illustrates Sayer's assertion that

> the same mechanism can produce different outcomes ... according to its spatio-temporal relations with other objects, having their causal powers and liabilities, which may trigger, block or modify its action. Given the variety and changeability of the contexts of social life, this absence of regular associations between 'causes' and 'effects' should be expected.[103]

In his analyses of specific formations and conjunctures, Marx starts by relating empirical agents – groups or individuals – with the classes and fractions of classes that register the contradictory tendencies around the processes of production; each generative mechanism has its own spatio-temporal tendencies, but has to adapt to the concrete conditions of the context where it actually

---

101   See Grüner 2005, pp. 24–5; also, Lukács 1978, p. 103. On the unpredictability of open systems: Bhaskar 2008, pp. 118–26. Gaddis also calls attention to this feature of history shared with the historical natural sciences. Gaddis 2002, pp. 35–52.

102   Marx 1976b, p. 876.

103   Sayer 2000, pp. 15–16.

develops.[104] This allows Marx to move between the empirical and the real, and thus to account for the actuality of the conjuncture in a concrete manner, in which space and time play an essential role. In these analyses, struggles for and against the state have particularly clear spatio-temporal determinations that are intimately related to the stratum of economic production. The Marxian analyses of the U.S. Civil War, the Paris Commune, and 'so-called primitive accumulation' are emblematic of this conception.

These cases have different delimitations: while the primary space of the analysis of the Commune is the city of Paris, the articles on the Civil War occur basically in the territory of the United States, and the specific *locus* of *Capital*'s explanation of the origins of capitalism is the English countryside. As for their temporal delimitations, the first takes place in the lapse of around two months, while the conflict between Union and Confederacy lasted for four years – of which Marx's writings refer to the first two. 'So-called primitive accumulation', on the other hand, develops between the last third of the fifteenth century – with the first mass evictions from common lands – and the last decades of the eighteenth century – with the advent of large scale industry.[105]

However, each of these processes cannot be explained by following these delimitations alone; on the contrary, Marx's conception of spatio-temporal differentiality becomes clear in his treatment of particular cases. Since the explanation of an open system implies the relation between several mechanisms – each of which, as we have already seen, produces its own spatio-temporal dynamic of scale, configuration and rhythm – these analyses highlight the multiplicity of social spaces and times needed in order to approach a historical process.

For instance, since *The Civil War in France* deals with a political event, the short duration of punctual events and individual figures play a more important role here than in other of his works. However, while the main events happen in Paris, they are not comprehensible without reference to the Franco-Prussian war and the National Assembly ('The Assembly of the Rurals') in Bordeaux; Marx's explanation of the rise and fall of the Commune resorts to the French and European scales. In terms of temporal scale, in this piece Marx emphas-

---

104   The last chapter of *Capital* Volume I, on the colonies, gives another example of this mediation of mode of production and spatio-temporal singular conditions: the availability of land for European settlers in the colonies prevented the formation of a surplus labour force, and hence the development of capitalist accumulation and concentration. Capitalist dispossession had to be promoted through direct coercive rather than indirect economic means. Marx 1976b, pp. 931–40.

105   Marx 1976b, pp. 878, 922.

ises the historical geography of state power in France – a two hundred year process of centralisation – as the background for the short time span of most of the writing, and he relates the transformations in this political process with the power shifts between social classes in this period, which in turn refer to the space-times of the stratum of production.[106] The French conjuncture of 1848–50 is a constant reference, especially in order to indicate the changes during the twenty years of Bonapartian rule. Marx analyses this conjuncture extensively in *Class Struggles in France* and his *18th Brumaire of Louis Bonaparte*, and probably the lack of a deeper economic and class analysis in *The Civil War in France* is due to Marx's implicit reliance on those previous works.

While the main spatio-temporal approach in this pamphlet was short-scale, the *longue-durée* and transcontinental scale prevails in *Capital*'s explanation of the origins of capitalism, where Marx relates four intertwined processes: first, the revolution in the form of appropriation of land into a regime of private ownership, which generated an early proletariat and the ascent of capitalist farmers; second, the emergence of a state that privileged capitalist interests through coercion and economic policies, and that especially benefited the rise of non-agricultural capitalists; third, the imposition of colonialism on the world scale. Finally, the fourth is a shorter process – it took place during slightly more than one century – which Marx summarises briefly: the agricultural revolution.

These processes responded to different mechanisms, and thus their space-times differed from each other in terms of scales, spatial configurations and rhythms; Marx's account of 'so-called primitive accumulation' seeks to explain the English case, but in order to do so it shifts spatially from that territory to the world market, noting the discontinuity and contradictions between the national and the international scales. Moreover, his explanation of the origins of capitalism indicates a profound and violent reconfiguration of social times

---

106   Marx argues that centralisation had been fundamental in the struggle against feudalism in France, but the state evolved into a parasitic entity with 'ubiquitous organs of standing army, police, bureaucracy, clergy and judicature – organs wrought after the plan of a systematic and hierarchic division of labour'. Marx 1986, p. 328. While generating national debt and heavy taxes, the state apparatus concentrated in Paris became increasingly a site of patronage and an engine of class despotism, especially after 1830, when the capitalists took the government from the class of landlords. Thus, through a highly asymmetrical production of its national space, Paris had become a centre of accumulation of political and economic power at the expense of the rest of the country: France was an epitome of uneven development. This was of course also an accumulation in terms of infrastructure. Thus Marx as puts it about the burning of buildings during the retreat of the Communards: 'the Commune knew that its opponents cared nothing for the lives of the Paris people, but cared much for their own Paris buildings'. Marx 1986, p. 351; see also pp. 329–30.

and spaces both in Western Europe and its colonies,[107] leading to the complex geography of centres and peripheries – based on asymmetrical flows of wealth – that characterises the modern world-system[108] and without which the establishment of wage relations would have not been possible.

Thus, the four-century period between the first laws of expropriation and the industrial revolution created the conditions for the emergence of several fractions of the capitalist class in England: there was a wealthy class of capitalist farmers – tenant farmers who hired waged-labourers to work in those lands and paid a part of the surplus product to their landlord – by the end of the sixteenth century. Non-agricultural capitalists, on the other hand, consolidated as an economic force in a much less gradual way than their rural counterparts, but also appealed to more complex mechanisms in order to achieve it. They drew from ancient forms of capital – usury and merchant's capital – and new production methods in manufacture, but also developed a combination of new state policies destined to benefit them as a class: colonial rule, national debt, the modern tax system and system of protection. By the end of the seventeenth century England had implemented this combination.[109] Hence, this period of formation of an English capitalist class took around two centuries, a period that set the basis of the modern national state-system. In addition to this, the legislation for the expropriation of peasants that started in the fourteenth century, encompassing laws against vagabondage, against trade unions and for the regulation of wages (to the benefit of capitalists), clearly outlined the state as a central agent in the service of capitalist transformation.

The agricultural revolution, in turn, emerged in the last third of the fifteenth century and extended over most of the sixteenth, thanks to 'the revolution in

---

107   The colonial system was essential in Marx's explanation of the origins of capitalism, because the colonies were markets for the metropolitan manufacturers, to which they – through looting, enslavement and murder – provided products (among them, the metals necessary for a money-driven economy) that generated capital. As Marx writes, sarcastically, 'these idyllic proceedings are the chief moments of primitive accumulation'. Marx 1976b, p. 915. On the historical necessity of capitalism to exploit labour in the colonies as well as in the central economies, see Grüner 2015; also Anievas and Nişancioğlu 2015.

108   The implementation of the colonial system went in hand with the consolidation of the territory of the Western European national states. The subordination of the colonies – through such means as the international credit system and metropolitan protectionism, when not simply through open violence – implied the competition between the strongest economic and military powers, and the definition of clear national boundaries. In this sense, Sassen argues that in Europe the concept of a territorial state was alien to the Middle Ages, and only came to be a well-established type of political organisation during the 1600s. Sassen 2008, pp. 41, 61–3.

109   Marx 1976b, pp. 905–7, 915.

property relations on the land … accompanied by improved methods of cultivation, greater co-operation, a higher concentration of the means of production
and so on, and because the agricultural wage-labourers were made to work at
higher level of intensity'.[110] The processes of the commodification of soil and
labour force – and, with them, of space and time – were decisively accelerated
due to these technical transformations.

Marx makes it clear that he does not consider 'so-called primitive accumulation' as a universally necessary pattern of transition to capitalism, but does
find that it was a model for the explanation of the emergence of this mode
of production in the Western European countries,[111] especially in France and
the Netherlands. Indeed, Marx finds common legislation, policies and imperial
behaviour between the English élites and their French and Dutch counterparts.[112] In this sense, this section of *Capital* develops a historical case study
of the origins of English capitalism, but also points towards an abstract model
of large-scale social transformation in which uneven development is a constitutive characteristic. In this measure, the abstraction from Marx's (theo-
retically-based) empirical explanation – which is not merely deducted from
the internal laws of a mode of production – also helps to explain other cases.[113]

Marx's analyses of the U.S. Civil War provide a yet more complex treatment
in terms of spatio-temporal forms; beyond the analysis of a conjuncture, as

---

110   Marx 1976b, p. 908.
111   In the French edition of *Capital*, the last modified by Marx, he clarifies this position: 'the
      basis of this whole development is the expropriation of the cultivators. *So far, it has been
      carried out in a radical manner only in England: therefore this country will necessarily play
      the leading role in our sketch. But all the countries of Western Europe are going through the
      same development*, although in accordance with the particular environment it changes its
      local color, or confines itself to a narrower sphere, or shows a less pronounced character,
      or follows a different order of succession'. Translated and quoted by Anderson 2010, p. 179.
      See also Marx's 'Letter to Otechestvenniye Zapiski' Marx 1989b [presumably written in
      November 1877].
112   The comparative history of these national cases (as open systems) would hence reveal the
      efficiency of the mechanisms described by this model as abstracted from its original Eng-
      lish reference. About comparative history – a central project for history as a science in the
      twentieth century – see Bloch 1928, pp. 15–50.
113   Based on these mechanisms of capital accumulation, Rosa Luxemburg maintains that
      capitalism requires the dispossession of resources from non-capitalist modes of produc-
      tion as much as it needs the exploitation of its own working class; according to her model
      of capital accumulation, an 'outside' – controlled through imperialistic militarism – is
      structurally necessary for capitalism. Parting from this thesis, David Harvey argues that
      'so-called primitive accumulation' is inherent to the structure of capitalism, which per-
      manently seeks to turn common and public property into capital assets. Luxemburg 2003,
      pp. 432–3; Harvey 2003, pp. 137–82.

in his analysis of the Commune, he elaborates a study of the social formation taking place in the United States. Blackburn indicates that for Marx this Civil War had three causes, all due to the need of the territorial expansion of the South: the exhaustion of their soil for agriculture; the need to keep their veto power in the Senate, which implied the minting of new slave states to match the new 'free' states; and the existence of a numerous class of restive young whites, which could generate domestic problems if they were not to find an external outlet.[114] With this multi-causal explanation, Blackburn tries to evade accusations of economism often formulated against Marx, who in any case explicitly denies that the war was motivated by the conflict between a protectionist and free trade system.[115]

However, we should observe – if we are not to unnecessarily consider Marx's analysis completely separated from his theory of history – that the three causes correctly indicated by Blackburn do not have the same explanatory importance. From this point of view, the basis of the conflict has to do with soil as means of production. Marx suggests that:

> The cultivation of the southern export articles, cotton, tobacco, sugar, etc., carried on by slaves, is only remunerative as long as it is conducted with large gangs of slaves, on a mass scale and on wide expanses of a naturally fertile soil, which requires only simple labour. Intense cultivation, which depends less on fertility of the soil than on investment of capital, intelligence and energy of labour, is contrary to the nature of slavery. Hence the rapid transformation of states like Maryland and Virginia, which formerly employed slaves in the production of export articles, into states which raise slaves to export them into the deep South. ... As soon as this point is reached, the acquisition of new Territories becomes necessary, so that one section of the slaveholders with their slaves may occupy new fertile lands and that a new market for slave-raising, therefore for the sale of slaves, may be created for the remaining section.[116]

The territorial problem was hence due to the struggle of two different spatio-temporal configurations of capitalist production as a conflictual unity within the United States,[117] both with a tendency to expansion, but differing in regard

---

114   Blackburn 2011, p. 9.
115   This position was originally quite popular in *The Economist* and other London-based newspapers. Marx 1984e, pp. 32–3.
116   Marx 1984e, pp. 39–40.
117   Marx 1984c, pp. 43, 50; Marx 1984a, p. 60.

to the relations between labour and capital – each represented a different mode of exploitation.[118] Since production under slave labour could only exploit the soil for relatively short lapses of time, open conflict was then a matter of time: the imminence of the exhaustion of their available soil precipitated the outburst of Southern hostilities when the presidential elections – along with the ongoing development of free labour in the Northwestern states – proved adverse to the interests of slave-holders.[119]

Marx uses these abstract spatio-temporal models in order to explain the singular, contingent geography of the United States and its specific political and demographical conditions. However, in his explanation the abstract spatio-temporal tendencies of capitalism have to adapt to the actual geographical conditions of the territory of the United States. The latter are particularly important to him, in order to demonstrate why slavery was not strongly supported in the border states. He finds that there is a relation between the number of slaves and number of free persons in respect to the political attitude about slavery: the bigger the proportion of slaves in a state, the stronger its tendency towards slavery.[120] In turn, this refers, as he notes, to a correlation between highlands and free labour, and between lowlands and slavery:

> the two lowlands separated by the mountainous country, with their vast rice swamps and far-flung cotton plantations, are the actual area of slavery. The long wedge of mountainous country driven into the heart of slavery, with its correspondingly clear atmosphere, an invigorating climate and a soil rich in coal, salt, limestone, iron, ore, gold, in short, every raw material necessary for a many-sided industrial development, is already for the most part free country. *In accordance with its physical constitution, the soil here can only be cultivated with success by free small farmers. Here the slave system vegetates only sporadically and has never*

---

118   Against the narratives of modernisation and progress that criticise slavery in terms of 'backwardness', Marx insists on the capitalist nature of modern slavery, noting that such barbarism was the condition for the achievements of capitalist civilisation. Marx 1982a, pp. 101–2; Marx 1973, pp. 224, 513. Banaji argues that modern slavery was a specific mode of exploitation within capitalism; he concludes that 'the slave-plantations were *capitalist* enterprises of a patriarchal and feudal character producing absolute surplus-value on the basis of slave-labour and a monopoly in land'. Banaji 2011, p. 71.

119   According to Marx, on the other hand, had the North not contained the expansion of slavery, the latter would have ended up swallowing the Northern industry, and reducing its working class to helotry. Marx 1984c, p. 50; Marx 1985, p. 416.

120   Marx 1984c, pp. 45–8.

struck root. In the larger part of the so-called border states, the dwellers of these highlands comprise the core of the free population, which sides with the North if only for the sake of self-preservation.[121]

The South, in particular, due to its lack of industry and its concentration of land for extensive agriculture meant for foreign trade, developed a spatial configuration without big urban centres: 'In densely populated and more or less centralised states there is always a center, with the occupation of which by the enemy the national resistance would be broken. ... The slave states, however, possess no such center. They are sparsely populated, with few large towns and all these on the seacoast'.[122] This meant that for the South the most important means of communication was the railway, rather than the highways, which in military terms made them more vulnerable if the Unionists took control of a couple of strategic points. In such a case, the Confederacy would be torn in two incommunicable camps.[123]

Marx's explanation of the causes and development of the U.S. Civil War thus prioritises the spatio-temporal conditions of economic production,[124] but also recognises the determinate role of politics and the military – the latter especially based on Engels's studies – as generating mechanisms with their own corresponding spatio-temporal scales and dynamics. Moreover, this explanation has its ultimate reference in the world scale, in the conflict between national sovereignty and world market. Marx notes that the effects of the North Amer-

---

121   Marx 1984c, p. 44. The emphasis is mine.

122   See Marx and Engels 1984, p. 193. This configuration without big urban centres implies a strong concentration of resources with luxury consumption by the slave-holders, which substitutes for the consumption by slaves; the urban economic centres needed by the Southern system were located in the Northern states and in Europe – hence the importance of the railways. Marx 1973, pp. 434, 528. This is the reason why Marx considers that the South could not be said to be a country on its own, sealed off from the North: while the latter had achieved a certain level of self-sufficiency due to its industrial development, its slave-holding counterpart depended on the wage-based capitalism of its neighbour and from abroad. As Marx affirms some years before the war, 'if ... the Negro states were isolated, then all social conditions there would immediately turn into pre-civilised forms'. Marx 1973, p. 224. See also Marx 1984c, p. 43.

123   Marx and Engels 1984, p. 194. This came to happen when the Northern army took hold of New Orleans, which isolated West Louisiana, Texas, Missouri and Arkansas from the Confederate government. Marx 1984f, pp. 201, 205.

124   In their private correspondence, Marx argues with Engels that these conditions would prevail in the outcome of the War in favour of the North, over the military conditions that at the time of this exchange tended toward the South. He concludes: 'It strikes me that you allow yourself to be influenced by the military *aspect* of things *a little too much*'. Marx 1985, p. 416.

ican conflict were felt in the whole capitalist world-system: the cotton shortage from the United States could not be replaced by British industry with Indian cotton, due to the lack of means of communication and transport in India, and to the bad conditions of its peasant working force. It would have taken years before India could produce as much cotton as provided by the United States.[125] The consequent rising price of this product seriously affected British textile production, a problem further aggravated by the contraction of the Indian and Chinese markets. Marx's analysis indicates that while during the first year of the war in the U.S., British exports around the world – except for Italy – declined, the French imports grew considerably, as did the imports from the Union.[126] A British military intervention – championed for some time by a part of the London press – might have changed the course of the war in favour of the South, but was dismissed due to the British dependency on Northern grain, the importance of investment in the Northern states (Marx also notes the importance of English letters of credit in the commerce of the United States with China and Australia), and the very high expenses of such a war.[127]

Marx's analysis of this case is thus particularly interesting because it reveals two different – interdependent yet competing – kinds of capitalist spatio-temporal development, and situates them in their specific geographical conditions. Once again, the formation of the world market is of the greatest importance for capitalist spatio-temporal development, but it is not merely a register of abstract social relations: material conditions such as topography or the decreasing fertility of the soil are determinants for its concrete functioning. Marx hence provides a complex explanation of the U.S. Civil War through several spatio-temporal planes (natural-geographic, economic, political, military), each with its own rhythms and configurations, and at both the national territory- and world-scales. This explanation relies on a combination of social forms which, although in general oriented towards the accumulation of capital, cannot be reduced to one single abstract mechanism.[128]

---

125   Marx 1984d, p. 56. Indeed, Marx later affirms that in India, 'as a result of the great demand for cotton after 1861, its production was extended at the expense of rice cultivation in some otherwise thickly populated districts of eastern India. In consequence, there arose local famines, because, owing to deficiencies in the means of communication, and hence the absence of physical links, failures of the rice crop in one district could not be compensated by importing supplies from other districts'. Marx 1976b, p. 473.

126   Marx 1984c, pp. 18–9 and Marx 1984g, pp. 63–5.

127   Marx 1984h, p. 111; Marx 1984i, pp. 128–9; Marx 1984j, p. 132; Marx 1984k, pp. 231.

128   In capitalism, such combination is ultimately achieved through subsumption, by which the labour-times of the different forms of production are synchronised – ultimately through universal clock-time. As elaborated in the first chapter, this is a central position

Epilogue

For Marx, historical explanation entails a dialectic between the abstract and the concrete, where the abstract models help one to grasp particular historical processes. This is not, however, a one-way process of knowledge, since the explanation of the latter in turn provides new concepts and models that contribute to theory at a more abstract level. There is a return from the abstract to the concrete, but the latter also opens the way for new abstractions that broaden the knowledge of social forms – and eventually, provide approaches to their transformation. Hence, against interpretations that downplay Marx's analyses of actual historical conjunctures, as Grüner says, 'those historical studies are not mere *applications* of a previously finished general theory on a particular case. On the contrary, each "case study" helps to *advance* the theory, to open new fields of knowledge for it and to provide new modes of production of such knowledge'.[129]

The consideration of determinations through spatio-temporal models introduces more precision into the elements for historical explanation enumerated by Fulbrook: it redefines the problems and questions posed to historical research, as well as the concepts and methods required to answer them. It highlights the need to organise existing sources according to different spatio-temporal processes in a formation, but also to assure the representation of such sources in it. Ultimately, it leads to forms of representation adequate to explain a complex totalisation.

As Tilly indicates, historical analysis should consider 'that space-time connections define social processes and that social processes operate differently as a function of their placement in space and time'.[130] Time and space are hence indispensable for social explanation due to their function as indexes of

of Harootunian's theory of historical time in his *Marx After Marx* (although, as noted above, he overemphasises the role of formal subsumption), Harootunian 2015b, pp. 55–72. On universal clock-time, see Martineau 2016, pp. 107–62. In turn, Martineau draws on Tomba's interpretation of Marx, according to which, 'in the world-market, the capitalist mode of production encounters traditional and unwaged forms of production, which are not specifically capitalist, and are inserted into the capitalist market in hybrid forms of subsumption. In this way, patriarchal forms of exploitation and new forms of slavery not only coexist with high-tech production, but also combine with it'. Tomba 2013a, p. 168. See also above, 1.3.

129   Grüner 2005, p. 24. The risk of not thinking the relation between the abstract and the concrete in a dialectical manner is to incur what Banaji calls *bad theory*, the 'substitution of *purely* theoretical explanations for historical research and/or recourse to a theory that is itself simply a string of abstractions'. Banaji 2011, p. 8.

130   Tilly 2006, p. 568.

the singularity of the studied case; the concrete analysis of a formation should determine the specific physical space and chronological time of the processes analysed – otherwise, we are not dealing with history.[131] Hence, as a historical event, it is firstly imperative to locate the first battle of the Civil War of the United States in Fort Sumter, South Carolina, on 12 April 1861, before relating it to other historical events and processes.

But beyond this purely formal criterion, historical explanation should account for the diverse *social* spaces and times as mechanisms with their own dynamics and active conditions in social relations. Thus, in order to explain the causes and consequences of the Civil War of the United States, as we have seen, it is necessary to take into account aspects such as the differences between the forms of capitalist exploitation in the Southern and the Northern states as well as the cycles of electoral politics in the country. The consideration of spatio-temporal models accounting for the diverse mechanisms thus contributes to Marxian historical explanation by helping to organise social relations in a particular formation, and by indicating hypothetical patterns of social activity and transformation derived from them. Marx's historical explanations are therefore always multi-temporal and multi-spatial, and they ultimately refer the perceptible social conflicts, through diverse mediations, to specific class antagonisms and modes of production in the particular formation.

The spatio-temporal development of the concrete social formations, as open systems, should be explained from the interactions and tensions of several forms, among which unforeseen elements (whose incidence is often seen as contingent) should also be taken into account.[132] Marx's explanation prioritises the strata of economic production and secondarily that of the political, incorporating other spheres according to the kind of social form he specifically analyses – his analysis of the Commune, for example, is particularly situated within the realm of politics. Every mode of production has inherent spatio-temporal tendencies, which are actually deployed according to other relevant mechanisms in the social formation.

---

131   This delimitation comes up in the title or subtitle of every historiographical writing, but can be implied by other textual means. We can consider this formal element as a transcendental condition of historiography.

132   '[World history] would, on the other hand, be of a very mystical nature, if "accidents" played no part. These accidents themselves fall naturally into the general course of development and are compensated again by other accidents. But acceleration and delay are very dependent upon such "accidents", which include the "accident" of the character of those who first stand at the head of the movement'. Marx, 'Letter to Kugelman, 17th April 1871', in Marx 1989a, p. 137.

The differentiation between levels of abstraction is thus methodologically fundamental. Accordingly, spaces and times become more concrete in the dialectical process of knowledge, corresponding to the level of totalisation to which they refer. The consideration of uneven and combined development – which is clarified by the spatio-temporal models – is then indispensable for the explanation of an actual social formation and its conjunctures. Moreover, this consideration has decisive implications for the phases of documentary research and historiographical representation.

CHAPTER 3

In Marx's Archive

He regards it as his task to brush history against the grain.[1]

∙∙∙

In general terms, we keep few pieces, those that we insert into a wider argument. But this rejected archive is not absent: it goes with us, beats under the text because it has convinced us about many things.[2]

∙∙
∙

In the epistemology of history, the documentary phase encompasses the operations required in order to transform a historical source into documentary evidence;[3] it thus provides the most basic criteria for the epistemic validity of a historiographical interpretation.[4] As Ricoeur argues, this phase deals not only with the selection and criticism of sources but also with the evaluation of the truth or falseness of the facts constructed and established by the historian,

---

1 Benjamin 1999, p. 257.

2 Caimari 2017.

3 Ricoeur uses the expression *documentary proof*; however, *documentary evidence* is epistemologically more accurate, given the more definite sense of the former expression. If the establishing of a fact is indicative (but not conclusive) of the occurrence or non-occurrence of an event, *evidence* better describes the relation between them, since – unlike the term *proof* – it leaves open the possibility of the eventual refutation of the fact. Ricoeur 2004, pp. 176–80.

4 This is precisely the reason why Hayden White suspends the consideration of this phase, opting instead for a formalistic approach where historians and philosophers of history *share* a common ground: 'in consideration of such thinkers, I will moot the issue of which represents the most correct approach to historical study. Their status as possible models of historical representation or conceptualisation does not depend upon the nature of the "data" they used to support their generalisations or the theories they invoked to explain them; it depends rather upon the consistency, coherence and illuminative power of their respective visions of their historical field'. White 2014, p. 4.

which should be 'capable of being asserted in singular, discrete propositions, most often having to do with the mentioning of dates, places, proper names, verbs that name an action or state'.[5]

Hence, source criticism is one of the cornerstones of historical knowledge. Yet although modern historians have always been aware of the active role of sources – this even includes the traditional methods of criticism of historians allegedly limiting their research to 'bare facts'[6] – it is particularly social historians in the twentieth century who have grappled with the implications of the social production of sources. In this line, the great medievalist Jacques Le Goff points out that

> the document is not a stagnated commodity from the past; it is a product of the society that has manufactured it according with power relations between forces. Only the analysis of the document as such allows the collective memory to recover it, and the historian to use it scientifically, that is, with full awareness of its causes.[7]

However, the predominantly institutional character of the documents calls not only for the awareness of each of the documents used, but also of the criteria by which those documents have been produced and preserved: the criticism of the archive – conceived as an epistemological and methodological moment rather than a passive collection of documents – is then the first step in this phase. Since dialectics does not assume that phenomena reveal reality immediately, but considers them as sediments and artifacts of the social praxis of humankind themselves,[8] the critique of the conditions of production of empirical data is an essential part of the process of knowledge in which such data partakes. Yet historical sources are even more complicated, because they are phenomena that refer to other phenomena; they pertain to the realm of the empirical, albeit in an indirect manner, as traces of the actual processes that have taken place.

Although Marx's methodological considerations stress the role of theory, his approach to sources available to him reveal his method of criticism at the documentary phase. This treatment is necessary in order to produce reliable information for the different levels of the abstraction of historical knowledge. Historical sources – and primary sources in particular – are the material from

---

5   Ricoeur 2004, p. 178.
6   Langlois and Seignobos 1904.
7   Le Goff 1991, p. 236.
8   Kosík 1976, p. 6.

which singular facts that integrate the realm of the empirical are elaborated, and this realm is necessary in order to know the actual processes and eventually the real mechanisms at work in a social context. In this sense, independent of which theories are used to question the sources, the limits of the archive – with its temporal and spatial determinations – are the limits of the possible historiographies based on it. Theory defines the kind of sources to be sought and the questions posed to them, but the sources cannot be reduced to the former; as Sayer states, the fact that observation is theory-laden does not mean that it is unilaterally determined by theory.[9] This point is fundamental to Marx's documentary critique.

The examination of this phase of Marx's conception of history in this chapter starts with a general description of his archive and method of source criticism – including his critique of ideology in the sources. The second section deals with several Marxian concepts and historical interpretations – his treatment of pre-capitalist modes of production and the Asian mode of production specifically, as well as his piece on Simón Bolívar – that have been accused of Eurocentrism, in order to clarify in what measure such spatio-temporal bias is attributable to Marx's theory, or to his archive.

Finally, the third section addresses historical processes analysed by Marx – the Paris Commune in *The Civil War in France*, the U.S. Civil War, and 'so-called primitive accumulation' – from the standpoint of more recent historiography, in order to examine the spatio-temporal explanatory possibilities of Marxian theory in light of more recent sources. Moreover, the productive use by these new explanations of different spatio-temporal operations for the examination of these cases (spatial analysis and internal displacement of focus, spatio-temporal scale shifting) contributes, as well, to the thesis in this book about the necessity of considering space and time in the formulation of historical explanations: that is, as indispensable mediations of every social totalisation.

3.1   Documentary Critique and Critique of Ideology

Marx is well aware of the spatial and temporal determinations of his theoretical activity, and specifically the ramifications of doing research in London, rather than in Germany or France:

---

9   Sayer 1992, p. 73. This irreducibility of the empirical to theoretical claims contradicts the relativist thesis of the incommensurability of paradigms. In this line, Adorno argues that there is a surplus in the object that cannot be reduced to the identity of the concept. Adorno 2004, pp. 183–86; see also Sayer 1992, pp. 65–71.

The enormous amount of material relating to the history of political economy assembled in the British Museum, the fact that London is a convenient vantage point for the observation of bourgeois society, and finally the new stage of development which this society seemed to have entered with the discovery of gold in California and Australia, induced me to start again from the very beginning and to work carefully through the new material.[10]

Although it is unlikely that Marx planned to stay in London for the rest of his life,[11] it was nonetheless a privileged place to investigate the development of the capitalist mode of production at his time. As Anderson remarks, not only was Marx in the only properly industrial capitalist economy, but also in the heart of the world's largest empire, from which he could be relatively well informed about non-Western societies and colonialism. As the economic and political centre of the British Empire, which produced huge amounts of paperwork and collected objects from all over the world, London was by then also a centre of information. Richards argues that this accumulation of data played a central role in the ideology of the Empire during Victorian times; institutions like the Royal Geographic Society, the Royal Society, the Royal Asiatic Society and, of course, the British Museum – all of them based in London – constituted an entire epistemological complex in the imperial mythology: an imagined imperial archive.[12]

However, since Marx's concept of history is not that of a 'past' left behind in unilinear time, his sources were not limited to the conventional archives. His analyses of current affairs required more recent sources, and thus fundamentally relied on an older, non-centralising institution: the postal service. This system was an important means for the circulation of information and knowledge, through which Marx kept himself informed about current events like the Paris Commune,[13] and which allowed him to obtain pamphlets, newspa-

10   Marx 1987a, pp. 264–5.

11   Against Marx's image as a political refugee forced to live in London, Karatani has argued that he was pardoned in Germany in the 1850s, but *chose* to stay for research reasons. However, this claim is not sufficiently sustained, nor explains why – as Sperber notes – Marx was making plans to return to Germany as late as 1861. Karatani 2003, pp. 135–6; Sperber 2013, p. 243.

12   Anderson 2010, p. 1; Black 2000. Richards 1993, pp. 14–15.

13   'What comforts me is the nonsense which the petite press publishes every day about my writings and my relations with the Commune; this is sent to me each day from Paris. It shows that the Versailles police is very hard put to it to get hold of genuine documents. My relations with the Commune were maintained through a German merchant who travels on business between Paris and London all the year round'. Marx 1989c, pp. 150–1.

pers – whole or in cuts – and books from different countries, especially from Europe. Newspapers were particularly important for the flow of information, and London was a privileged hub for this kind of material.[14] Private venues in London collected information from countries and regions abroad; during the U.S. Civil War, for instance, Marx attended a place called the 'American Coffee-house', where he had access to newly arrived periodicals from the United States. This proved to be important because, according to him, the British papers often suppressed useful information about the war.[15]

However, the seat of the Empire also had its limitations as a vantage point, the most obvious being the spectre of Eurocentrism – now a commonplace accusation against Marx by scholars in post- and de-colonial studies[16] (and an issue I address in the next section). At this point, I have argued that the Marxian conception of history as a decentred, multi-temporal and multi-spatial totalisation is incompatible with such ideological constructs. But did Marx's archive prevent him from overcoming them?

An examination of Marx's historical sources is a useful starting point to address this matter. In his more historiographical texts, he cites three kinds of sources: books, official reports, and newspapers.[17] These kinds of sources, however, serve different functions in Marx's explanation of historical processes, especially with regard to temporality. Most of the longer-term processes – especially modes of production – are constructed on the basis of already existing historiography (that Marx reinterprets by conceptually problematising it), while processes from the point of view of shorter-term temporalities – con-

---

14   'Besides railways and steamboats, the electric telegraph contributed decisively with the acceleration of circulation in the nineteenth century press: dispatches began to be sent routinely by wire to London newspapers from provincial centers or from abroad by means of press agencies such as Reuters (1851), the Press Association (1868) and the Central News Association (1870)'. Wiener 2015, pp. 212. Marx and Engels often exchanged newspapers via mail, although from their correspondence it appears that Marx, in London, was better situated than Engels, in Manchester, who more often asked Marx for these materials.

15   Marx 1985a, p. 305; Marx 1985b, p. 429. About the British press, see King 2007.

16   Chakrabarty 2000, pp. 47–71; Lander 2006, pp. 209–43. See below, 3.2.

17   Specifically, the main sources in this section are those which deal with the explanation of particular spatio-temporal cases in *Capital, Grundrisse, The Civil War in France*, and Marx's articles on the U.S. Civil War. The English language edition of the *MECW* provides a list of these sources: 'Index of Quoted and Mentioned Literature', in Marx and Engels 1984b, pp. 430–44; Marx and Engels 1986a, pp. 741–59; Marx and Engels 1986b, pp. 568–76; Marx and Engels 1987, pp. 564–5; Marx and Engels 1996, pp. 818–52; Marx and Engels 1997, pp. 540–6; Marx and Engels 1998, pp. 920–32. Other historical manuscripts are very occasionally referenced, as in the case of the eccentric note on the Duchess of Orkney. Marx 1976b, p. 884.

junctures, particularly – generally utilise testimonies, reports and newspapers. Official sources, which often contain statistical information, also allow Marx to address diverse social situations in specific moments, from the point of view of national territories.

Regarding the processes of expropriation in *Capital*'s chapters on 'primitive accumulation', Marx cites mostly British authors – which is to be expected in a historical analysis centred on the development of English capitalism – and a notable part of his secondary sources constitute the latest available research, published after 1850. When he quotes other European historians, he does so to indicate similar processes in neighbouring territories, hence observing a common logic of capitalism beyond the particular conditions in each. The section on precapitalist formations in the *Grundrisse*, on the other hand, is largely based on Niebuhr's *Römische Geschichte* (second edition, 1827), especially in regards to the ancient and Germanic forms of appropriation. This three-volume book is abundant with ethnographical details, and for decades was an unavoidable study on the matter, especially due to its thorough criticism of sources, to which Ranke – the founder of modern documentary criticism – was openly indebted.[18] Marx also cites Dureau de la Malle's *Économie politique des Romains* (1840), another book detailing around a thousand years of Roman civilisation. The availability of studies based on a considerable amount of data from primary sources, comprising several centuries, facilitates the observation of broader tendencies and the construction of more abstract models – particularly modes of production. Large aggregates of data from sources are essential for the method of abstraction, whereas an insufficient amount may lead to models of strictly anecdotal validity. The higher the level of abstraction of the conceptual totality to be constructed, the more 'serialised' the utilised sources should be.

While testimonies and narratives of singular events are more important when analyses deal with shorter conjunctures, when Marx considers longer spans of time he also addresses punctual events, incorporating them into the less observable long-term processes.[19] The testimonies of ancients like Juvenal, Cicero and Cato are used to illustrate and explain structures in the *Formen*

---

18   Iggers 1968, pp. 65–6.

19   Although in his letters Marx affirms the use of testimonies in some of his analyses, for example regarding the cases of the U.S. Civil War and Paris Commune, he did not cite them due to the format in which these studies were written – and also to protect his interlocutors, as in the case of the Parisian events of 1871. On Marx's and Engels's unpublished sources, see Thompson 2000, pp. 42–3.

section of the *Grundrisse*, while those of Thomas More, Francis Bacon and Edmund Burke, among others, help to elaborate Marx's histories of commerce, finance and the privatisation of land ownership. Testimonies such as these are regularly used by Marx as illustrations that help to make the effects of wider social tendencies more representative.[20]

As opposed to testimonies, which usually account for singular events, official reports enable one to determine patterns, because they are composed and archived precisely in order to address situations of a similar type; they not only help to illustrate a process, but to find spatial and temporal tendencies in it.[21] The production of these kinds of sources grew as the state assumed new functions of social control over the population, eventually giving rise to the science of statistics.[22] The censuses of the United States in 1860[23] and of England and Wales in 1861 allowed Marx to differentiate the spatial tendencies within the respective national cases. His interpretation of these tendencies in each of the regions of the United States (North, South, Intermediate and Northwestern states) regarding the contradictions between slave and salaried labour was based on the first census, while the second one was a main source for his analysis of the labour force in *Capital's* chapter on the general law of capitalist accumulation, along with the reports on the state of public health and statistics for agriculture in Ireland.[24]

In this use of official reports, *Capital* followed in the steps of Engels's 1845 *The Condition of the Working Class in England*. Along with the aforementioned reports on public health, other documents by commissioners and inspectors dealt with the situation of transportation, agriculture, banking, child labour, etc. Most of the official reports cited in *Capital* are British, with occasional counterparts from the United States, France and Germany. Temporally, most

---

20   On the role of testimony for historiography, Ricoeur 2004, pp. 161–6; also Osborne 2013, pp. 190–201.

21   The use of series of quantitative data is one of the most important methodological contributions of twentieth-century social history, particularly in the fields of economic and demographic history. Burke 1990, pp. 74–9.

22   The very concept of *population* is a product of this process. Foucault 2004; and Foucault 2009.

23   The editors of volume 19 of the *Collected Works* indicate that Marx obtained this census's data through a publication by the British newspaper *The Times*. See Marx 1984b, p. 45 footnote a.

24   This chapter of *Capital* is particularly attendant to space, both at the level of the differences between industry and agriculture in the British counties, and at the *lived* experiences of the working class.

of these documents are contemporary with Marx's writing of *Capital* – the late 1850s and 1860s – with the exception of reports on factories, from which he utilises data from the 1840s for his chapters on the working day and in the fragment on the cotton crisis in Volume III.

While Marx occasionally cites French, Dutch or German official publications, he generally uses these sources in order to compare them with the British documents that are overwhelmingly prevalent in his analyses, from which he presents the history of English capitalism as representative of the Western European path to capitalism. Among the publications of legislative acts, the 1810 edition of the English *Statutes of the Realm* is particularly important for Marx's account of the laws against the expropriated between the sixteenth and nineteenth centuries. This source reveals the tendency of the British élites to respond with increasingly violent repression of the problems created by the dispossession of the peasantry, but it does not show the concrete implementation of the laws in different regions and conjunctures. Therefore, and especially in terms of space, the section on 'primitive accumulation' deals in a general fashion with these processes in Britain.

Finally, Marx constantly draws upon periodicals in his writings. *The Economist* is an ubiquitous interlocutor in his *oeuvre*, as a source both of data to be reinterpreted and explanations to be refuted. On the other hand, although cited in *Capital* – where they especially served as illustrations – newspapers for mass consumption were, as mentioned before, particularly important for Marx's analyses of then-current situations and of short-term processes. Unsurprisingly, the editors of the volumes of the *Collected Works* corresponding to Marx's analyses of the U.S. and French civil wars find numerous references to the press in the respective countries during these conjunctures. These sources were not made explicit by Marx due to the original formats of these publications: newspaper articles in the case of the U.S. Civil War, and a pamphlet in the case of the Paris Commune.

The variety of kinds of sources in Marx's writings are indicative of the differentiality of times in his approach to the processes he analyses; even in his smaller-scale studies, Marx combines different spatial and temporal scales in order to explain concrete conjunctures. Sources possess their respective levels of abstraction, and the predominance in a text of a certain kind of source depends on the principal scale of the historical process to be analysed – newspapers do not usually interpret *longue-durée* processes, for example – as well as the moment of their issue. Analytical studies of particular conjunctures and historical periods, for example, take more time to get edited and published and hence are not useful as main sources when addressing events currently in progress.

In any case, the balance of Marx's sources shows an overwhelming majority of Western European – and particularly British – authors published in the nineteenth century. This is understandable given the intellectual world in which Marx works, but of course suggests a spatio-temporal bias for the formulation of his theory and analyses of social formations. Since Marx's method does not pretend to speak for the subaltern, but *does* intend to demonstrate how the logic of capitalistic production creates subalternity – basically, but not exclusively, class oppression – the critique of sources is fundamental to the kind of history Marx is writing. Moreover, most of his sources are apologia for capitalism,[25] hence making it indispensable for him to read through their omissions, distortions and involuntary confessions; his treatment of sources follows the systematic process of the critique of ideology, representative of an hermeneutics of suspicion.[26] And just as a substantial part of *Capital*'s method consists in indicating the inner contradictions of bourgeois political economy – its *immanent critique*[27] – his treatment of sources confronts the document with the class standpoint of its author. This procedure does not assume the mere falsity of the document's content, but sheds new light on it.

Hence one of the strategies Marx follows is to criticise the insufficiency of the interpretations of these authors in relation to the information within their own expositions. His *Ethnographic Notebooks*, where he engages in a reading of texts from several Western European observers of peripheral societies, is a clear example of this kind of criticism. In his notebooks on Phear's book, Marx mocks this author's affirmations that the social structure of the villages in West Bengal is feudal and that the 'private family' is the basic unit in 'Indoaryan' societies.[28] The latter thesis had also been assumed by Henry Maine (from whom Phear draws some of his information in order to build his prototypes of 'Aryan' villages), who sought to justify the imposition of capitalist private property in India. Marx is especially critical of Maine, indicating that his conclusions are

---

25   In Marx's lifetime, documents from popular classes and other subaltern social sectors were quite limited, a limitation that led researchers of popular cultures in the twentieth century to the formulation of oral history.

26   Ricoeur 1970, pp. 32–7. Grüner explains that 'Marx starts by *accepting* the "text" of bourgeois political economy as a *partial* truth and then questions its "silences" and inconsistencies. ... Marx produces his own theory, his own *critical interpretation* of capitalism ... by constructing upon those "voids" of classical economy'. Grüner 2005, p. 30.

27   Antonio 1981, pp. 330–45. Echeverría argues that *Capital*'s method of critique of political economy corresponds to what Ginzburg calls an 'evidential paradigm', a reading that reveals what is hidden through the observation of a text from the point of view of its symptoms. Echeverría 2003–4, pp. 29–34.

28   Marx 1974b, pp. 256, 281.

drawn from the wrong theoretical assumptions – such as considering the state as an autonomous entity in relation to society – and are rather soft on the clergy, lawyers and higher classes.[29]

Marx also regularly criticises one of his most important sources of statistical information, *The Economist*, by deconstructing its analyses of data. He states about an article in late 1861:

> from statistics given as to the population and the area of the United States, he [the writer of the article] arrives at the conclusion that there would be room enough for the establishment of at least seven vast empires, and that consequently, 'the dream of universal dominion' ought to be banished from the hearts of the Unionists. The only rational inference which *The Economist* might have drawn from its own statistical statements, viz., that the Northerners, even if they liked to do so, could not desist from their claims without sacrificing to Slavery the vast States and Territories 'in which Slavery still lingers, but cannot maintain itself as a permanent institution' – this only rational conclusion he successfully contrives not even to touch upon.[30]

Remarks like these criticise the inconsistency of the conclusions by relating them to the subject position of the authors. Although Marx often dismisses authors by simply questioning their intelligence, when he criticises authors that he respects, such as Smith or Ricardo, he relates their limitations to their class positions.[31] This kind of criticism is related to what Langlois's and Seignobos's *Introduction to the Study of History* – the manual of 'positivistic' historiography *par excellence* – called negative internal criticism, where the good faith and accuracy of the authors are evaluated.[32] However, while these French historians reduce this aspect of criticism to the possibility of superficial cognitive or moral problems such as 'error or mendacity', Marx's critique departs from a conception where knowledge is mediated by the subject's conditions. Hence

---

29   Krader 1974, p. 32; Marx 1974a, 326–30.

30   Marx 1984a, p. 60.

31   We can see the contrast between Marx's creative insulting and his historicising criticism in his description of Bentham as a 'genius in the way of bourgeois stupidity', on the one hand, and his comments on Aristotle's inability to conceive labour as a universal measure and on Franklin's definition of man as a tool-making animal, on the other. Marx 1976b, pp. 759, 151–2, 444.

32   Burke 1990, pp. 6–11. Langlois and Seignobos 1904, pp. 155–90. Since Marx very rarely worked with archival sources, he did not need to do external criticism of his sources – the procedures ensuring the legitimacy of the document.

not all knowledge is accessible to any one person, and Marx is especially attent-
ive to the ideological closures at work in discourses about capitalism.

Marx's other strategy is to stress the social contradictions admitted in texts
by his theoretical and political adversaries, and then elaborate on them. In
regards to this approach, Ginzburg indicates that 'reading historical testimonies against the grain, as Walter Benjamin suggested – that is, against the intentions of the person or persons producing them (even if those intentions must
of course be taken into account) – means supposing that every text includes
uncontrolled elements'.[33] These elements are precisely what allows Marx to
formulate his historical analyses as what would later be called *counterhistor-
ies*, against interpretations of history that legitimise the existing relations of
exploitation and domination.[34]

Thus, at the beginning of his analysis about the origins of capitalism, Marx
says he quotes Thomas B. Macaulay's *History of England* 'because as a systematic falsifier of history he minimises facts of this kind [the expropriation of
peasants] as much as possible'.[35] In the same fashion, his use of official reports
about the situation of the working class in England takes advantage of their
condition as instruments of state policy, which makes them unlikely to be
sympathetic towards socialism. Similarly, he used official reports in order to
describe the disastrous results of the British policies that led to the 1866 fam-
ine in India.[36]

One of the sources Marx uses in order to document the abuses of the
European powers during the colonial expansion is Stamford Raffles's *History
of Java*, where this former British lieutenant-governor of Java describes the
corruption and cruelty of Dutch colonialism. But Marx, backed by William
Howitt's *Colonisation and Christianity*, argues that this violence was constitutive of the colonial system and thus common to all the colonisers. Furthermore, he maintains that capitalists behave in the colonies as they would, if they
had the chance, in their mother countries; *Capital* thus affirms that the merit
of Wakefield's theory of colonisation lies in showing the truth about capitalist
relations in the metropolitan countries.[37]

As indicated before, Marx is aware of the spatial and temporal determinations of his sources, and his critical reading is thus a basic part of his historiographical interpretations. However, the ideological critique of sources is

---

33   Ginzburg 2012, p. 4.
34   Tomba 2013b, 408.
35   Marx 1976b, p. 877.
36   Marx 1978, p. 218.
37   Marx 1976b, pp. 916–17; 932.

a merely negative form of knowledge (because it tells one about the limitations of the source, but does not provide positive knowledge in its place), and
working mostly with secondary sources led to inevitable limitations, given the
state of the historical knowledge in Marx's period. When he did research based
on secondary sources, Marx cross-checked them, as can be seen in his reading
of Maine, in which Marx corrects some of the data of this author by reference to authors like Strange, Morgan and Niebuhr, both for documentary and
theoretical reasons. The obvious problem with this approach was its ultimate
dependence on observations that could not be directly refuted – an *archive*
rather than a *source* problem. As Wood has indicated, some of Marx's historical observations are quite wrong, 'for reasons having less to do with his own
shortcomings than with the existing state of historical scholarship at the time
of his writing'.[38]

3.2   The Imperial Archive and the Limits to Interpretation

Indeed, we can clarify the reach of Marx's theory and method by examining
some of his particular analyses in terms of the conditions of his archive. Marx
deliberately analyses most non-capitalist societies from the point of view of
his study of capitalism; as Wood states, his 'discussion of precapitalist forms
is, after all, part of a discussion of capital'.[39] Basso argues that, because of this
preeminence of capitalism as the point of reference for pre-capitalist forms,
Marx investigates them in a non-critical manner, but Basso's argument is inaccurate: the method in the *Grundrisse* turns to the analysis of previous modes of
production explicitly in order to explain capitalism, and consequently Marx
is aware of the possibility of obfuscating the differences and specificities of
each individual pre-capitalist mode of production.[40] Against this methodological possibility, Marx repeatedly acknowledges the diversity of pre-capitalist
modes of production.[41]

    However, the limited availability of sources leads Marx to an incorrect eval-
uation of the relevance of pre-capitalist modes of production, especially in
the *Grundrisse*: he overestimates the representative power of the 'classical' or

---

38   Wood 2010, p. 79. See Karl Marx 1974a, pp. 285–336.
39   Wood 2010, p. 80.
40   Basso 2013, p. 338. Sartre develops some of the implications of this method, which he calls
       regressive-progressive. Sartre 1963.
41   See Banaji 2013, p. 131.

'ancient' mode of production, while on the other hand is unable to develop an accurate theory of the Asiatic mode of production, which remains a residual category for non-European forms whose history was largely unavailable to Marx and Engels. Hobsbawm's judgment on the sources of Marx's pre-capitalist forms of appropriation in the *Grundrisse* is indeed quite conservative: while he finds Marx's and Engels's knowledge of classical antiquity and the European Middle Ages good and their knowledge of the rise of capitalism outstanding, their knowledge of the ancient and medieval Middle East is unimpressive. On the other hand, he considers (wrongly) that they are well informed about India, but not about pre-history, pre-Colombian America or Japan, and know virtually nothing about Africa.[42]

Wood's evaluation of Marx's theory of pre-capitalist social formations, under the light of current research, is even less positive. The formations called 'Oriental' or 'Asiatic' in the *Formen* predominated in ancient civilisations, although not particularly in Asia, while recent scholarship and archaeological discoveries, on the other hand, have determined that the 'ancient' form was not prevalent in Greek or Roman societies – or anywhere else.[43] And beyond its insufficiency to explain the transition to feudalism, the Germanic type has an essential problem: the sources available to Marx about these peoples are Greco-Roman, and present a distorted and often mythologised version of the German tribes, exaggerating the individualism and equality within them – archaeology suggests that the thesis of the isolated households is incorrect, and that there were considerable inequalities of wealth between their members.[44]

Marx's theory of pre-capitalist forms has thus been seriously challenged by the development of scholarship after a century and a half of groundbreaking archeological discoveries and the emergence of other new sources. The Asiatic mode of production is the most polemical within this theory, particularly after Said's intervention in *Orientalism*: although Marx's formulation of this mode of production entails the disavowal of a Eurocentric unilinear conception of history, *Orientalism* emphasises the ideological connotations of such a construct.

---

42   Dunn 2011, p. 123. Banaji 2011, p. 349. Spivak interprets the formulation of the pre-capitalist forms in the *Grundrisse* as 'an attempt to fit historical presuppositions into a logical mold'. Spivak 1999, p. 81. Hobsbawm 1965, p. 26.

43   Wood 2010, pp. 80–3. Also against Marx's conception of the spatial morphology of the ancient forms of appropriation, recent scholarship argues that there were crucial differences between the centre-and-periphery model of cities in the Roman world and the more locally differentiated cities in the less unified Greek world. Scott 2013, pp. 9–10.

44   Wood 2010, pp. 83–5. In spite of this, the Germanic form has numerous features in common with the *peasant mode of production*. See Wickham 2005, pp. 536–9.

While Said's interpretation of Marx is far from rigorous,[45] it begins a long discussion in post- and de-colonial studies about the validity of Marx's conception of history.

Marx bases his 1853 remarks (and arguably those in the *Grundrisse*) about land property in Indian communities on François Bernier's description of seventeenth-century Mughal India,[46] while references to this region in Marx's work from the 1860s (*Theories of Surplus Value, Capital* Vol. I and the drafts of *Capital* Vols. II and III) especially rely on Richard Jones's writings on Oriental societies. This utilitarian political economist, disciple of Bentham and Ricardo, uses Bernier's account of India, but adds the idea that the craftsmen of the imperial court were unproductive labourers – a feature that explains the alleged lack of dynamism in the oriental cities – and extends his typology to Oriental countries more generally.[47]

As indicated in the previous chapter, the expression '*Asiatic mode of production*' is first coined by Marx in his 1859 *A Contribution to the Critique of Political Economy*, but is elaborated on in the *Grundrisse* as a communitarian form of appropriation. The main features of this mode of production – which Marx never systematises – are: 1. a self-sufficient network of rural communities, producing both food and handcrafts and supplying surplus to the central authorities (who managed water resources and public works); 2. a despotic bureaucracy or caste that centralises power for political and military purposes; and 3. the collective ownership of land, productive property, and 'hydraulic' works.[48]

Drawing on empirical research, different authors have denied the validity of each of these features; this is particularly the case for India, the country which this mode is primarily supposed to explain. In this vein, Banaji maintains that the insufficiencies of the 'Asiatic mode of production' are due to Marx's dependence on English sources which, for instance, exaggerate the isol-

---

45 Ahmad 1994, pp. 159–219.

46 O'Leary insists that in his first articles on India, Marx uncritically reproduces the features of Bernier's descriptions, which had a specific political motivation: to convince Colbert – Louis XIV's finance minister – to dissuade the king from declaring all French land as royal property; in order to do this Bernier relates India's alleged economic decline to the Mughals' disdain for private property. In spite of this, as O'Leary observes, the 'three interrelated features of Hindustan as described by Bernier – monarchical ownership of all the land, a service nobility and parasitical cities – provided the core of the "empirical" assumptions upon which the future models of oriental society would be built by occidental political economists'. O'Leary 1989, p. 57. On Bernier's impact on Marx's early writings on India: Lindner 2010, pp. 29–31.

47 O'Leary 1989, pp. 106–18, 78. Jones 1852, p. 61ss.

48 McFarlane 2005, pp. 284–5.

ation and self-sufficiency of the Indian villages, a 'stereotyped formula' which is recycled from one report to another. Additionally, the existence of a class of powerful landed proprietors in the cases of the Mughal, Byzantine and Tang empires, as opposed to Marx's position that the Asiatic despot was the exclusive proprietor and autarkical ruler, are further proof of the invalidity of the 'Asiatic mode of production'.[49]

O'Leary, one of Marx's harshest critics, even argues that Marx prioritises second hand stereotypes over the careful reading of administrative sources and Bernier's originals, and points out that a close reading of Bernier shows several important inconsistencies with Marx's main narrative. He also indicates that during the writing of the *Grundrisse* Marx wrote a piece acknowledging the existence of intermediate landed proprietors in India, which he then ignored until the 1870s. O'Leary concludes that Marx uses his sources selectively, ignoring contrary evidence in his source materials;[50] hence the limitations and overall inadequacy of the concept of the Asiatic mode of production is not primarily a consequence of limitation of sources, but of Marx's criteria for selecting the appropriate data in his sources.

There is no doubt, as Ahmad confirms, that this is a serious error of judgment on Marx's part, 'a theoretical error and a violation of the very materialist method which he did more than anyone else to establish in the sciences of the social as such'.[51] And yet, it is also clear that it was not possible for Marx to construct an alternative model from fragments and contradictory versions; the only alternative to this *cul de sac* would have been to do empirical research directly, or wait for new, more consistent scholarship to be written. Marx chooses to construct his Asiatic model on the basis of feeble evidence and is wrong – at least as regards the generality of Asian societies.[52]

Although by the 1860s Marx arrives at a position where neither capitalism has a centre nor history an exclusive path of development, he does not reevaluate his previous research on Asian societies until the 1870s, when he does

---

49   Habib 2002, pp. 14–58; Zingarelli 2016, pp. 31–2. Banaji 2011, pp. 17–19. The author quotes
      Dumont's analysis of nineteenth-century English administrative literature in India.
      Dumont 1966, pp. 67–89.
50   O'Leary 1989, pp. 262–7 and 103–4.
51   Ahmad 1994, p. 241.
52   Of course, the generalisation of a mode of production for the totality of Asia cannot
      be sustained rigorously. However, the prominent Egyptologist and methodologist Ciro
      F.S. Cardoso argues that the Asiatic mode of production adequately explains ancient societies such as the Egyptian. Zingarelli argues for this thesis, while Wood, on the other hand,
      includes Minoan and Mycenaean Greece – along with the ancient empires of Asia – within
      this model. Zingarelli 2016, pp. 27–76; Wood 2010, pp. 81–2.

so through his readings of Morgan and Kovalevsky, having by then learned to read Russian and studied peasant societies extensively.[53] O'Leary concedes that Marx changes his mind about these matters in the late 1870s 'as a result of reading the latest history and anthropology' but – not surprisingly – he scarcely comments about this phase of Marx's work: it does not support his claim according to which 'Marx abused his sources when analysing Indian history'.[54] By then, in contrast to his previous uncritical reception of authors such as Bernier and Jones, Marx systematically criticises the colonial bias of the existing sources.[55] However, he did not systematise these enquiries.

Bolívar y Ponte, Marx's encyclopedia entry on Simón Bolívar, is also regularly presented as an example of Marx's alleged Eurocentrism. Interestingly, the English, French, German and North American encyclopedias Marx used when preparing for this piece presented openly favourable opinions of Bolívar, as does one of Marx's three cited sources – John Miller's *Memoirs*. Marx's negative depiction proceeds from two of Bolívar's former officials: Hippisley – a colonel who left Bolívar's army after it experienced financial problems – and, particularly, Ducoudray-Holstein, a general who, along with a considerable section of the Independence army, stopped recognising the authority of the 'Liberator' after the defeat at Ocumare in 1816.[56]

But the most striking feature of this article is the absence of Marx's historical materialist method. His account is that of a traditional 'bare facts' historian: he focuses on notable military events, mentions the big names and factions in politics, and places a lot of attention on Bolívar's personality. There is no exploration of social and geopolitical relations. Scaron points out that Marx missed the opportunity to use *The Memoirs of General Miller* as a source about race relations and social classes in New Granada, but the same could even be said of Ducoudray-Holstein's more vitriolic book.[57] Thus this article does not even attempt to go beyond the level of the pseudo-concrete; *Bolívar y Ponte* is as un-Marxian a historical interpretation as one could possibly get.

So why does Marx go against most of the sources available to him and why does he not apply his materialist method when dealing with Bolívar? There is

53   Shanin 1983, pp. 1–94.

54   O'Leary 1989, pp. 124, 87.

55   Lindner 2010, p. 36.

56   Marx 1982b, 219–33. Draper 1968, p. 70. It is understandable that these countries tended
      to favour the dissolution of the Spanish empire. Hippisley 1819, pp. 426–50. Masur 2008,
      pp. 258–60.

57   Scaron 1972, pp. 12–13. See especially the introduction to Ducoudray-Holstein 1831, pp. vii–
      lxx.

a huge logical leap in interpreting Marx's anti-Bolivarism as Eurocentrism.[58] Independently of how one evaluates Bolívar's fight for the independence of South America, such interpretation assumes that Bolívar was somehow representative of the whole population of that subcontinent, rather than a wealthy New Grenadian creole. For his part, Aricó does not consider that Marx's position is due to Eurocentrism, but hypothesises that Hegel's concept of 'non-historic peoples' colours Marx's approach to the events of the Independence.[59] Since the events in this narrative appear as contingent, their outcome certainly suggests that chance, rather than military and political skill, favoured Bolívar's success. In Aricó's version, the Eurocentric residues in this piece thus do not come from Marx's documentary sources, but from the Hegelian philosophy of history.

This account is problematic, since in the *Grundrisse* – one to two years before the Bolívar entry – Marx had already started his attempts to explain forms of community which did not necessarily have a state (the Hegelian criterion of historical rationality), as in the case of the Germanic form. Why would Marx return to a form of Hegelian speculation when there were already empirical sources from which he could draw? O'Leary argues that Marx's main influence when thinking about Asia in the 1850s was the empirically-oriented accounts of the utilitarian political economists, rather than the tradition of political theory and typology from Aristotle to Hegel,[60] and it is arguable that Marx breaks away from Hegel in a materialist direction precisely through the critique of the kind of reasoning behind a concept like 'non-historic peoples', a concept that underpins Hegel's speculative philosophy of history.

Aricó's hypothesis, like those that openly accuse Marx of Eurocentrism and anti-Latin American bias,[61] misses a basic textual and contextual aspect of this piece. The revision of other biographical entries (including those regarding other characters in Latin American history) in the *New American Cyclopaedia* reveals that the treatment Marx gave to Bolívar went by the standards of this publication. The format of the entries called for a traditional historiographical approach: it is undeniable that contingency prevails in Marx's narrative, but this is also true of every other biographical entry written by Marx in this

---

58   Examples of this stereotyped approach can be found in Roque Baldovinos 2007, pp. 843–6; and Güendel 2011, pp. 98–100.

59   Aricó 2014, pp. 58–63.

60   O'Leary 1989, p. 81.

61   On the contrary, Marx's condemnation of European interventions in 1861 in Mexico and 1865 in Jamaica, for instance, are unequivocal. See Marx 1984h, pp. 71–8; and Marx 1987b, 198–9.

volume. This lack of historical materialist explanation is evident for example in the entry on Robert Blum,[62] one of the 'martyrs' of the 1848 German revolution that Marx explains in the *Manifesto* as a class conflict. Aricó's hypothesis attributing the absence of class struggle in the entry to an assumption by Marx of the lack of rationality of Latin American formations during their wars of independence thus shows itself to be false.

Marx's penchant for gossip in the Bolívar entry can also be observed, for instance, in those about the German- and British-born generals Bennigsen and Beresford,[63] and was probably seen by the editors as making the reading more pleasant in light of the numerous dates and names of battles. In this sense, although Marx is completely responsible for his evaluation of Bolívar, the kind of approach in this entry has to do more with editorial interests than with Marx's own philosophical positions. Due to its isolation in Spanish language editions from other entries,[64] a tradition within Latin American scholarship has exaggerated the importance and singularity of this article in Marx's oeuvre.

Draper's interpretation of Marx's antipathy to Bolívar seems to be the most balanced among the commentators on this piece. Draper argues that Marx does not deny the 'progressiveness' and legitimacy of the independence movement led by Bolívar, but criticises him because of his authoritarianism, which reminds him of Louis Bonaparte. Hence, Draper concludes, 'Marx remains, to this day, one of the few champions of the democratic aspirations for which the northern South Americans fought *against* their "Liberator". He does not accept the rationalisations for dictatorship, which have not changed much in a century and a half'.[65]

Although under quite different circumstances, in the cases both of the Asiatic mode of production and the entry on Bolívar, Marx chooses to contradict some of his sources, relying on others instead. These choices lead to a bad model for explaining Asian societies and to a very limited account of an important historical figure. However, since Marx did not follow his method when writing *Bolívar y Ponte*, the first is arguably more problematic in theoretical terms. Marx does sketch the concept of an 'Asiatic mode of production' over

62   Marx 1982c, pp. 80–2.

63   Marx and Engels write about Bennigsen: 'his excessive passion for the fair sex at that time made more noise than his warlike exploits'. Marx and Engels 1982a, p. 76; about Beresford, Marx and Engels 1982b, pp. 289–90.

64   Aricó and many after him read *Bolívar y Ponte* through Scaron's compilation of Marx and Engels's fragments dealing with Latin America, his *Materiales para la historia de América Latina*.

65   Draper 1968, p. 77.

a long time.[66] While these cases have Eurocentric elements, this is not due to Marx's method and theoretical positions, but in spite of these positions.

Moreover, it is worth recalling that Marx's accounts of non-European economic forms were not exoticising: as for the imagery of the Indian peasant starving next to a thriving bull – often depicted as a sign of superstition and backwardness – Marx uses the explanation that it is more difficult for those economies to replace an ox than a man, and this was thus rational behaviour in terms of the survival of the community. He applies the same criterion when he addresses the practice of 'widow burning' in India, which he explains in relation to the interests of the priests, rather than for cultural reasons – the properly orientalist account of such traditions.[67] Marx's Hegelian awareness of the historical determination of his own conditions of knowledge (and, as stated, of the biases in his sources) leads him to ground his project of a science of history on the method of abstraction – which opens the possibility of a spatio-temporally multilinear history – rather than on an evolutionist scheme. As argued in section 1.2. above, historical diversity is to be understood from this abstract anthropological unity as a point of departure. From the basis of this unity, Marx emphasises the historical specificities of different social forms, as can be seen in his critical remarks about Phear's and Maine's articles on India, where he insists on the necessity of not imposing European concepts, such as *feudalism* and *state*, on other formations.[68]

Marx's archive limits his possibilities for interpreting societies spatially and temporally far away from him, but it also provides him with opposing views and sometimes contradictory versions, between which he sometimes does not have enough empirical criteria to decide with certainty. Due to his central interest in the study of capitalism, non-capitalist societies are not of primary interest to Marx during most of his lifetime. And just as his analyses of pre-capitalist formations are subordinated to the study of capitalism, his attention and time management trend towards the latter as well. Marx worked for many years to

---

66   As Sayer affirms, 'we quite rationally place considerable weight upon theoretical claims and we are obliged to take their refutation seriously. Conversely, we neither place much confidence in claims about contingent matters nor worry much if they are refuted'. Sayer 1992, p. 144.

67   Marx 1978, p. 314. Marx 1974a, pp. 325–6. Ironically, post-colonial studies exoticises Indian cultural difference as a radical alterity to Western Europe. For a Marxist critique of the postcolonial turn in authors like Guha and Chakrabarty, see: Chibber 2013; and especially Kaiwar 2015.

68   Marx 1974b, pp. 256–7; Marx 1974a, pp. 326–30. On the contrary, Marx does find it appropriate to characterise the Japan of his day as 'feudal'. Marx 1976b, p. 878.

establish the basis for a new, materialist conception of history, and tried to apply it accordingly, but his personal limitations (economic difficulties, frequent illness and relatively early death) and the priority of the study of the capitalist mode of production prevented him from developing a definitive version. Naturally, the research derived from a philosophical and scientific conception cannot depend on the work of a single person. In this sense, further historical investigations productively draw from Marx's theory and evaluate his specific hypotheses under the light of new sources.

3.3   Beyond Marx's Archive

The development of historical and social scientific research after Marx has regularly led to the re-evaluation of his explanations, and attention to the spatio-temporal elements opened by new sources has proven to be particularly fruitful for enriching the mechanisms at play in the cases that Marx analyses. Since space and time are (ontologically) fundamental in the organisation of the social totalisations, attention to their development should lead to a better understanding of the specific conjunctures, as exemplified in the next pages through discussions of 'so-called primitive accumulation' and the civil wars in France and the United States. Furthermore, as indicated in the previous chapter, such revisions are important not only for the specific explanations they offer, but also for the advancement of the theory itself – especially through the formulation of models.

The United States Civil War is probably the most studied among the specific processes analysed by Marx, and since his explanation heavily depends on social spaces and times, it is particularly useful to approach it in relation to recent studies. While the idea of the inevitability of the conflict due to the expansionist character of the South – Marx's fundamental thesis about the cause of the conflict – was widely accepted until the late 1920s, Craven's and Ramsdell's analyses challenge this position, arguing that the Southern economy had more flexibility and capacity to reform itself than had been previously presumed, and thus that there were alternatives to the war. Following this revisionist line, Runkle concludes that while Marx is probably right to state that slavery needed to spread in order to survive, the exhaustion of the soil available for slavery was far from imminent, and hence the conflict could have been avoided.[69]

---

69   Genovese 1989, p. 243. Runkle 1964, p. 136.

Similarly, while Genovese agrees with the revisionists that the advent of the war was not triggered by an immediate crisis of land scarcity, he also demonstrates that even reforms to the slave system depended on its expansion. However, he argues that a peaceful solution to the contradiction between the North and South would have been impossible due to the psychology of the slaveholding ruling class: the defence of slavery was for the slaveholders the defence of their honour and dignity.[70]

In any case, contrary to the widespread assumption in this literature, an emphasis on culture or politics as the immediate cause of the war does not exclude Marx's interpretation based on the conditions of production as the framework for this conflict. Following the stratified conception of history described in Section 1.1., culture and politics mediate and help to negotiate the basic conflict at the level of production. The prospect of the scarcity of land could have determined the actions of the agents long before its actual advent. In this sense, in favour of Marx's explanation (albeit not referencing him), Foner argues that beliefs that limiting the expansion of slavery would lead to its extinction were common in the United States from the 1840s. Among others, Foner cites one of the editors of the *New York Tribune*, Horace Greeley, who affirmed in 1856 that 'to restrict Slavery within its present limits is to secure its speedy decline and ultimate extinction'.[71] According to Ransom, 'observers outside the South uniformly viewed the cotton kingdom as eagerly seeking new land. By the 1850s this view had become an obsessive fear'.[72]

The tension rose to an unsustainable level for the Southern élite with the election of the anti-slavery candidate Abraham Lincoln. The cycles of federal (electoral) politics, not the actual exhaustion of slave-state soil – a thesis Marx never makes – was then the immediate cause for the declaration of secession in the South, though the contradiction between two competing forms of capitalist accumulation determined the interests of those at war. This complementarity of economic and political dimensions is highlighted by Ransom, whose general

---

70   Genovese convincingly argues that the Southern economy needed to expand to the newer territories of the Union, and that Mexico, the Caribbean and Central America would also be under threat of becoming slave territories. Genovese 1989, pp. 247, 249–50; also 269–70. Thus, the Marxian claim that pirate expeditions to these countries was favoured by the White House under Pierce and Buchanan is not only backed by empirical evidence, but also by structural explanation. Marx 1984e, pp. 37–8.

71   Quoted in Foner 1995, p. 116. As this journal was Marx's main source of information about the United States, it is arguable that he based his interpretation of the Secession process on points of view such as Greeley's.

72   Ransom 1989, p. 59.

explanation of the causes of this war coincides with Marx's, but renders Marx more concrete by delving into the role of western lands in this contradiction.

Based on the economic reconstructions of the prices of slaves and exported cotton, Ransom argues that the opening of the western settlements was detrimental to the interests of slave-holders:

> had there been no western land, the price of cotton would not have fallen, and the value of slaves would have been greater ... Restricting settlement of western lands would have increased rents for slave-holders, and the political debates and votes on homesteading and the Graduation Act in the 1840s and 1850s suggest that both slave-owners and landowners in the South realised this.[73]

In Ransom's interpretation, the Southern slaveholders wanted to expand, but did so especially in order to acquire not *land*, but *territory*, i.e., to gain political influence that would let them have more control over the prices of slave labour and land. In this explanation, as in Marx's, the problem of the overpopulation of 'poor whites' is another important element for Southern expansion, although its growth was lower than that in the North. Ransom concludes that even if the South had been able to expand to Cuba and Central America – a very optimistic scenario for Southern interests, given their repeated failed military attempts to do so – and hence to temporarily solve the problem of 'poor white' overpopulation, their domestic political problems would have persisted unless new slave states could be minted.[74]

Ransom's analysis thus leads him to consider the impact of the recently-settled western territories on the economic and political conditions in the United States as the central cause of the outbreak of war.[75] Although formulated in terms of prices and profit – phenomenal and highly mediated forms of value and surplus value, from Marx's perspective – this economic analysis is nevertheless compatible with Marx's explanation (which Ransom does not cite), based on the contradiction between two opposing regimes of capitalist exploitation within a single social formation.[76] With this displacement,

---

73 Ransom 1989, pp. 55, 57.

74 Ransom 1989, p. 60. On the history of the Southern attempts to seize Central American and Caribbean territories, see May 2002.

75 Although Marx does consider the role of the Northwestern territories in his interpretation, he does not interpret them as the decisive element for the U.S. Civil war, as Ransom does. See above, 2.3.

76 Banaji contends that plantations were 'commodity-producing enterprises characterised

Ransom's explanation presents the incorporation of the western territories two decades before the War as the spatio-temporal transformation that ultimately led to the crisis of the North-South contradiction.

On the other hand, for the Paris Commune, Marx's use of newspapers and letters as sources for *The Civil War in France* contrasts with the approaches since the 1960s that have clarified aspects such as the composition of the Parisian labour force and the social base of the communards, through the use of 'serialised' sources – such as censuses and secondary elaborations – that have allowed them to transcend impressionistic reconstructions of the conjuncture.[77] More recently, the analyses by Gould and Harvey highlight the importance of the social-spatial organisation of Paris in the development of this event. Also, while Marx's class analyses about 1848 France are only implicitly referenced in his *Civil War in France*, and his contextualisation of the Commune prioritises the history of the state,[78] these recent authors analyse both events as part of the historical development of the Second Empire.

Serial sources would have allowed Marx to elaborate a more precise analysis of this conjuncture and to avoid some theoretically vague formulations about this event. For example, Marx states that the proletarians of Paris had taken over the direction of the city, and consequently depicts the Commune as a 'working men's Government', and the Communards as 'plain working men' and proletarians,[79] but Tombs, based on Rougerie's analysis in 1964 of the statistics and court records of captured insurgents, affirms that the communards 'were skilled workers; they were fairly evenly spread over the age-range 20–40 …; and

---

by speculative investments … in the production of *absolute* surplus-value *on the basis* of landed property'. This form of enterprise thus differs from the classic capitalist form of enterprise, in that the former is compatible with a constant composition of capital, and hence with stagnant or declining levels of labour productivity; in sum, 'the slave-plantations were *capitalist* enterprises of a patriarchal and feudal character producing absolute surplus-value on the basis of slave-labour and a monopoly on land'. Banaji 2011, pp. 69, 71. Italics in the original.

77   The printed sources of this piece have been established by the editors of the Marx and Engels Collected Works, thanks to Marx's own notebook with newspaper excerpts on the Commune from 18 March to 1 May 1871. Marx and Engels 1986c, pp. 665–7. For the classics of the 'serial' approach, see Rougerie 2004; Rougerie 1964.

78   Written as a political communication from the International Workingmen's Association, very shortly after the fall of the Commune, the basic methodological problem of *The Civil War in France* is that the more abstract levels of its social analysis are absent or implicit, and its brief history of state centralisation does not account for the complexity of the class struggle in 1871 Paris. Marx, pressed to publish this document, does not elaborate beyond the immediate level of the conjuncture, and even then remained within the political (or, more precisely in this case, state-) stratum.

79   E.g., Marx 1986, pp. 334, 336.

they worked mostly in long-established and small-scale Paris craft industries'.[80] While this does not refute Marx's account of the process – his concept of *proletariat* does not exclude skilled workers, nor is it limited to the labour force of big industries – it better captures the social base of the movement and its possibilities.

In this sense, Roger Gould's spatial approach significantly refines the explanation of this conjuncture. Through the analysis of a range of documents from post-Commune trials against presumed Communards, Gould concludes that community was more decisive than class in the organisation and mobilisation of the Commune, and that the Commune was thus fundamentally a movement for municipal liberties. He argues this by establishing neighbourhood networks and solidarities as the main criterion for the organisation of the Communard battalions – even sometimes in conflict with the orders from the central command of the Paris National Guard. Also, his analysis suggests that class was a more significant factor in the centre of Paris than in the peripheries, where the Commune had stronger support. In addition to this, Gould locates solidarities between working- and middle-class neighbours by analysing a sample of civil marriage records from four adjacent Parisian districts (*arrondissements*) in 1869.[81]

As previously argued, Gould's opposition between class and social space – specifically addressed by him through the category of *community* – simplifies a multi-level historical relation in which concrete spaces do not directly express the abstract class structure.[82] Also, against Gould's argument about trans-class solidarities, Harvey indicates that while the differentiation between workers and small owners was at the time porous, the fact that workers aligned with 'respectable' witnesses such as lawyers, doctors or other local notables for a rather uncommon ritual does not demonstrate the existence of solidarities between members of different classes. Ultimately, even if that had been the case, such trans-class solidarities do not deny the primary class divide: it is dubious, Harvey writes, that bankers and financiers, landlords, merchant capitalists, industrialists or other members of the bourgeoisie turned up as witnesses in Gould's data.[83]

---

80   Tombs 1999, p. 111. Writing about the elected members of the Commune, Edwards considers that 'what is striking is how small a number came from the new heavy industries that had grown up on the outskirts of Paris'. Edwards 1973, p. 28. This makeup of the Commune's leading body is consistent with Harvey's indication that Haussmann's urban reforms had by 1870 deindustrialised Paris. Harvey 2005, pp. 162–3.

81   Gould 1995, pp. 175–87, 81–90.

82   On the relations between real and actual space-times, see above, Chapter 2.

83   Harvey 2005, p. 237. Against Gould, Harvey argues that concubinage, rather than mar-

Besides his reservations about the inferences drawn from the records of civil marriages, most of Gould's evidence on the importance of spatial proximity, neighbourhood institutions and the *arrondissements* as vectors of solidarity, are, as Harvey indicates, consistent with his own Marxian explanation of the changes in the Parisian space relations from the point of view of the accumulation of capital, particularly the impact of the urban reforms under Haussmann as producing 'a city in which the circulation of capital became the real imperial power'.[84]

For all its nuances, it is impossible to ignore the relations between politics and spatial class segregation in Paris. While Rougerie, based on the 1872 census, describes the districts of the Eastern periphery as predominantly inhabited by workers and day labourers (*ouvriers, journaliers*),[85] Harvey notes that these districts – where radicals, socialists and revolutionaries led the numerous public meetings and the bourgeois reformers were banned – were crucial in the agitation that led to the Commune. The analysis of the elections of March 1871, with a notoriously high voter turnout and overwhelming support in the East for the Commune – as opposed to the low number of voters and contrary voting tendency in the West – corroborate this tendency.[86]

The Commune thus faced challenges from without the city – the Versailles and Prussian armies – as well as from some of its own districts. But things were complicated even among the Communards, for there were discrepancies as to the political and economic transformations that were sought.[87] Marx's explanation in *The Civil War in France*, by focusing on the social and symbolic opposition between Paris and Versailles, thus underestimates the social contradictions and political disagreements within Paris and among the leaders of the Commune.[88] Hence, the spatial composition of the city reveals conflicts and solidarities that help explain the development and outcome of this process.

---

riage, was the norm for working-class couples, except when they looked for social mobility. Harvey 2005, p. 237. Rougerie, on the other hand, has questioned the representability of Gould's sample for being too small. See Rougerie 2004, pp. iv–v.

84   Harvey 2005, pp. 108–9; see also 239.

85   Rougerie 2004, pp. 17–19. Merriman indicates that these districts not only received workers from the centre of Paris displaced by Haussmann's reforms, but also became home to newcomers from the provinces. Merriman 2014, pp. 7–8.

86   Harvey 2005, pp. 234, 296. See Rougerie 2004, p. 144.

87   'Conspiracies against the Commune were afoot from the beginning. Within a couple of weeks, anti-Communard organisers began to distribute armbands (*brassards*) – conservative rallying marks that were at first white, the color of the Bourbons, and later tricolor – in conservative neighborhoods. Those who had them awaited the day they could come into the open and crush the Commune'. Merriman 2014, p. 72; also p. 79.

88   Perhaps Marx's later (better) knowledge of these internal conflicts led to this sceptical

In addition to the operations of displacement and analysis in the two previous cases, the widening of scale is a third spatio-temporal strategy allowed by new sources. This is indeed the path followed by Alex Anievas and Kerem Nişancioğlu's recent book that addresses the decades-long debate between Brenner and Wallerstein about the origins of capitalism. While the latter insists that the accumulation of surplus secured the existence of a world-economy on the global scale, Brenner affirms that capitalism fundamentally began with new agrarian class relations that emerged in late medieval and early modern Western Europe.[89]

Anievas and Nişancioğlu, on the other hand, maintain that the origins of capitalism 'can only be understood in international or geopolitical terms, and that this very "internationality" is constitutive of capitalism as a historical mode of production'.[90] Unlike Wallerstein's world-systems theory, these authors emphasise the role of the modes of production in the dynamics of the geopolitical system from which capitalism emerged; and they do this by analysing this world-system from the point of view of its uneven and combined development. Against Brenner, *How the West Came to Rule* argues that the conception of capitalism as necessarily tied to a single form of exploitation obfuscates the many forms on which actually existing capitalist social relations and labour regimes have thrived.[91]

Accordingly, they argue that the changes in the sphere of production that led to 'classic' English capitalism are not properly explicable without the consideration of complex transcontinental political and economic relations. England's very isolation, which is central to Brenner's thesis of the Anglo-centred origin of capitalism, is shown by Anievas and Nişancioğlu to be a product of the Habsburg-Ottoman conflict: while Christian continental Europe was in tension with the Ottomans in the Southeast and the Mediterranean, Northwestern

---

evaluation ten years after the publication of *The Civil War in France*: 'aside from the fact that this was merely an uprising of one city in exceptional circumstances, the majority of the Commune was in no sense socialist, nor could it have been. With a modicum of COMMON SENSE, it could, however, have obtained the utmost that was then obtainable – a compromise with Versailles beneficial to the people as a whole. The appropriation of the Banque de France alone would have rapidly put an end to the vainglory of Versailles, etc., etc'. Marx, 'Letter to Nieuwenhuis, 22 February 1881', in Marx 1992, p. 66. Emphasis in the original.

89   See Wallerstein 1974; Aston and Philpin 2002; Denemark and Thomas 1988, pp. 47–65. This debate is regularly assumed to be a prolongation of the debate between Sweezy and Dobb about the transition to capitalism. See Wood 2002, pp. 35–43.

90   Anievas and Nişancioğlu 2015, p. 2.

91   Anievas and Nişancioğlu 2015, pp. 30–1.

Europe had the margin to develop 'the peculiar fusion of interests among the landed nobility, capitalist tenants and the state in England, which proved crucial to the success of the English ruling class in enclosing land'.[92] Moreover, *How the West Came to Rule* concludes that territorialised state sovereignty – a co-constitutive process with capitalist social relations in Europe – developed through the conflict between Amerindians and Europeans. Later the Atlantic triad of American land, African slave labour and English capital made the overcoming of English agrarian capitalism through the Industrial Revolution possible.[93]

The internalist conception of the origins of capitalism – along with the strictly typological concept of capitalism – is thus shown to be insufficient in order to account for the historical development of this mode of production. Marx's own explanation exposes the centrality of colonialism in this development[94] and hence the necessity of a longue-durée, world-scale approach. This, however, has only been possible through the existence of a vast quantity of relatively recent studies in the social and economic history of the Mongol and Ottoman empires, as well as the Americas and Africa between the fifteenth and seventeenth centuries. In this sense, Anievas's and Nişancioğlu's archive (of secondary sources) is strikingly more diverse in geographical terms than Wallerstein's, enabling them to formulate a more systemic and non-Eurocentric account of the origins of capitalism than Wallerstein and Brenner. Crucially, analyses of peripheral social formations by Marxist scholars Irfan Habib, Jairus Banaji, John Haldon and Halil Berktay, among others, offer empirical data and explanations which dovetail with this book's spatially and temporally uneven explanation that clarifies the conditions of production of diverse formations, not by comparison between them as isolated cases, but through their relations within a complex, decentred totality.

The recent investigations of the modes of production at work in the Mongol, Spanish and Ottoman empires, and their impact on European formations, thus allow an expansion of the temporal and spatial scopes of Marx's explanation

---

92   Anievas and Nişancioğlu 2015, p. 120.
93   'Not only did the widened sphere of circulation implied by the transatlantic triangular trade offer numerous opportunities to British capitalists to expand their domain of activities, but the combination of different labour processes across the Atlantic enabled the recomposition of labour in Britain through the Industrial Revolution. The development of the productive forces – and the real subsumption of labour under capital as such – was thus built on the exploitation of a transatlantic subaltern class made up of Amerindians, African slaves and Europeans'. Anievas and Nişancioğlu 2015, p. 275. See also Anievas and Nişancioğlu 2015, pp. 139–41, 158–62.
94   See above, 2.3.

of the origins of capitalism. But as we have already observed, the same is the case with his discussions of the U.S. Civil War and the Paris Commune: Marx's accounts not only have considerable influence on these discussions, but scholars following Marxian theory and method continue to develop more consistent and detailed historical explanations, drawing on newly available sources. This operation of confronting Marx's theories with new sources allows us to conceive of a Marx whose theories and explanations can benefit from demographic and agrarian history, in a dialectic that either makes his formulations more concrete or refutes them. This is the necessary alternative to the 'bad theory' that Banaji criticises.[95]

Research on the conjuncture – the most concrete level of a socio-historical totality – can thus have important implications for the more abstract levels. Marx's was not a top-down methodology where the more abstract concepts remain unchanged, but a conception of knowledge in which the (critically treated) empirical data helps to shape the concepts. Systematic temporalisation and spatialisation contributes to the knowledge of relevant mechanisms for the explanation of actual historical formations, but also to the clarification and reformulation of the concepts and theories at more abstract levels, as has been observed in the spatio-temporal operations in the processes in this section: an expansion of scale in the case of 'so-called primitive accumulation', a displacement of focus to a specific area in the case of the U.S. Civil War, and an analysis of the spatial-demographic composition of the city in the case of the Paris Commune.

Epilogue

Since the theoretical construction of modes of production – as *historically-specific abstractions of necessary/internal relations* – relies on the accuracy of the information about their social conditions as much as on the theoretical framework, the criticism of sources and archives is essential for historical explanation as conceived by Marx. In this sense, besides the traditional modes of source criticism, ideology critique is Marx's original manner of 'brushing history against the grain' in order to reveal the social – and among them, the spatio-temporal – determinations of the sources. However, like other kinds of criticism, ideology critique only provides a negative knowledge that cannot substitute for the availability of valid sources. Sources are often grasped as

---

95   Banaji 2011, pp. 7–8.

providing the empirical foundations for historical research, but it is necessary to see them in equal measure as limits to historical interpretation.

In contrast, prominent Marxist authors like Lukács and Hobsbawm minimise the role of sources in Marx's conception of history. In *History and Class Consciousness*, the former proposes that:

> let us assume for the sake of argument that recent research had disproved once and for all every one of Marx's individual theses. Even if this were to be proved, every serious 'orthodox' Marxist would still be able to accept all such modern findings without reservation and hence dismiss all of Marx's theses *in toto* – without having to renounce his orthodoxy for a single moment. Orthodox Marxism ... refers exclusively to *method*.[96]

Similarly, Hobsbawm suggests that

> the general theory of historical materialism requires only that there should be a succession of modes of production, though not necessarily any particular modes, and perhaps not in any predetermined order. Marx thought that he could distinguish a certain number of socio-economic formations and a certain succession. But if he had been mistaken in his observations, or if these had been based on partial and therefore misleading information, the general theory of historical materialism would remain unaffected.[97]

Although both authors explicitly formulate these theses as a *reductio ad absurdum* reasoning and do not back them, by separating theory and method from historical content these positions are nonetheless formalist,[98] and thereby distort Marx's dialectical conception of knowledge. While Lukács protects the foundations of historical materialism (Level 1 in Figure 2) against empirical knowledge, Hobsbawm does the same for the general theory of the modes of production (Level 2 in Figure 2). As observed above, while the differentiation of levels of sociohistorical knowledge is necessary, this does not prevent abstract concepts and theories from being reassessed by knowledge at the more concrete levels.

---

96   Lukács 1971, p. 1.
97   Hobsbawm 1965, pp. 19–21.
98   As regards to the critique of methodologism in *History and Class Consciousness*, see Rose 2009, Chapter 1.

Marx's explanations of specific processes bear the mark of the conditions of their writing and of the archives at the time. In this sense, while he contributes substantial historical knowledge, his theory and method for social analysis transcend his biographical and archival limitations through the work of numerous researchers after him, particularly in the case of non-Western and non-capitalist formations. This is possible because – contrary to visions that portray his conception of history as a closed system – for Marx historical knowledge calls for periodical discussion and eventual reformulation on the basis of the new state of knowledge, as he did time and again during his lifetime in his practice as a researcher.

As seen in this chapter, Marx devolves into Eurocentric interpretations in the cases of the Asiatic mode of production and his biography of Bolívar, when he does not follow his own critical method and theory. However, we have also observed that the Marxian-based consideration of social spaces and times enables the clarification of some of the problems he addresses through a more limited and sometimes contradictory archive. In this sense, Marx's critical reading of Western sources since the writing of the *Grundrisse* and the 1857 wars in India and China shows a growing awareness on his part of the social spatio-temporal determinations of his archive, ultimately enabling him to reject colonialism and develop an internationalist form of politics incompatible with the evolutionist, Eurocentric, and world-historical assumptions that prevailed during his lifetime.

CHAPTER 4

Narrative as Presentation

Without such temporal-spatial expression, even abstract thought is impossible. ... Every entry into the sphere of meaning is accomplished only through the gates of the chronotope.[1]

∴

Ricoeur describes the third epistemological moment in his philosophy of history, the *representative phase*, as 'the putting into literary or written form of discourse offered to the readers of history'.[2] This phase is not limited to the writing of historiography, but refers to the narrative, rhetorical or imaginative elements that constitute its literary form, and are present all along the process of research; the intertwined character of the phases of historical knowledge should, in any case, prevent us from isolating form from content in socio-historical research.[3]

Although an exaggerated emphasis on literary form has led to a trend in the philosophy of history to conceive of narration as the sole determining factor of socio-historical research, to consider narrative form as a prison-house of historical knowledge,[4] such excesses should not minimise the importance of analysing *how* history is presented through historiographical discourses. The 'representative' phase has its own particularities, which do not simply 'mirror' the processes in the previous phases, and awareness of the textual mediations of historical discourses undeniably enriches our understanding of the ontology and epistemology of history.

From a critical realist conception of historical knowledge such as Marx's, narrative form should correspond to the structure of the object of knowledge. Since space and time are inescapable categories for the explanation of historical processes, narrative must account for the complexity of their relations

---

1 Bakhtin 1981, p. 258.
2 Ricoeur 2004, p. 136.
3 Ricoeur 2004, pp. 234–6.
4 Arguments for such a 'postmodern history' are championed, to name two examples, by Jenkins 2003 and Ermarth 1992.

in its subject matter, and hence be able to express the uneven and combined development of a particular social formation through the prism of a concrete conjuncture. The problem of historiographical narrative is thus aesthetic – rhetorical and narratological – but primarily it is epistemological and, as will be argued, political. Specifically, in order to explain historical processes from a narrative vantage point, Marx's conception of history implies a narrative form which makes possible the spatio-temporal explanation of the hierarchy of causalities between social mechanisms.

Since history is not reducible to historiography, the thematisation of this phase grapples with the relations between them, showing the ontological and epistemological foundations of the processes of the textualisation and nar-rativisation of history. Although, particularly since the 1920s, there have been rich and substantive discussions by Marxist authors – most notoriously Lukács, Bloch, Benjamin, Brecht and Adorno – concerning the problems of aesthetic and literary form, the prevalence in historiography of the cognitive over the aesthetic suggests a different field for its corresponding narrativity.

In the Marxian conception of history, this necessity of an epistemological mediation of the relation between history as *res gestae* and historiography as *historia rerum gestarum* introduces the problem of historical *representa-tion* as a problem of the *presentation* of the results of the research. Properly spatio-temporalised research requires a narrative form capable of accounting for these dimensions of its subject-matter. In Tomba's words:

> Global society, whose proper name is the world-market, requires a histori-ographical paradigm that is adequate to the combination of a plurality of temporal strata in the violently unifying historical dimension of mod-ernity. The postmodernist juxtaposition of a plurality of historical times, where forms of peasant-slavery exist alongside high-tech production in the superannuation of the dualism between center and periphery, not only explains nothing, but is obfuscatory. The mosaic of temporalities and forms of exploitation, even when it speaks of inter-relation, poses the diverse times as being in a state of reciprocal indifference, when the real problem is their combination by means of the world-market's mechan-isms of synchronisation.[5]

Following Tomba, this chapter looks at problems of Marx's conception of space-time in historiographical presentation, in particular through the rela-

---

5   Tomba 2013a, p. xiv.

tion between narrativity and chronotopes. In the following pages I argue that the latter is the narrative element that makes history intelligible as a totalisation. The first section thus problematises Marx's concept of presentation (*Darstellung*) from the perspective of Ricoeur's theory of the double dimension of narrative: the configurative and the episodic dimensions, referring to the synchronic and the diachronic, respectively. This allows us to criticise Hayden White's narrativism from a realist and materialist theory of narrative based on Marx's theory of history and his historiographical writings.

The second section analyses Marx's poetics of space-time in distinct modes of production in terms of its metaphors and tropes, showing the relation between the configurative dimension and the explanation in history at the level of closed systems. Finally, the last section analyses the narrative aspect of Marx's studies of specific conjunctures, and how the chronotope makes different emplotment options possible. In this sense, the chronotope at the episodic dimension, as I will argue, is the element that most evidently relates the cognitive, aesthetic and political aspects of historiography and historical knowledge.

4.1   Presentation, Chronotopes, Narrative

We can take Marx's distinction between method of inquiry and method of presentation as the starting point for the discussion about representation and narrativity in historical discourse. In the postface to the second edition of Volume I of *Capital*, its author indicates that

> of course, the method of presentation must differ in form from that of inquiry. The latter has to appropriate the material in detail, to analyse its different forms of development and to track down their inner connection. Only after this work has been done can the real movement be appropriately presented. If this is done successfully, if the life of the subject-matter is now reflected back in the ideas, then it may appear as if we have before us an *a priori* construction.[6]

In general, the distinction between the methods of inquiry and presentation corresponds to that between the moments of the second and the present chapter of this work;[7] therefore, the clarification of the concept of *presentation* is indispensable at this point, in order to understand how Marx conceives

---

6   Marx 1976b, p. 102.
7   In a similar manner, Ankersmit distinguishes between historical research (*Geschichts-*

what philosophers of history often call the 'problem of representation' and its implications for space-times in historical narratives. His depiction of the relation between the two methods asserts that the presentation should properly explain the mechanisms that determine its object of study; the appearance of necessity in the presentation thus comes from adequately grasping how the object of study works, and is therefore not imposed on the object. As Kosík maintains, 'the presentation is an *explication of the thing* precisely because it presents the thing in its *necessary internal* development and unfolding'.[8] Furthermore, Derek Sayer indicates that in Marx's presentation the succession of forms, as the ascent from the abstract to the concrete, follows the order of the hierarchy of conditions of possibility.[9]

In contrast with positions that assume a chasm between history as a chaotic *thing in itself* and historiography as an operation of ultimately arbitrary assignment of sense upon the former, the starting point of this dialectical approach is a triadic perspective where history has to pass through the mediation of a theoretical-methodological process in order to attain its proper intelligibility. Thus, the presentation does not seek to merely represent history as it happened – as in the most disingenuous version of realism, typically criticised by neo-Kantian or Nietzschean conceptions – but to show the results of the conscious, active production of knowledge. The relation between history and historiography is hence not aporetic,[10] but mediated by a historically determined praxical process.

Marx does not engage the past as the sole object of his science of history, but constructs different spatialised temporalities in relation to the corresponding mode of production; indeed, his above reference to his method of presentation

---

forschung) and historical writing (*Geschichtsschreibung*), where the former 'deals with the selection, interpretation and analysis of historical sources and with how this analysis may help us explain causally (or otherwise) what the evidence has taught us about the past', and in the latter 'the results of historical research are integrated into a historical narrative or representation. ... The problems encountered at the level of the establishment of historical fact – both practical and theoretical – are essentially different from the task of integrating these facts into a unified historical text'. Ankersmit 2012, p. 60.

8   Kosík 1976, p. 16.

9   'The commodity is analysed before money, and money before capital, the first form in either pair being a condition of the second; the concept of value is developed before that of surplus-value, and that of surplus-value before those of its transmuted forms (profit, rent, interest) for the same reason'. Sayer 1979, p. 101.

10   Ricoeur contends that it is in the representative phase 'that the major aporias of memory return in force to the foreground, the aporia of the representation of an absent thing that occurred previously and that of a practice devoted to the active recalling of the past, which history elevates to the level of a reconstruction'. Ricoeur 2004, pp. 136–7.

refers to his theory of the capitalist mode of production, and thus to the level of closed systems. However, Marx's concept of 'presentation' calls for greater precision in order to address more concrete levels, and to do this, it is necessary for it to address the problems of narrativity. Narration is thus accountable for the contingency inherent to open systems – i.e. social formations and conjunctures – as combinations of different mechanisms. As I will argue, narration necessarily completes presentation in order to explain actual history.

In this discussion about the relation between history and narrativity, it is important to examine the premises of one of the most important Marxist theories of narrative: Jameson's *The Political Unconscious*. He affirms that

> history is *not* a text, not a narrative, master or otherwise, but that, as an absent cause, it is inaccessible to us except in a textual form, and that our approach to it and to the Real itself necessarily passes through its prior textualisation, its narrativisation in the political unconscious.[11]

History as an absent cause, he indicates, refers to the mode of production as the synchronic system of social relations as a whole. Jameson takes this thesis from Althusser, who argues that *Darstellung* is the 'concept whose object is precisely to designate the mode of *presence* of the structure in its *effects*, and therefore to designate structural causality itself'.[12] In his interpretation, presentation is not a re-presentation because there would not be an outside cause which the former would express; the structure is nothing outside its effects.[13] Thus, for instance, value does not represent labour because, as Hartley comments, 'it is nothing but the retroactive process of this presentation of abstract human labour in the value-form'.[14]

In Jameson's quote, therefore, history as an absent cause is an inner limit to narrative discourse, rather than an outside referent. The problem with this approach is that, if it is to maintain itself within the coordinates of the Marxian conception, it needs a 'positive' theory of history – this is precisely what Jameson elaborates through his discussion of the mode of production. The absent cause has to be theorised *beyond* its textual presentation; hence, it is the political unconscious rather than history that is immanent in textualisation and narrativisation as their effects. The theory of history would then belong to a dialectic of the objective, which would be the complement of the dialectic of

---

11   Jameson 2002, p. 20.
12   Althusser and Balibar 2009, p. 208. See also Jameson 2002, p. 21.
13   Althusser and Balibar 2009, p. 209.
14   Hartley 2003, p. 120.

the subjective in *The Political Unconscious*.[15] The use of the concept of 'absent cause' thus does not dissolve the categories of essence and appearance – as Althusser wants – but transposes their dialectical relation to the social totalisation, beyond the realm of symbolisation (which is nonetheless necessary in order to grasp it).

As regards the problem of the relations between explanation and presentation, it is productive to return to Ricoeur's theory of time and narrative – and in particular his distinction between the episodic and configurative dimensions of narrative. The former is constituted by events and moves forward in a linear representation of time and, in accordance with the events in an open system not being deductively predictable,[16] its function is to aggregate contingencies and peripetheia that lead to a conclusion that is not logically present in the previous premises.[17] The configurative, on the other hand, 'transforms the succession of events into one meaningful whole which ... makes the story followable. ... The configuration of the plot imposes the "sense of an ending" ... on the indefinite succession of incidents'.[18] In other words, *the configurative dimension sets the conditions of possibility of the narrative* within the diegetic universe, including its spaces and times. We should therefore not univocally relate space to the configurative and time to the episodic, since both dimensions of narration have spatial and temporal components. Rather, the configurative and episodic correspond, respectively, to the synchronic and diachronic, which are analytical approaches and not ontological categories.[19]

The narrative configuration should not be conflated with fiction (nor does narrative, as will be argued, substitute explanation), although some authors in the narrativist line perpetuate this misunderstanding.[20] Such a position, as

---

15   Jameson 2002, pp. 21, ix.

16   Bhaskar 2008, p. 119. See also above, 2.1.

17   Ricoeur 1984a, pp. 66–7.

18   Ricoeur 1984a, p. 67.

19   Andrew Sayer indicates that geography's concern for space provides this discipline with a stronger orientation towards the configurational dimension, but this should not be assumed on the basis of an equation between space and synchronicity (as this author implies), since, analytically speaking, there are synchronic times as well as diachronic spaces. Sayer 2000, p. 143. On the temporality of the synchronic, see Jameson 2012, pp. 79–80.

20   Thus, Carr for example affirms that 'history unavoidably contains elements of fiction' – an inaccurate assertion, since it is not clear whether those elements necessarily make history fictional (not claiming to be true) or they are just common in both history and fiction. This author leans towards the first option, but the ambiguity of such a formulation is symptomatic of the confusion created by assuming *fiction* to be a synonym for *narrative*. Carr 2014, p. 200.

Ricoeur argues, makes it impossible to differentiate historiography's claims to truth from the lack of them in literary fiction,[21] and hence obfuscates the specific epistemological aspects of both historiography and fiction. Narrative is not an exclusive quality of fiction (in which the suspension of disbelief is assumed), but a fundamental feature of historiography: the fact that both share narrative features does not dissolve the differences between these genres and their relations to reality.

Through an interesting hypothesis – which lamentably, and typically in this philosopher, ignores space – Ricoeur suggests that the plot of a historiographical narration, as 'a synthesis of the heterogeneous, embracing intentions, causes, and accidents,'[22] integrates the Braudelian moments of the structure, the conjuncture and the event. Therefore, while the episodic dimension refers to the short-time span, the configurative deals with the long-time of structures – and with the time of the conjuncture we could add, since Ricoeur and Koselleck at first mention this intermediate scale but then ignore it – hence referring this narrative relation to endurance and efficacy as well. This heterogeneous synthesis, whose literary form is the plot, has thus both explanatory and narrative functions.[23]

In this case, narrative allows the interplay of scales and consequently the differentiation and hierarchisation of space-times – including the mechanisms that set them in motion. This characteristic is epistemologically fundamental because, as we have noted,[24] the lower the stratum of history, the larger the spatio-temporal scale in which it functions (e.g., the scale at which the relations of production function is larger than that of the political transformations). In Ricoeurian terms, narrativity cannot substitute the *modes of explanation/understanding*, but can account for the causal relations that the latter establish – a position consistent with the Marxian conception of the relation between inquiry and presentation. Moreover, this narrative interplay can be

---

21   'This equating of narrative configuration and fiction, of course, has some justification inasmuch as the configuration act is … an operation of the productive imagination, in the Kantian sense of this term. Nevertheless, I am reserving the term "fiction" for those literary creations that do not have historical narrative's ambition to constitute a true narrative. If we take "configuration" and "fiction" as synonyms we no longer have a term available to account for the different relation of each of these two narrative modes to the question of truth'. Ricoeur 1984b, p. 3.

22   Ricoeur 2004, p. 246.

23   Ricoeur indicates that the *synthesis of the heterogeneous* in historiography brings 'coordination between multiple events, or between causes, intentions and also accidents within a single meaningful unity'. Ricoeur 2004, p. 243.

24   See above, 1.1.

productively approached through the concept of *chronotope* as the narrative counterpart to the spatio-temporal models that help to explain historical processes.

However, Mikhail Bakhtin's original formulation of this concept is problematic: while for him the chronotope is 'the place where the knots of narrative are tied and untied', and 'it can be said without qualification that to them belongs the meaning that shapes narrative',[25] he admits that his use of it was only a first attempt to investigate time and space in literature. Thus, his essay *Forms of Time and of the Chronotope in the Novel* does not engage in the definition and development of the concept, but rather applies it to narratives from different historical contexts (Greek and chivalric romance, ancient biography, Rabelaisian novel, etc.). This leads to a vague and open concept, to which further determinations have to be given in order to make it empirically operational and theoretically pertinent.

His initial reference to Einstein and his consequent call to treat space and time as narratively inseparable suggest that the chronotope constructs a *world* – an 'ultimate perceptual horizon'[26] – where these categories are not simply formal markers, but act in their unity as active agents of the narrative, rather than a form external to its contents. This aspect is nonetheless underdeveloped in Bakhtin's work, in which the chronotope appears assimilated to a diegetic space-time (road, castle, salon, etc.) supposed to condense and articulate the relations of characters and objects in the narrative. He analyses the kinds of space-times necessary for each kind of narrative, but the characteristics he finds are related to contents alone, not explained in terms of form.[27]

Since narrative is the means by which language allows the subject to grasp space-times, the rhetorical construction of the chronotope – its literary form in general – should be at least as important as its explicit contents; narratology can hence productively contribute to a more concrete concept and characterisation of the chronotope. Although Hayden White's narratological approach to historiography may initially seem far from the scope of the chronotope, it becomes essential to it if we endorse Gaddis's interpretation, according to which

---

25 Bakhtin 1981, p. 250.

26 Jameson 2002, p. 98. On the construction of the world in a phenomenological sense, see the first chapter of Part Two in Husserl 1982, pp. 51–62.

27 See for example his characterisation of the chronotope in the travel novel. Bakhtin 1981, pp. 103–4.

writing about 'emplotment' and 'formist, organicist, mechanistic, and contextualist' modes of explanation, what he's [White's] really describing is the historian's liberation from the limitations of time and space: the freedom to give greater attention to some things than to others and thus to depart from strict chronology; the license to connect things disconnected in space, and thus to rearrange geography.[28]

Clearly, such liberation from chronology and geography needs certain limits, since *the historiographical chronotope should present the spatio-temporalised explanation of real structures* – a necessity that will lead us to differentiate between a configurative and an episodic dimension in the chronotope. However, Gaddis correctly points out the centrality of emplotment in the construction of the chronotope; the latter should thus be approached through the interplay of the configurative and episodic dimension in the text and, to the extent that historiographical presentation aspires to explain the logic of the social mechanisms, the chronotope should refer to the spatio-temporal models that account for the social forms it refers to: it should account for its scales, spatial configurations and rhythms.

White argues that the deep structural forms of the historical imagination correspond with the four basic tropes for the analysis of language: metaphor, metonymy, synecdoche and irony. These tropes, he believes, underpin every possible historiographical style (a singular combination of modes of emplotment, argument and ideological implication),[29] and are the basic elements of this kind of narrative. However, they are pre-narrative, and therefore already present in the (synchronic) configurational dimension of the emplotment, independently of its episodic dimension. As such, tropes complement the abstract concepts that configure the spatio-temporal tendencies at the level of the presentation of modes of production.

Literary figures form part of the *analogical grammar* of theories, which is 'the indispensable stock of metaphors, analogies, models etc., available to a field of inquiry or theoretical approach which helps to generate hypotheses and solutions ... and lend the approach plausibility'.[30] As such, they should not be considered external to theoretical activity; on the contrary, improving the metaphors used by science is an essential task for its development.[31] Hence,

---

28   Gaddis 2002, pp. 19–20.
29   White 2014, pp. 29–30.
30   'Grammar', in Hartwig (ed.) 2007, pp. 2007, 223–4.
31   Sayer 2000, p. 78. See also Sayer 1992, pp. 62–65; and Bhaskar 2008, p. 194.

insofar as theories account for the functioning of generative mechanisms, their tropes should be adequate for their explanation.

Theories thus have a tropological facet, but the conditions they set are only tendencies to be fulfilled or contested by the contingent narrative events in the episodic dimension. Although White attributes emplotment to the theoretical moment, his differentiated treatment of historians and philosophers of history suggests that this realisation is secondary for the latter: while he analyses the works of historians through the criterion of emplotment, those of philosophers are primarily characterised through their prevailing tropes.[32] Following the characterisation of tropes in *Metahistory*,[33] a metaphorical construction then represents a space-time through another one, while through metonymy the chronotope as a whole is built into the projection of one of its parts. A synecdochical operation would integrate two or more space-times into a single chronotope, while irony calls the possibility of the specific chronotope into question.

Some previously mentioned cases in this investigation are useful to exemplify the construction of space-times through tropes. A relation between two different objects, metaphor is revealed by Castells's use of computers and information science as a model for the analysis of the space-time of globalisation, mentioned in the introduction. When Marx speaks about Versailles and Paris in his *The Civil War in France*, he does so in a metonymical way, in general (though not always) assuming, for the sake of exposition, that each of them function coherently, as a unitary actant. However, as this example shows, for Marx this operation needs to be complemented. The opposition between these symbolic cities is an example of a synecdochical construction, where the parts are integrated into a qualitatively different whole: as symbols of the oligarchy and the working class, respectively, they configure France during this conjuncture as a contradictory field of struggle. Finally, Jameson's description of Gehry's house in Santa Monica is a good example of an ironic chronotope: the juxtaposition of heterogeneous spaces, and Jameson's own indications about

---

32   Michelet, Ranke, Tocqueville and Burckhardt are characterised through their respective romantic, comic, tragic and satirical emplotments, respectively; Marx, Nietzsche and Croce are characterised, respectively, by their use of metonymic, metaphoric and ironic tropes.

33   White 2014, pp. 30–7. It is important to recall that there are several other theories with different definitions and numbers of tropes. On this theme, see Jameson, 'Figural Relativism; or, the Poetics of Historiography', in Jameson 2008a, pp. 169–70. White's fondness for four-fold classifications, as is also the case in his theory of genres of emplotment, can be traced back to the Kantian transcendentalism underlying his philosophy. See Ankersmit 2009, pp. 34–53.

1.   a, b, c, d, ... n
2.   A, b, c, d, ... n
3.   a, B, c, d, ... n
4.   a, b, C, d, ... n
5.   a, b, c, D, ... n

FIGURE 3   Events and narrative causality
             SOURCE: WHITE 1985, P. 92

the incommensurability of the experiences in them, suggest the impossibility of totalising into a coherent narrative.[34] The cognitive mapping of this post-modern space-time is thus inherently ironic.

But if the individual tropes and concepts are at the basis of the chrono-tope in the configurational dimension, the relation between causes and effects only actually emerges with the sequence of events in the episodic dimension. White explains this through a chronological-syntactical arrangement – presented above in Figure 3 – where the capitalised letter shows the privileged status of the event in terms of its explanatory force (this should not be confused with a configurative moment; it involves decisive change through a new event).

According to this figure, Series 1 is a chronicle – a mere sequence without a proper explanation – while in Series 2 the decisive factor happens in the begin-ning, thus configuring a deterministic narrative. Series 5, where the last is the determining event, corresponds to an eschatological or teleological account, exemplified by White through Augustine's *City of God* and Hegel's *Philosophy of History*. In order to account for a history beyond (apparently) isolated facts, an event should here be understood in the wider sense – that is, not as an atomistic fact, but as the depiction of a synchronic moment in the narrative.[35]

Figure 3 therefore shows different possibilities of causal structuration in a narrative. However, it follows a unilinear chronological path which is clearly incompatible with the spatio-temporal dynamics of Marx's conception of his-tory. In this sense, Harootunian praises White's (occasional) use of the concept of *chronotope* because it substitutes the linearity of the historical period for a multidimensional image of history.[36] While agreeing with this criticism of uni-linearity, it is fair to suggest that although the episodic dimension tends to the linear representation of time, narratives do not necessarily have to be unilin-ear; on the contrary, they can tell a story from different, complementary and

---

34   Jameson 1991, pp. 108–29.
35   White 1978, *pp.* 92–3. About historical events as narrative events, see Ricoeur 1984a, pp. 208–25.
36   Harootunian 2015a, pp. 146–9. See also White 2010, pp. 237–46.

even contradictory points of view. Examples of this abound in literature and films, e.g. Waters's novel *Fingersmith* and Cunningham's *The Hours*, as well as the films *Rashomon* and *Pulp Fiction* by Kurosawa and Tarantino, respectively.[37]

Chronotopes and emplotment are thus not mutually exclusive; rather, a complex chronotope sets the conditions for a complex and multilinear emplotment. Such a story can adopt different strategies of emplotment and combine them under a main line of narrative development. For example, forms of tragic, romantic or comic emplotment can easily coexist under the primacy of satire; the novel does this regularly, as Bakhtin indicates, characterising it as a hybrid form that

> orchestrates all its themes, the totality of the world of objects and ideas depicted and expressed in it, by means of the social diversity of speech types and by the differing individual voices that flourishes under such conditions. ... These distinctive links and interrelationships between utterances and languages, this movement of the theme through different languages and speech types, its dispersion into the rivulets and droplets of social heteroglossia, its dialogization – this is the basic distinguishing feature of the stylistics of the novel.[38]

Historical narrative has no need to be any less complex than this, as any reader of Hobsbawm's classic trilogy on the ages of *Revolution, Capital* and *Empire*, or Braudel's *Mediterranean*, would testify. In its simplest manner, the chronology of events in a process of uneven development can be described through Figure 4, where d and d' correspond to two different events with a common cause and in the same chronological moment, while e and e' share the latter but each of them develops in a different line.

The written narrative is expressed through a single line, but it also has textual devices that account for the complexities of times and spaces. For example, as long as this structure is properly explained and the space-times are well differentiated, the order of the narrative can be: a, b, C, d, e, f, d', e', f'; or it can be d, e, f, d', e', f', a, b, C; or C, d, e, f, d', e', f', a, b.; etc. The chronological and narrative order are not necessarily the same order: e.g. when the latter is expressed by

---

37 Ricoeur 1984a, p. 67. *Pulp Fiction*, for example, consists of several short stories that, although narrated in a non-linear order, consist of events and characters relating to each other that make up a common narrative universe. As for *Rashomon*, which presents different versions of a crime according to different characters in the story, see Redfern 2013, pp. 21–36. These films are hence examples of non-linear narratives.

38 Bakhtin 1981, p. 263.

         d, e, f
1.   a, b, C<
         d', e', f'

FIGURE 4   Events in a narrative of uneven development

a detective story, the explanation of the hidden details of the traumatic event in the past is delivered at the end, or as the development of the causes leading to an event that appears at the beginning of the tale. It is also important to observe that, although Figure 4 is simplified for the sake of clarity, each line refers to a space-time with its own rhythms and directionalities (cyclic, linear, etc.).

   The episodic dimension introduces discontinuities into the space-times of the narrative by indicating the transformations of the configurative dimension: whenever there is change in these spatio-temporal conditions, a re-configurative moment appears in the story. The adequate presentation of spatio-temporal models (with their scales, spatial configurations and rhythms) thus depends on the configurative dimension, but the transformations of the chronotope are developed in the episodic dimension. Marx's theory and sociohistorical analyses provide examples of the relations between chronotopes and spatio-temporal explanation.

4.2   Poetics of Theory

While historiography requires the integration of both the configurative and episodic dimensions of narrative, social theory dwells in the former; in this sense, synchronic explanation is pre-narrative. In Marx's case, the level of the mode of production is then the central problem to be examined through the configurative dimension. Although studies about literary forms and metaphors in Marx's work have been around since at least the 1970s, investigations about these aspects of *Capital* have flourished in the last decade.[39]

   Theological and teratological metaphors are highlighted as constituting a structure that provides additional depth to Marx's explanation of capitalism: in this sense, McNally convincingly contends that Marx establishes a new, radical poetics in which the monstrous plays a central critical role, and Dussel, closer to

---

39   On Marx's poetics in general: Silva 1975; Prawer 1978; Dussel 1993; Wolff 1988. On *Capital* especifically: McNally 2012; Jameson 2014; Roberts 2017; Pepperell 2010. I would like to thank Alex Fletcher for this reference.

the theology of liberation, reinterprets Marx's critique of commodity fetishism as a critique of idolatry – thus Marx's 'metaphorical theology' is negative and fragmentary, but explicitly anti-fetishist. These interpretations are not mutually exclusive, as we can infer from Roberts's analysis of Volume I of *Capital*, in which he finds both Christian religious imagery and monstrous mythology from Dante's *Inferno*; moreover, he argues that Volume I shares its literary form with this aspect of the *Divine Comedy*. Whether this form of representation affects Marx's conceptual and substantive understandings is a further problem which the rest of this chapter tackles.[40]

The most influential interpretation of Marx's philosophy of history from the standpoint of literary form, White's *Metahistory*, differentiates 'grammar' from 'syntax': while the former organises the data of history into the concepts of base and superstructure, the latter deals with their rules of transformation, and ultimately with the Utopian narrative of the successive modes of production leading to communism. In this interpretation, Marx's 'grammar' is metonymic, but his 'syntax' is synecdochic, which in terms of emplotment means that the former tends to be tragic, and the latter tends towards comedy. Furthermore, the imageries in each would be mechanistic and organicist modes of argumentation, respectively.[41]

Metahistory's reading of Marx contrasts with the argument of this work. In regards to what White calls 'grammar', I maintain that the 'base' does not work mechanically on the 'superstructure' but, as a lower stratum, acts as a condition of possibility of the latter. As for the order of the 'syntax', by assuming that the Marxian conception of history was already established by *The German Ideology* – around 1845 – White incorrectly assumes a de-temporalised and de-spatialised version of Marx's philosophy of history, whereby history is a continuum.[42] In opposition to such continuity, this investigation argues that Marx breaks from the world-historical, unilinear narrative in the second half of the 1850s.

We should then examine this matter in more detail in order to adequately understand the construction of Marxian chronotopes. Let us first return to Marx's analysis of precapitalist modes of appropriation in the *Grundrisse*, in which we originally find 'the natural unity of labour with its material presuppositions', such that the worker 'relates to the objective conditions of his

---

40   McNally 2012, pp. 115–16; Dussel 1993. Harvey's critique of Roberts accepts the existence of this form, but argues that it does not have an influence on the theoretical contents of Marx's *Capital*. See Harvey 2017.

41   White 2014, pp. 310–11.

42   White 2014, p. 303.

labour as to his property'.[43] The clan community is the presupposition for the communal appropriation of land and other conditions for subsistence. In its earliest form, there is a balance between community and earth, the latter being 'the great workshop, the arsenal which furnishes both means and material of labour, as well as the seat, the base of the community'.[44]

Although Marx constructs the chronotopes for modes of production mainly through abstract terms related to geometry and movement, he uses metaphors to supplement his explanations. As for these, childhood- and animal-related terms are common in Marx's depiction of the communitarian forms. The characterisation of Greek antiquity as an infantile stage already appears in Marx's praise of classic art in the introduction to the *Grundrisse*. On the other hand, the recurrence of terms derived from *Tier* or *Herde* (for instance, *Herdswesen*: herd-like existence and *Menschenpack*: human pack) insists on the closeness of these forms to animality. Marx characterises these forms as a *unity* of humans between themselves and with nature – a plenitude that contrasts with the isolation required and promoted by capitalism, where individual workers are deprived of their objectivity. In contrast with these forms, the capitalist mode of production is metaphorised as a *complete emptying-out,* and with the religious connotations of a *sacrifice of the human end-in-itself.* The *separation* (*Loslösung*) of workers from land and property thus leads to the *agglomeration,* the *stockpiling* (*Anhäufung,* rather than *Akkumulation*) of workers and instruments at particular points.[45]

But it is not capitalism that threatens the precarious balance of these other forms of property and production. While Marx downplays their internal contradictions, he sees the development of their forces of production as the factor which leads to their *dissolution* (*Auflösung*). Dissolution is the permanent threat to these communitary forms, and as such it appears constantly under both its noun and verb forms in the pages dedicated to the forms preceding capitalism in the *Grundrisse.* Since the Asiatic form is the oldest, its unity is stronger: its members cannot be *separated* from their land, because they are 'rooted to the spot, ingrown' (*festgewachsen*). Again, a metaphor related to nature appears as a temporal marker of an earlier moment. The possibility of

---

43   Marx 1973, p. 471.

44   Marx 1973, p. 472.

45   On geometry and movement, see above, 2.2. On the animal-related terms: Marx 1973, pp. 110–11, 488, 496, 497; Marx and Engels 1983, pp. 44–5, 396, 404. On the unity of pre-capitalist societies: Marx 1973, pp. 495–6. On the 'emptying out' in capitalism: Marx 1973, p. 488; Marx and Engels 1983, p. 396. On separation and stockpiling: Marx 1973, pp. 512, 508; Marx and Engels 1983, pp. 419, 415.

the dissolution of the communitarian form emerges from its own tendency towards separation (of agriculture from manufacture, of individuals from property). The master-servant relation appears then to *ferment* the original forms of property and production.[46]

Marx's rhetorical construction of communitary modes of production is based on a periodisation that permanently relates them with capitalism. Insofar as these modes of production are conceptualised in opposition to their posterity – they are characterised as *forms which precede capitalist production* – their whole construction contains an implicit narrative, given by their inner tendencies. Childhood and animality are temporal metaphors that refer to stages before adulthood and humanity, hence implicitly depicting capitalism as a more developed form: this metaphorics is related to the evolutionist line in the introduction to the *Grundrisse*, according to which the anatomy of the human explains that of the ape.[47]

In this sense, the spatiality of the communitary forms in the *Formen* is based on the opposition between unity and separation, wherein the former means an equitable spatial distribution of the resources – even undifferentiated, as in the case of the Asiatic form – in opposition to the unevenness of capitalism, where labour processes and social wealth are concentrated in places different from one another. Likewise with the pre-capitalist temporalities: their cycles of reproduction should repeat once and again, lest they succumb to nature or turn into non-communitary forms. The fragility of the unitary forms thus has tragic features; indeed, their dissolution comes in terms of a *hybris*, an excess that threatens the balance of their reproduction. This comes with the development of particular interests and relations of domination: with the master-servant relation particular groups substitute for the communitary unity, and thus the *principium individuationis* prevails over unity, just as Nietzsche describes the decline of ancient tragedy.[48]

Concerning the metaphors about capitalism, Dickman asserts that in the first volume of *Capital* Marx

> reaches backward into the Greek mythology of the Cyclopses, to describe monster machines, like a gigantic hammer that even Thor could not wield; and into Hindu mythology, to allude to the proletariat being crushed beneath the wheels of the chariot of Juggernaut. He digs deep into

---

46   On dissolution: Marx 1973, p. 495; Marx and Engels 1983, p. 403. On ferment: Marx 1973, p. 501; Marx and Engels 1983, p. 408.

47   See above, 1.2.

48   Nietzsche 1993.

the grave of the occult, conjuring vampires and werewolves, that suck the blood of workers and devour their flesh. Along with the occult, there is the alchemist's retort, into which lead is transformed into gold. He employs the imagery of the processes of nature: the biological metabolism of man and the physical world; the metamorphosis of the larva in a chrysalis, to emerge as a butterfly. There are nature's flora and fauna: the body with its members, organs and cells; the nut and its kernel, spider and its web, honey bee and its hive. There is the world of machinery, like the clock-work with its cogs and wheels. And man is crippled by this same machine, consumed by it; and is transformed, himself, into a machine for the pro-duction of surplus-value. ... Our fetishism of commodities is compared to an ancient tribe's creation of a fetish to worship as a god. And finally there is the metaphor of war, beginning with the class struggle between the working class and the capitalist class that lies at the heart of capitalism. There are its battles and armies; its barrack-like discipline; its unending list of working-class casualties.[49]

These metaphors describe a world of destruction, where constant transform-ation is the rule. Destruction of labour power, raw materials and even com-modities – through consumption or the waste of goods for which there is no demand – is correlated with production. Capitalism thus appears as a negative force and production as a process of destruction: while metaphors of nature prevail in the fragments about pre-capitalist social forms, capitalism is asso-ciated with the monstrous, especially with werewolves and undead creatures, and alienation appears both as a separation and as an inversion.[50] In the lat-ter case, prosopopoeia – personification – functions as the literary figure that accounts for the power of social products over their producers, with commod-ity fetishism being the most notorious example. There, not only are the char-acters merely personifications of economic relations, but inanimate objects appear to evolve grotesque ideas and intentions of their own.[51] The use of this

---

49   Dickman 2014.
50   About production as destruction, see Jameson 2014. About the monstrous in the first volume of *Capital*, see McNally 2012, p. 109. Silva convincingly argues that Marx's construc-tion of syntactical structures through the inversion of terms is meant to show the unity of opposites in their reciprocal relations. Hence, for example, the young Marx argues that as the dominion of private property begins with the property of land, in late feudalism it is land that inherits the firstborn son rather than the opposite. Silva 1975; Marx and Engels 1988, p. 63.
51   Marx 1976b, p. 179; pp. 163–4.

trope corresponds to a theoretical stance that criticises a world where impersonal forces act as if they were subjects.

Inversion is itself a temporal concept,[52] and since capital is a process rather than a thing, the basis of the valorisation of value is described through images that capture the passage of matter from dispersal to solidity: labour power thus moves from its original *fluid state* to value as a *coagulated state*, a *congealed mass of human labour*. Jelly (*Gallerte*) and 'crystals of this social substance' (*Kristalle dieser ihnen gemeinschaftlichen Substanz*) are other terms with which Marx refers to value in *Capital*, thus referring to production as a *process of transformation* into a solid state:[53] the results of alienated relations achieve a stability that, in light of the continuous transformation of the world by capitalism, is only ever relative.

As argued in the second chapter, Marx provides a much more temporalised account of capitalism than the other, earlier modes of production. In this sense, while the stability of the other modes depends on their lack of development in order to avoid dissolution, in Volume I of *Capital*, as Jameson indicates, the verb *to extinguish* (*auslöschen*) describes a permanent temporal condition of capitalism; *separation* and *expansion*, on the other hand, characterise its space.[54] As Harvey productively interprets it, the metaphor of the *annihilation of space by time* in the *Grundrisse* illustrates the spatio-temporal compression due to capital's tendency to accelerate its turnover cycles, while indicating the destructive character of capitalist production.[55]

Marx thus constructs the chronotope of capitalism through conceptual and metaphoric language, as an unstable stability and as an uneven field of forces where capital is concentrated and centralised among fewer proprietors, while growing masses of people (including capitalists who lose to larger-scale capital) are pauperised. In his words, 'capital grows to a huge mass in a single hand in one place, because it has been lost by many in another place'.[56] This image relies on the conception of movement, and beyond its metaphoric function – after all, 'hands' is not to be taken literally – it describes a landscape of

---

52   Temporal in the sense that it supposes that the inverted situation is not immediate, but a product of social relations. However, such inverted states are not opposed to pre-existing states of plenitude, but refer strictly to the negation of human praxical possibilities. See above, 1.1.

53   Marx 1976b, pp. 142, 128; Marx and Engels 1962, p. 52. As Leslie explains, Marx uses the image of crystallisation with a precise chemical sense, from which he draws an analogy between the social and chemical world. Leslie 2016.

54   Jameson 2014, pp. 93, 110.

55   Harvey 1991.

56   Marx 1976b, p. 777.

an uneven distribution of resources in a geographical space: capital as a movement between 'places' – be they cities (e.g., industrial to financial-based cities),
regions or countries. These centre-periphery relations produce an uneven and
unequal chronotope.[57]

Capital does not focus on the growing wealth of successful capitalists, but
on the growing misery of those directly and indirectly (i.e. unemployed working people) exploited. In Volume I, the literal transcription of testimonies from
factory inspectors and medical reporters serves as a literary realist strategy,
turning bureaucratic documents into vivid accounts of how the tendencies of
capitalism destroy the immediate conditions of working people – and especially their bodies. The consequences of the labour processes and the conditions for their reproduction are therefore presented at the scale of the phenomenal experience, not only as abstract problems; descriptions of illness, degrad-
ation and death abound in its pages. Regarding the consequences of capitalism
on English agricultural labourers, Marx quotes:

> 'Sutherland ... is commonly represented as a highly improved county ...
> but ... recent inquiry has discovered that even there, in districts once fam-
> ous for fine men and gallant soldiers, the inhabitants have degenerated
> into a meagre and stunted race. In the healthiest situations, on hill sides
> fronting the sea, the faces of their famished children are as pale as they
> could be in the foul atmosphere of a London alley'.[58]

Hence Marx's poetics of modes of production is irreducible to a metonymical
operation, since the latter cannot, on its own, account for the contradiction and
uneven development that structure his chronotopes. Moreover, even if we were
to accept White's (wrong) mechanistic interpretation of the relation between
base and superstructure, this relation is secondary in respect to the logic of the

---

57   Marx also observes processes of displacement – now referred to as 'gentrification' – as
      structural effects of the capitalist production of space: '"improvements" of towns which
      accompany the increase of wealth, such as the demolition of badly built districts, the erec-
      tion of palaces to house banks, warehouses etc., the widening of streets for business traffic,
      for luxury carriages, for the introduction of tramways, obviously drive the poor away into
      even worse and more crowded corners'. Marx 1976b, p. 812.

58   Marx 1976b, pp. 380–1. Regarding the inadequate conditions of housing, Marx quotes: '"in
      its higher degrees it [i.e. overcrowding] almost necessarily involves such negation of all
      delicacy, such unclean confusion of bodies and bodily functions, such exposure of animal
      and sexual nakedness, as is rather bestial than human. To be subject to these influences is
      a degradation which must become deeper and deeper for those on whom it continues to
      work"'. Marx 1976b, p. 813.

value-form and the world it produces. Although *Metahistory* contributes useful tropological and narratological elements for the analysis of social theory and historiography, its account of Marx's literary forms is insufficient.

The interpretation of *Capital* as an ironic text is more challenging. Pepperell and LaCapra develop interesting analyses of this matter, the former, in particular, considering that the sole intent of this book is to disclose the inconsistencies of bourgeois political economy and to deconstruct the Hegelian category of totality – which she defines rather arbitrarily as a metaphor – through the use of parody. For Pepperell, Marx's theory of value is a parody in which Marx 'intends the argument not to be taken seriously'.[59]

If this interpretation were correct, the object of *Capital* would be political economy rather than capitalism. This contrasts with numerous affirmations from Marx about how his book unveils the functioning of the mode of production based on capital, and sidesteps the epistemologically realist dimensions of his work on political economy. That Marx considers that knowledge in a historical moment is conditioned by the 'limitations of the practical experiences available to members of his society',[60] does not invalidate such knowledge, but situates it as a product of determined conditions – as is already the case in Hegel's philosophy. Following this line it is arguable, against Pepperell's antifoundationalist interpretation, that historicisation itself necessarily relies on an ontology, and that in capitalism labour plays the role of praxis in Marx's ontology of social being: *Capital* not only explicates positive dimensions of capitalism, but is also based on ontological assumptions.

In any case, the tropology of the configurative dimension is only a preliminary element of the narrative chronotope, whose inner tendencies – as part of the analogical grammar for the explanation of the mechanisms in question – it helps to characterise. The presentation (*Darstellung*) of the chronotope at the configurative level requires the episodic dimension in order to develop a properly historiographical narrative. It is the in episodic that the problems of periodisation and emplotment, as well as the relations in historiography between the epistemic, the political and the aesthetic, are productively clarified.

---

59 LaCapra 1983; Pepperell 2010, p. 79. In contrast, Tomba characterises the poetics of *Capital* as a sort of estrangement effect (*Verfremdungseffekt*): 'the literary style of *Capital*, its metaphors and its sarcasm are functional to the change of perspective that is able to disorient; to render foreign what is familiar'. Tomba 2013a, p. 122. Similarly, McNally analyses how the concept of the *fetishism* of commodities ironises the stereotype of superstitious non-European societies by indicating the superstition behind the everyday functioning of capitalist economy. McNally 2012, pp. 126–7.

60 Pepperell 2010, p. 90. On Marx's realism, for example, Marx 1978, p. 303; Marx 1973, p. 90. See above, 2.1.

4.3   Emplotment as Politics

As argued in the second chapter, the explanation of an actual individual social form requires the consideration of the various mechanisms at work in its development. Even as different strata and spheres have observable tendencies, the interaction between them – each with its own space-times – produces unpredictable outcomes. In historiographical narrative, this contingent character of actual history thus requires the episodic dimension to account for the development of the process as story. A narrative explanation is thus one that retrospectively accounts for the contingencies of a historical process while relating them to the generative mechanisms that help to explain such development.

As Jameson indicates, class struggle is Marx's central narrative device;[61] in the analysis of specific conjunctures, however, this conflict is embodied by empirical actors, which in the actual situation means that it has determinations beyond those directly linked to the stratum of forces and relations of production – however determinant these factors may in the last instance be. While in his interpretation of the Paris Commune Marx identifies the struggle between the bourgeoisie and the working class as a form of the conflict between Versailles and Paris, his analysis of the U.S. Civil War is built on the opposition of two capitalist forces based on different forms of exploitation: slave versus wage labour, South versus North.

Collective actants – impersonal and supra-personal characters – thus unite heterogeneous social groups. 'The South' in the context of the Civil War encompasses for Marx the slave-owners and 'poor whites' – but not the slaves – while 'the North', in turn, refers to industrial capitalists as well as the salaried working class. Paris and Versailles symbolise spaces led by opposing social classes, although each of them is not on its own. These actants, named here after their geographical referents, are metonymical constructions insofar as they reduce plurality to one of its parts – both in the sense of the leading social force and their belonging to a space. The characters in the narrative of 'so-called primitive accumulation' are more diffuse, but since these chapters account for the birth and tribulations of the working class, they would therefore constitute a sort of Gothic tale of horrors for the populations enduring dispossession.

Marx's narrative thus depends on a double tropic operation: it integrates the social actors through metonymy, but this integration has meaning only to the extent that they are part of a wider conflict where the whole is different than the addition of its constituent parts. In *The Civil War in France*, his praise

---

61   Jameson 2010, p. 550.

of the independent and empowered Parisian *communard* women accompanies his scorn of the *cocottes* and their protectors, which symbolised the old world championed by Versailles. The old French state appears as a parasitic creature[62] and, again, the opposition between life and death arises in this text: the Assembly of the Rurals is 'the representative of everything dead in France, propped up to the semblance of life by nothing but the swords of Louis Bonaparte. Paris all truth, Versailles all lie: and that lie vented through the mouth of Thiers'.[63]

The same consideration of contradictory unity is made explicit in Marx's work on the U.S. Civil War: in spite of what their differences might suggest, the North and South, he warns, cannot be considered as separate countries, because they competed for the same territories. The only way one could survive is if it vanquished the other,[64] a situation that inevitably unified them and made separation an implausible solution to their conflict. As with his narrative of the Commune, Marx's analyses of the war in the United States ultimately define their chronotope by reference to the state-form – albeit in necessary reference to the world market. The abstract chronotope of the capitalist mode of production guides these accounts, and their specific spatio-temporal narrative characteristics are developed on top of it. Centre-periphery spatial configurations, to name an example, are common in both cases, but they now appear as concrete historical conditions that configure the (episodic) development of the conjuncture.[65]

While the chronotope of 'so-called primitive accumulation' is specifically the world market, this narrative focuses on the consequences of this expansion on British territory. The medieval English state is a central actor in this process, through the action of different successive kings and their legislations for the dispossession of the immediate producers from their soil. The metaphors Marx uses here are not only monstrous but brutal; the history of this expropriation,

---

62   Marx 1986, p. 341. When Marx writes about the 'heroic, noble and devoted' women of the Commune who 'give up their lives at the barricades and on the place of execution' (Marx 1986, p. 350), it is impossible not to recall the *pétroleuses* who resisted the occupation from the Versailles army. See Thomas 2007. Also, Linton 1997, pp. 23–47; Eichner 2004. On the state as parasite: Marx 1986, p. 328.

63   Marx 1986, p. 342.

64   Marx 1984a, p. 60.

65   In this sense, the level of a social formation functions at the configurative dimension, while the conjuncture does so at the episodic dimension. Albeit pertaining to different levels of abstraction, both the mode of production and the social formation work in a synchronic manner, i.e., on the basis of mechanisms that follow certain rules – while the episodic dimension accounts for changes in such mechanisms.

he indicates, 'is written in the annals of mankind in letters of blood and fire'.[66] Accordingly, this part of *Capital* echoes numerous testimonies abounding in details about the consequences of this process of ruthless enslavement, plunder, murder and torture on the bodies of the expropriated in Great Britain and around the world. Moreover, Marx ironises abundantly by recalling bourgeois humanitarian and religious commonplaces about capitalism and its origins.[67]

The account of the origins of capitalism is structured by the explanation of the different processes and agents that led to the consolidation of that mode of production in England and Northwestern Europe. Unlike texts like *The Class Struggles in France* and the *18th Brumaire*, which kept a more linear narrative, the section on 'so-called primitive accumulation' proceeds by separating each of the processes – each with different spatio-temporal determinations, but protagonised by Western European forces – that unveil 'the secret of primitive accumulation' – precisely the name of the first chapter of this section. Although the explanation focuses on English capitalism as its final result, the spatio-temporal differentiality of the account suggests paths to peripheral capitalism (as in the Americas and Southeast Asian colonies) as well: it is a multilinear narrative – perhaps Marx's most complex account of an actual process.

Narratively, *The Civil War in France* follows a more linear episodic order, with the first section explaining the immediate political context after the Franco-Prussian war that defines the characters, both collective and individual (with several pages dedicated to Thiers in particular), while the second refers to the uprising of Paris against the National Assembly. The third, in turn, does a brief *flashback* in French political history in order to explain the changes set in motion by the Commune. The fourth closes the narrative, drawing conclusions from the defeat of the Parisian forces, especially by Prussian intervention: as a small scale narrative, the role of this foreign army in a critical moment is the decisive element for the outcome of this conflict. The closing paragraphs, referring to the solidarity of the International Workingmen's Association with the Commune, and the support of other European governments with Thiers's counterrevolution, project the opposition between Paris and Versailles as a synecdoche to the whole of Europe.

On the other hand, the ongoing character of Marx and Engels's writings about the Civil war in the United States and their publication in newspapers during the years of 1861 and 1862 led to a corpus that was never unified by

---

66   Marx 1976b, p. 875.
67   For instance, after describing the devastation and depopulation in Java by the Dutch, Marx
      concludes: 'That is peaceful commerce!' Marx 1976b, p. 916.

these authors into a single piece. Even so, they all amount to a coherent narrative, where some of the articles have a more long-scale structural (narratively configurative) character, and function as the backbone for others that focus on more specific themes – the shortage of cotton, electoral or military events, for example. Hence, Marx's articles in *Die Presse* on 25 October and 7 November 1861[68] establish the configurative chronotope from which he and Engels develop other narratives – on military, commercial or electoral matters, among others – related to this theme. These premises of the narrative set up its final outcome (which had not yet arrived at the time when these articles were written: although Lincoln's election was the event that unleashed the tensions between the slave- and wage-labour regimes, Marx considers that the same conditions that produced the war long before it started would lead to the victory of the North), even when military events suggested the contrary.

Hence, in the Marxian construction of chronotopes at the configurative dimension, metonymy and synecdoche are mutually necessary, although not in the sense that White argues: the metonymical 'grammar' is not, according to our considerations, a phase of a synecdochical 'syntax' that articulates the modes of production one after another.[69] This unity of opposites in historiography corresponds to what Jameson, inspired by Aristotle, characterises as *destiny*, which leads to recognition of the *Other*: the moment of taking sides in this oppositional narrative, which in turn generates political confrontation. His third figure, that of the *Absolute*, refers to historical experience as the totalisation of History as system and as event, which in narrative terms entails the problem of the construction of the chronotopical totalisation – the experience of globalisation is the central reference in Jameson's essay.[70]

In these terms, the diversity of Marx's narrative choices can be understood as defined by such taking sides, which makes the subject position explicit in the otherwise seemingly impersonal theoretical analysis of the conjuncture.[71] A significant part of the narrative form depends on the delimitation of the space-times of the story: even in the fairytale form, for instance, the formula 'and they lived happily ever after' represses the necessity of the death of the characters by

---

68 Marx 1984e, pp. 32–42 and Marx 1984c, pp. 43–52.

69 White 2014, p. 310.

70 Jameson 2010, pp. 475–612.

71 Bourdieu's distinction between position and position-taking is here especially useful: each subject (qua *habitus*) occupies a position within their social field, but through their practices can assume different options in regards to the contradictions in such a field. Thus, the habitus has an initial *disposition* towards certain attitudes and practices, but eventually can take distance from them. Bourdieu 1996, pp. 231–4.

closing the narrative before such existential ends arrive.[72] It is hence useful to recall Jameson's affirmation that periodisations are 'representational choices which can neither be proven nor falsified, which correspond to starting points in the void, without presuppositions, or in other words that they can be false but never true, and that they can only be motivated politically but not by the "facts"'.[73]

Let us assess this position by examining some of Marx's narratives. In them, the fortune of the oppressed classes defines the tone and style: thus, in spite of the bloody repression by the reactionary forces against the Commune, Marx suggests that the conflict between the Old and the New will continue, and that socialism will eventually be able to overcome this contradiction: he thus avoids a tragic closure of this narrative. Certainly, the same events described in a different manner can serve as the basis for other narrative forms – for example depicting the rise and fall of the Commune through a comic form where an original order is restored after a temporal disruption. Eventually, a shift of scale in the periodisation would allow a *happy ending* for either of the two conflicting narratives: in the short scale, the restoration of the pre-Commune order is a triumph for the bourgeoisie, but in the large scale, by considering the possible expropriation of the expropriators as a reappropriation by the community, the *happy ending* would be for the proletarians. Yet it is also arguable that Marx might formulate this possibility not merely because of narrative means, but because in his work the mechanisms that generate class struggle have not been exhausted, and thus the massacre of the Communards does not mark the end of the political conflict in Europe, in spite of constituting an important episode of it. Theory sets limits to historical narrative, which is hence not exclusively determined by the political point of view of the narrator.

Since historiography always deals with the *history of* ... (of a city, an individual, a social class, an institution, etc.), its periodisation depends on the concrete development of the historiographical object – what Danto indistinctly

---

72   This importance of delimitation in narrative is also exemplified by an anecdote from Žižek about religious film censorship in the former Yugoslavia. In his account, by cutting some of the references to Christ in *Ben Hur* and ending the film shortly after the main character's triumph in the horse-race, the censor completely changed the meaning of the movie – for the better: 'although undoubtedly he had not the slightest notion of the tragic existentialist vision, he made out of a rather insipid Christian propaganda piece an existential drama about the ultimate nullity of our accomplishments, about how in the hour of our greatest triumph we are utterly alone. And how did he pull it off? He added nothing: he brought about the effect of "depth", of a profound existential vision, by simply *mutilating* the work, by depriving it of its crucial parts'. Žižek 1994, pp. 127–28.

73   Jameson 2014, p. 76.

calls a *temporal whole* and *temporal structure*[74] – whose story it tells. Against the Althusserian epistemology at the base of Jameson's appreciation of periodisation, a Marxian realist perspective would not depend on the *a priori* constitution of a theoretical object – in (a false) opposition with the *reception* of the latter[75] – but would research the mechanisms at work in the specific spheres of an object and their relation with the social formation where it exists. Otherwise, Marx's periodisations in *The 18th Brumaire* and *The Civil War in France*, which are not directly based on the development of the productive forces but on the shifting balances of power in the state and politics, would have to be considered merely polemical formulations rather than explanations of actual processes, and would have no relation with the theory of history or that of capitalism in particular.

However, a specific historiographical object can be periodised differently, according to the aspect that the narrative explanation wants to emphasise. For example, the account of a city will vary whether the interest is focused on its architectural, economic, political or demographic aspects. The *reception* of the reference (the particular city, in this case) is the first moment in the methodological construction of the object, which should not only synthesise its internal determinations and diverse mechanisms, but also its relation with the complex totalisation in which it develops: in Marxian historiography, the object always plays a role in regards to the respective mode of production.[76] In any case, the problem of *reference* is not simply ideological; a theory which cannot account for the empirical – i.e. relate the latter to its abstract categories – cannot be considered a scientific approach. A historiographical object hence consists of several interrelated forms whose apprehension helps to make it more concrete and better explain it. When Marx deals with Paris in *The Civil War in France*, he

---

74 'Any term which can sensibly be taken as a value for x in the expression "the history of x" designates a temporal structure. Our criteria for identifying a, if a be a value of x, determines which events are to be mentioned in our history'. Danto 2007, p. 167; also p. 248.

75 Jameson's quoted stance above follows Balibar's in *Reading Capital*, according to which 'the determination of the objects of these histories must await that of the relatively autonomous instances of the social formation, and the production of concepts which will define each of them by the structure of a *combination*, like the mode of production. We can predict that these definitions, too, will always be *polemical* definitions, i.e., they will only be able to constitute their objects by destroying ideological classifications or divisions which benefit from the obviousness of the "facts"'. Balibar 2009b, p. 281. On theoretical apriorism, also Balibar 2009b, p. 279.

76 This is also true about *longue-durée* objects that transcend more than one mode of production. Thus Marx sketches histories of 'antediluvian' forms such as money and commercial capital, in Volume III of *Capital*, Marx 1981.

does it primarily from the point of view of the political mechanisms at work in that conjuncture, and this perspective leads the narrative, marking its defining turning points and limiting the possible forms that the story can take.

As a spatio-temporal operation, periodisation refers to the transformations of the narrative space-time through the narrative sequence: beyond the configurative chronotope – which was addressed in the previous section – there is an episodic chronotope which accounts for the narrative as a whole. Such an episodic chronotope sets the conditions for the emplotment, by determining not only the spatio-temporal conditions of the narrative (as defined by the spatio-temporal models for social explanation), but its delimitations as well. In a narration, the configurative chronotope can go through one or several transformations, or through none at all, but there is always an episodic chronotope as far as there is a narrative spatio-temporal delimitation.

In this sense, the periodisation of the military conflicts in the United States and Paris might seem to be obvious if we take for granted that the respective beginnings and endings of open hostilities between the sides were necessarily the beginnings and endings of the stories. But the conditions for the emergence of these wars nonetheless predate them (and in the case of the Commune, the substantive social conflict was not solved with the war), and hence Marx extends their respective chronotopes beyond the narrated events. Marx's account of the U.S. Civil War starts with the bombardment of Fort Sumter near Charleston in 1861, but the configurative chronotope which frames the conflict goes back to the distribution in 1787 of states dedicated to slavery, and to the negotiations about this matter in 1820, 1854, and 1859.[77] The constant struggles between the two blocs of states for the appropriation and formation of new states – whose reasons Marx explained[78] – conform to the chronotope through which this author narratively explains this war. Thus, the chronotope periodises, but is not limited to the events included within its own periodisation.

Marx's chronotopes are always structured on the basis of a conflict, with uneven social relations leading to uneven development: Paris and the rest of France at the end of the war with Prussia, and the North and South in the United States after Lincoln's election, configure the chronotopes in the respective narratives, with the accumulation of capital as the ultimate background of these processes. On the other hand, the chronotope of 'so-called primitive accumulation' – delimited by the expanding world market between the thirteenth and eighteenth centuries – is reconfigured through the depiction of the

---

77   Marx 1984e, p. 35.
78   See above, 2.3.

violence deployed in order to separate workers from their means of subsistence, and thus narrates the origins of the chronotope of capitalism. At the end of this section of *Capital* the original configurative chronotope has undergone a transformation into another, with class struggle at its base. In these cases, chronotopes are determined in order to explain the mechanisms behind the historiographical objects – here, conjunctures.

Having stressed the epistemological component of historiographical narration (against Jameson's claim that periodisation is a merely representational problem, thus downplaying its cognitive dimension), it is nonetheless imperative to state – with Jameson's argument about the role of the *Other* in narrativity – that side-taking is a necessary component of narrative, and that this is unavoidable due to the subject-matter of historiography: fractured societies cannot be neutrally described since, as Horkheimer argues, their conceptualisation always assumes a position within the field that it seeks to explain.[79] Partiality in historiography is thus inevitable, both because of the inherently political character of social theory – as observed in the relation between the conceptual and non-conceptual in Figure 1 – and because of the very essence of narrative: whereas abstract conceptualisation can barely conceal its political side-taking, narration cannot at all.

Social explanation – which in historiography requires a narrative form – is dependent on a subject position towards the formation it references.[80] In this sense, Marx and Engels's project of a scientific socialism implies that action can be inferred from analysis: the interpretation of the world should be the basis for its transformation, as his eleventh thesis on Feuerbach famously claims. The concept of an *explanatory critique* – which maintains the possibility of a unity

---

79   See Horkheimer 1982, pp. 188–243. In a similar line, Sayer affirms that 'realism does not require some kind of denial of "subjective" influences or standpoints and researchers' social context. On the contrary, it requires us to examine those standpoints so as to guard against forms of projection and selection which misrepresent our objects. Realist social science requires reflexivity'. Sayer 2000, p. 53.

80   In a piece written in the late 1970s, Jameson argues that a properly Marxist hermeneutic should address history as the confrontation of two distinct social forms or modes of production (that of the historian and that of his subject-matter). While he indicates that the individual character in the reading of a culturally or temporally distant artifact should not be dismissed, he nonetheless ignores the *class mediation* in this relation, thus opposing two modes of production as if they were monolithic units. Moreover, Jameson's dismissal of the concept of 'social formation' weakens the possibility of a concrete historicised approach to objects from artifacts different than researchers' contexts. Jameson 2008b, pp. 451–82 (especially pp. 475–80). As we will learn, Jameson himself provides a more productive explanation of the production of narratives through his critique of White's formalism.

of facts and values in social enquiry[81] – is at the crux of Marx's epistemology. The historical character of historiography as a social discourse – that is, its condition as a product of human praxis in a concrete social formation – defines it not only as a cognitive and aesthetic but as a political problem as well. For Marx, narrative explanation is therefore necessarily an explanatory critique.

Marx's account of 'so-called primitive accumulation' serves as an example of explanatory critique. Its very name is an ironic – even sarcastic – gesture to Adam Smith's theory of the origins of capitalism, which Marx replaces with another explanation that, based on an array of sources, shows the barbarism necessary for the emergence of the mode of production based on capital – a narrative explanation which is possible by making the point of view of the dispossessed visible. The explanation of the human costs generated by the mechanisms of capital accumulation is possible by approaching the social totality from its underside; this explanation is thus at the same time a critique formulated from the perspective of those who have not profited from these processes of dispossession.

As a socially produced discourse (form of praxis), the tropes and emplotment in a historiographic narration are conditioned by the side-taking implicit in the chronotope. Narrative is neither simply a logical nor aesthetic act: it is produced by a subject and thus implies an ideological closure.[82] Jameson's historicised critique of White's narrative formalism, following a case study by Greimas, argues for the necessity of the consideration of the social conditions underlying the utterance of the narratives: although there are different logical possibilities for the utterance of a discourse, its real possibilities are limited by the social position of the utterer. Therefore, he argues that 'what is missing [in White's method] is the mechanism of historical selection – that infrastructural limiting situation – to which it falls, out of the complete *logical* possibilities, to reject those that cannot empirically come into being in that determinant historical conjuncture'.[83]

---

81   'Values play a role not only in the choice of problems to investigate, but also in the adoption of strategies that specify the kinds of theories to pursue, the kinds of concepts they will deploy, the kinds of possibilities they are capable of identifying, and various methodological matters that concern the procuring of relevant evidence'. Lacey 2007, p. 199.

82   Considered as praxis, social scientific explanation already-always entails both cognitive and evaluative elements. In this sense, when approached from a dialectical perspective, the discussion of whether or not values can be inferred from facts is redundant: this is not a problem of logic, but of the pragmatics of discourse. See Edgley 1998, and Bhaskar 1998, pp. 395–408 and pp. 409–17.

83   Jameson 2008a, p. 168. Greimas's example analyses a Lithuanian folktale where a single actant could have logically united the functions of a father and priest, but this variant was

The *18th Brumaire* indeed relies on numerous satirical resources, and *The Civil War in France* has an epic tone. In both cases, mechanisms are explained in order to account for the conjuncture, but the narratives have different forms, because the approach to the events precludes some of the possible emplotments for a concrete narrator. A socialist narrator can tell the story of a failed revolution as a tragedy or as a coming-of-age tale, but her political perspective would make it quite difficult, if not impossible, to frame such a theme under the overall form of a comedy – unless it was a satire, which is not properly a comedy. Even so, satire would have been an odd choice of emplotment for the narration of a process like the Paris Commune, one that ended with the massacre of thousands of working-class people. Far from this, Marx's (theoretically-justified) chronotopical opening of this narrative – with the possible future of a triumphant working class – avoids concluding the account of this political experience with a pessimistic message.

The chronotopical operation which enables certain emplotments thus relies on the explanation of the mechanisms at work in the analysed historiographical object, but is also a political intervention in its own right. Temporalisations, as Osborne maintains, open different political possibilities in relation to capitalism[84] and – specifically in the case of historiography – the chronotope opens the possibility for appropriations of historical experiences from different social positions in struggle. Therefore, narrative explanation always implies taking a stand in the struggle for memory, wherein the narrative spatio-temporalising resources are essential.

The materialist analysis of historiographical narratives should then account for this imbrication of the cognitive, political and aesthetic, with the chronotope articulating these aspects. Narrativity thus completes the role of (synchronic) presentation in Marx's dialectic by accounting for actual history; there can be no explanation of an open system without an account of the contingency inherent to the complexity of the interaction of mechanisms in a given social formation. This is the reason for Marx's affirmation that 'reflection on the forms of human life, hence also scientific analysis of those forms, takes a course directly opposite to their real development. Reflection begins *post festum*, and therefore with the results of the process of development ready to hand'.[85]

---

precluded in the Catholic context – where the tale was produced – due to the mandate of priests' celibacy.

84   Osborne 2010, pp. 200–1; see above, Introduction. Also, Davis 2008.
85   Marx 1976b, p. 168. Hence also, as Jameson has pointed out, in Marxism 'the concept of historical necessity or inevitability is ... operative exclusively *after the fact*'. Jameson 1971, p. 361.

Epilogue

In his preface to *The Class Struggles in France*, Grüner observes how 'in this intensely *narrative* Marx, with his elegant and at moments relentlessly ironic style, we find all the theoretical and reflexive power of *Capital* and the *Grundrisse*, as well as the irresistible seduction of the great writer'.[86]

Indeed, Marx's writings about actual historical processes demonstrate that although structural explanation and narrative are different from each other, they are not – as historians and philosophers of history held during the twentieth century – mutually exclusive. On the contrary, narrative is the necessary means to seize the transformations of the diverse social mechanisms and their interactions in space and time; metaphors and other tropes are a substantial part of the formulation of scientific theories, as is literary form, additionally, for their application to actual contexts. The account of each mechanism is the problem of presentation, but its development in an actual formation is a matter of narrativity; narration thus completes presentation. In this sense, it is clear from the consideration of the levels of abstraction in Marx that – in history – narrative does not have to substitute for explanation, but can be, as with Marx's case studies, a kind of explanation based on several synchronicities: the narrative explanation of a conjuncture.

Although the linguistic turn in the philosophy of history elevated tropology and emplotment to the status of the only significant element of historical *discourse* – a concept that would substitute that of historical *knowledge* – a narrative explanation should first of all account for the real mechanisms and their transformations in the analysed social formation. Historiographical narrative should show how the hierarchised combination of the diverse mechanisms lead to particular consequences. Yet beyond this epistemological consideration, contents from sources cannot simply be fit into *any* previously assumed narrative form for pragmatic reasons: literary form has its own (historical) political mechanisms that set the rules for their use by social agents based on their subject positions.

However, as Tomba contends in the quote cited at the beginning of this chapter, the complexity of the relations between subject positions cannot be apprehended by simply juxtaposing their standpoints without a previously projected order. Guha, for example, argues for breaking from the coherence and linearity he affirms are inherent to narrativity, and which he claims 'dic-

---

86   Grüner 2005, p. 4. Emphasis in the original.

tates what should be included in the story and what is left out'.[87] Disruption and 'making a mess of its plot' is the way in which a new historiography would become multi-voiced, though the precise form resulting from this disorder is hard to predict. Consequently, finding an order in this presumed chaos would be a relapse into 'the regime of bourgeois narratology'[88] whose main narrative is that of the unilinearity of historical development and Eurocentric progress.

Such a merely negative – or rather nihilistic – approach is not only wrong in its simplification of narrativity to unilinearity, but by disavowing coherence, it disallows the explanation of its complex and contradictory object. Moreover, it relies on a problematic conception of history that takes memory as its model.[89] Jameson interprets similar positions in political terms:

> I suspect, indeed, that there are only a finite number of interpretive possibilities in any given textual situation, and that the program to which the various contemporary ideologies of pluralism are most passionately attached is a largely negative one: namely to forestall that systematic articulation and totalisation of interpretive results which can only lead to embarrassing questions about the relationship between them and in particular the place of history and the ultimate ground of narrative and textual production.[90]

This finite number of interpretive options is thus bound, as mentioned, with the narrative forms available for each subject position in relation to the contradictions in a determined social formation. The chronotope encompasses periodisation, but is more complex than this: through both its configurative and episodic dimensions, it articulates the epistemological, the political, and the aesthetic in historiography, making explicit through tropes and emplotment the side-taking which social theories tend to keep implicit.

Marx does not fully develop the implications of his theory of history for his historiography. However, since the presentation should make intelligible the functioning of the social totalisation, it is clear that a chronotope constructed on the basis of contradiction is necessary in order to explain the spatio-temporal dynamic of contradictory societies. Furthermore, while the concept of history implies the integration of the multiplicity of human experience into a single narrative, it is arguable that a totalising narrative is the necessary liter-

---

87   Guha 2009, p. 316.
88   Guha 2009, pp. 316–17.
89   Osborne 2013, pp. 190–6.
90   Jameson 2002, p. 16.

ary form for the totalising actual social form *par excellence* which is capitalism. In this sense, Marx's narrative of 'so-called primitive accumulation' as well as his account of the worldwide effects of the U.S. Civil War are examples of how narration can rely on different subplots and present them in a multilinear manner. At the same time, they show that narrative can be the means for the explanation of the complexity of the relations between processes in different space-times – even as it acknowledges its own side-taking.

Towards a Politics of Spatio-Temporal Totalisation

> If, then, today we detect a stagnation in our movement as far as these
> theoretical matters are concerned, this is not because the Marxist
> theory upon which we are nourished is incapable of development or
> has become out-of-date. On the contrary, it is because we have not
> yet learned how to make adequate use of the most important mental
> weapons which we had taken out of the Marxist arsenal on account
> of our urgent need for them in the early stages of our struggle. It is
> not true that, as far as practical struggle is concerned, Marx is out-
> of-date, that we had superseded Marx.[1]

• • •

> Always historicize![2]

• •
•

The analysis of Marx's work in this investigation has demonstrated, in the spirit
of Luxemburg's epigraph, that the explanatory possibilities opened by Marx's
conception of history are still far from exhausted. Politically and scientific-
ally productive concepts and approaches emerge from both his theoretical and
conjunctural writings – although Marx does not thoroughly develop the methodological issues and implications in the latter. Vilar's characterisation of historical research based on Marx's conception as an ongoing project – an *histoire
en construction*[3] – is therefore accurate; to the extent that his work is read and
adapted in accordance with diverse and changing historical circumstances, the
precision of its concepts and overall reach of its theory will continue to grow.

In this sense, the expansion of the capitalist world market since the 1990s,
commonly known as 'globalisation', makes the consideration and development
of the Marxian categories of social space and social time – which are not just

---

1   Rosa Luxemburg, quoted in Aricó 2014, p. 7.
2   Jameson 2002, p. ix.
3   Vilar 2011, pp. 47–80.

formal indicators but active, determinant elements in the development of historical forms – necessary in order to account for such a complex, multilinear process. Their elaboration by recent Marxist and post-Marxist authors thus responds to the need to account for the complexities of this reconfiguration of the world-system. Marx was one of the first theorists of globalisation; its later development also, in turn, throws light on his views on capitalism.

But, in addition to this historical condition, such proliferation of analyses based on the categories of social time and social space are explained at the most abstract level through Marx's concepts of praxis and totalisation (read through Lefebvre and Sartre), which lead to the conclusion that space and time are both necessary dimensions for the organisation of the social world and of our thoughts about it. A social totalisation is always mediated by space and time, and the consideration of these categories therefore enhances our knowledge about a particular social form. The Marxian operation of historicising does not consist in the mere location of a social phenomenon within geographical and chronological coordinates, but rather explains it in relation to the concrete totalisation wherein it takes place. Historicisation is not just a formal operation (although this is a necessary preliminary moment), but refers a social phenomenon to its corresponding social structure.

This work has argued for the importance of a realist reading of Marx – a necessary perspective in times when the (usually anti-Marxist) intellectual field of the philosophy of history has little relevance for social and historical research[4] – that examines his contributions to the different moments of historical knowledge: the ontology of history and the epistemological phases of theory, archive and presentation.[5] From this realist point of view, the process of totalisation in the world corresponds with knowledge as a process of re-totalisation that renders the former intelligible; ontology and epistemology form part of a dialectical unity.

As forms through which the world is organised and categories that help to explain it, social space and social time traverse all the ontological and epistemological moments. At the most abstract level – the ontology of history and social being – such forms are produced by the combinations of individual

---

4   Ironically, current philosophers of history like Carr and Ankersmit continue to dismiss dialectics and Marx's philosophy of history by referring to stereotypical Cold War depictions by authors like Walsh and Mink. See Ankersmit 2012, pp. 14–16; Carr 2014, 103–4.

5   For Haldon, 'historical materialism, while embedded within the philosophical terrain of a realist materialist epistemology, is less a philosophy itself than it is an empirical theory'. Haldon 1993, p. 26. However, it is misleading to assert this primacy of 'empirical theory', given the ontological framework that underlies the epistemological phases, as observed in the first chapter.

praxes, and are explained by generative mechanisms in different strata and spheres of social life. Marx's method of totalisation, based on social forms rather than stages, is outlined in the *Grundrisse*, but is developed and consolidated through his theoretical and political approaches to non-Western European countries – ultimately leading to his view of the 'Russian path' to socialism, without previous capitalist development. On the other hand, the concepts of 'subsumption' and 'abstract labour', elaborated in the 1860s, are central to the explanation of the historical expansion of capital, and are necessary in order to theoretically relate the diverse times and spaces in this process of uneven and combined development.

This ontology of multilinear history thus enables us to account for the diverse forms of human organisation through the theory of history – provided, of course, that such forms are duly studied in their specificity. The concept of history – which ultimately assumes the unity of human experience – entails the interplay between different levels of abstraction and concreteness, where real mechanisms are abstracted from the social phenomena, but then explain the latter concretely through concepts and models constructed in the process of abstraction. Such mechanisms have spatio-temporal tendencies – which can be synthesised into spatio-temporal models – whose consideration is necessary in order to explain the particular organisation of actual social formations. Elements of these spatio-temporal models are found in Marx's conceptualisations of modes of production, which thus allow better, more accurate explanations of the activities and transformations in each of these forms.

The ontological difference between mode of production and social formation therefore allows us to grasp the relations between the levels of abstraction in a totalisation, where a mode of production is abstract but real, whereas a social formation is actual: it is more concrete, with more determinations to explain. Epistemologically, to the extent that modes of production – qua mechanisms – are closed systems, their outcomes are necessary, but insofar as social formations – qua open systems – develop in relation with other mechanisms, a certain level of contingency is always present in history. Marx's characterisation of the pre-U.S. Civil War southern states, for example, discloses a capitalism that developed on the basis of geographic and demographic conditions very different from those in Northwestern Europe. The analysis of capitalism at the level of the mode of production is thus necessary, but insufficient in attending to the particular formations where it prevails; thus, a properly spatio-temporalised explanation must account for the diversity of the modalities of the expansion of capitalism by relating it to other mechanisms.

Regarding the documentary phase, by undertaking his work in London Marx had a huge amount of sources from which to elaborate his theories and analyses of specific cases. However, this imperial archive had the drawback of its own conditions of possibility: its sources were produced in asymmetrical social relations, and thus tended to reflect the dominant class, gender and colonial positions of their times. Marx was very conscious of bourgeois ideology in his sources and denounced the violence of colonialism behind the 'civilising' claims of his Western European sources, but the critique of ideology is a negative procedure that cannot substitute for the positive contents of the sources, and thus the spatio-temporal bias of Eurocentrism in his archive was a permanent problem for Marx's research – a major drawback of working on some issues mostly with secondary literature.

Thus, while he does not hold an exoticising view of non-European societies, his archival limitations lead him to the problematic theory of 'the Asiatic mode of production', which Marx abandons when new scholarship in the 1870s showed that Indian communities followed other patterns of social development. Research by authors based on sources unavailable to Marx, but following his theory and method (e.g. the work of Eric Williams, John Haldon, Jairus Banaji, and Chris Wickham), accounts for non-Western and non-capitalist formations, and shows Marx's post-*Grundrisse* materialist conception of history to be non-Eurocentric. In this line, I have argued that recent literature clarifies and makes some of Marx's explanations of historical processes more accurate by drawing on operations such as spatial-demographical analysis (as in the composition of the *Commune*), the displacement of focus to peripheral processes (such as the role of the Western territories in the crisis that led to civil war in the United States) and the widening of spatio-temporal scales (to explain the origins of capitalism). Social spatio-temporalisation thereby proves to be a productive avenue to more nuanced and accurate historical explanations.

Operations such as these are possible when we consider the concrete processes as totalisations whose contradictions can be explained through the same concepts. It is then only partially true when Ricoeur states that in changing scales one sees different things: indeed, this change brings different phenomena to light, but it does not refer to different objects, as he affirms, contrasting historical to architectural, optical and cartographical scale – a problem with both ontological as well as epistemological implications. Ricoeur's opposition between microhistory and macrohistory[6] too quickly dismisses the possibility of shifting from one scale to the other in an investigation, which we have seen is a characteristic of Marx's analyses. Without this interplay of scales, there is

---

6   Ricoeur 2004, pp. 215–16.

always the risk of not accounting properly for the relations between agency and social structure, which is precisely one of the strengths of the concept of history as a totalisation.

Finally, this investigation has maintained that the presentation of historical knowledge should integrate the synchronic explanation of abstract real mechanisms and the diachronic account of the results from these mechanisms' manifestations in actual formations (which necessarily entail contingency). Marx considers the explanation of a social process to be not just a re-presentation, but a presentation of results produced by the mediation of theory. This presentation, he indicates, should show the necessary in the movement of the form, in a manner that makes it appear as an *a priori* construction. Yet this concept of presentation must incorporate narrative in order to explain actual historical processes. In Ricoeur's theory, therefore, the synchronic and diachronic modes of explanation are related, respectively, to the configurative and episodic dimensions of narrative.

The reconstruction of Bakhtin's concept of chronotope, through Hayden White's theory of tropes and Ricoeur's narratology, provides us with the appropriate totalisation for the historiographical narrative. While tropes and concepts lie at the base of the configurative chronotope, the episodic dimension of the chronotope relies particularly on emplotment – which is directly related to the periodisation established by the chronotope. In historiographical narrative, the form of emplotment must be non-linear in order to account for the complexity of the actual historical processes. The novel as characterised by Bakhtin, as opposed to the premodern genres analysed in *Metahistory* as models of emplotment, thus appears as the literary form closer to the needs of narrative explanation required by Marx's conception of history.

Insofar as historiography has authority in the struggle for collective memory between conflicting social agents, the historiographical chronotope is closely defined by the subjects that formulate it – not every literary figure or form is possible for a specific subject when referring to a particular kind of process or event. The formulation of the chronotope is then an action of side-taking by a subject that narratively articulates the cognitive, the political, and the aesthetic, although the first prevails to the extent that the primary function of historiography in a realist conception is to account for the mechanisms at work in a historical process. The aesthetic aspect of the historical narrative contributes to its political efficacy, as Marx well knew when he wrote his depiction of France in *The Eighteenth Brumaire of Louis Bonaparte* as a satire, thus undermining the legitimacy of that reactionary government, or when he wrote (with Engels) the *Manifesto* in an epic tone, calling the proletariat to the revolution.

Marx formulates his conception of history within the social conflicts of his day and his and Engels's view of scientific socialism: his approach seeks to explain history such that the working classes can have more clarity and control over their own social conditions. Historical research and historiography thus contribute in at least two complementary directions to the struggle of the oppressed: on the one hand, by elaborating a knowledge – through the analysis of the conjuncture – that helps to transform the power relations where they are subaltern; on the other, by producing a memory from their perspective that motivates them into the transformation of their conditions.

Historical knowledge cannot isolate itself from its own historical conditions; even its most abstract level, the ontology of historicity, emerged with the development of capitalism and its antagonisms. This aspect enables us to highlight a final, and fundamental, difference between Marx's and Ricoeur's respective ontologies of history: while the former researches history as a means for political emancipation, the latter, in contrast, considers that the primary function of history is the remembrance of and homage to our dead. Thus although Ricoeur characterises historical research as both a scientific and literary discipline, his perspective is ultimately ethicist: an approach that dissolves social conflict into an abstract Otherness. The Marxian conception, on the other hand, by conceiving history primarily through – or rather *as* – contradiction, asserts the inherently political – besides scientific and literary – character of historiography.[7]

The critical character of Marx's approach is enriched by its spatio-temporalisation that makes the asymmetrical relations, dynamics and distributions of the social agents visible: in contrast with Ricoeur's ethicism above indicated, it prioritises the recognition of the vanquished 'enslaved ancestors' and the violences they endured,[8] while equally drawing continuities with current conflicts. Marx's conception of history as an ongoing process, constituted by a diversity of space-times, points to its transformation – which a conception of history that deals exclusively with the past does not.

The conception of history as a complex totalisation would then be capable of identifying the diversity of social actors and potential resistances to capitalism, as well as possible solidarities at the local and the global scales. Following the politics of such a properly spatio-temporalised totalisation, labour has the potential for emancipation, but it is not limited to the wage-labour relation; besides the traditional industrial working class, peasants and other subaltern

---

7 Ricoeur 1990, pp. 118–19. On the opposition between ethics and politics, see the critique of Dussel's Levinasian Marx in Bosteels 2012, pp. 299–310.

8 Benjamin 1999, p. 260.

classes resisting imperialism, for example, have the potential to develop altern-atives to capitalism. Marx's late interest in the Russian communes testify to the anti-capitalist possibilities of this kind of social organisation, but this can be said about his positions on Ireland and the anti-colonial rebellions in India and China as well. In this sense, the recent attention to Marx's conjunctural writings – sometimes described as 'journalistic' – have allowed us to observe this political line of reasoning, often obfuscated in the history of Marxism but necessary in order to think alternatives beyond capitalism in our globalised world-system.

The philosophical and theoretical potential of Marx's concept of history is then best realised by putting it in dialogue with current problems, as Luxem-burg states. This investigation has argued that the 'best Marx' for the production of critical knowledge of history is the one whose conception – at the ontolo-gical, theoretico-methodological and presentational levels – empowers us to shed light on the heterogeneity of historical processes through an integrative and spatio-temporalised totalisation, rather than a reductive perspective. This knowledge can then serve to think the development of capital in a more con-crete and accurate manner, and act politically in consequence. If this work has contributed to this conception, it can thus claim to have helped, however mod-estly, to advance both the field of the philosophy of history and the politics of emancipation based on Marx's work.

Bibliography

Adorno, Theodor 2000, W. *Introduction to Sociology*, Stanford: Stanford University Press.

Adorno, Theodor W. 2004, *Negative Dialectics*, London and New York: Routledge.

Agamben, Giorgio 1993, *Infancy and History*, London and New York: Verso.

Ahmad, Aijaz 1994, *In Theory. Classes, Nations, Literatures*, London and New York: Verso.

Althusser, Louis 2005 [1965], *For Marx*, London and New York: Verso.

Althusser, Louis and Etienne Balibar 2009 [1968], *Reading Capital*, London and New York: Verso.

Amin, Samir 1976, *Unequal Development. An Essay on the Social Formations of Peripheral Capitalism*, Sussex: Harvester Press.

Anderson, Kevin B. 2010, *Marx at the Margins. On Nationalism, Ethnicity and Non-Western Societies*, Chicago and London: The University of Chicago Press.

Anievas, Alex and Kerem Nişancıoğlu 2015, *How the West Came to Rule. The Geopolitical Origins of Capitalism*, London: Pluto Press.

Ankersmit, Frank 2001, *Historical Representation*, Stanford: Stanford University Press.

Ankersmit, Frank 2009, 'White's New Neo-Kantianism', in *Refiguring Hayden White*, edited by Frank Ankersmit, Ewa Domańska et al., Stanford: Stanford University Press.

Ankersmit, Frank 2012, *Meaning, Truth, and Reference in Historical Representation*, Ithaca: Cornell University Press.

Antonio, Robert J. 1981, 'Immanent Critique as the Core of Critical Theory: Its Origins and Developments in Hegel, Marx and Contemporary Thought', *The British Journal of Sociology*, 32, 3: 330–45.

Aricó, José 2014 [1980], *Marx and Latin America*, Leiden and Boston: Brill.

Arrighi, Giovanni 2002, *The Long Twentieth Century: Money, Power, and the Origins of Our Times*, London and New York: Verso.

Aston, T.H. and C.H.E. Philpin (eds.) 2002, *The Brenner Debate. Agrarian Class Structure and Economic Development in Pre-Industrial Europe*, Melbourne: Cambridge University Press.

Bakhtin, Mikhail Mikhailovich 1981, *The Dialogic Imagination*, Austin: University of Texas Press.

Balibar, Étienne 2009a, 'On the Basic Concepts of Historical Materialism', in Louis Althusser and Etienne Balibar, *Reading Capital*, London and New York: Verso.

Balibar, Étienne 2009b, 'The Elements of the Structure and Their History', in Louis Althusser and Etienne Balibar, *Reading Capital*, London and New York: Verso.

Balibar, Etienne 2014, *The Philosophy of Marx*, London and New York: Verso.

Bambach, Charles 2009, 'Neo-Kantianism', in *A Companion to the Philosophy of History and Historiography*, edited by Aviezer Tucker, London: Blackwell.

Banaji, Jairus 2011, *Theory as History. Essays on Modes of Production and Exploitation*, Chicago: Haymarket.

Banaji, Jairus 2013, 'Putting Theory to Work', *Historical Materialism*, 21, 4: 129–43.

Bartolovich, Crystal and Neil Lazarus (eds.) 2002, *Marxism, Modernity and Postcolonial Studies*, Cambridge: Cambridge University Press.

Basso, Lucca 2013, 'Between Pre-Capitalist Forms and Capitalism: The Problem of Society in the *Grundrisse*', in *In Marx's Laboratory. Critical Interpretations of the Grundrisse*, edited by Riccardo Bellofiore, Guido Starosta et al., Chicago: Haymarket.

Basso, Luca 2012, *Marx and Singularity. From the Early Writings to the* Grundrisse, Chicago: Haymarket.

Baudrillard, Jean 1975, *The Mirror of Production*, St. Louis: Telos.

Benjamin, Walter 1999 [1968], 'Theses on the Philosophy of History', in *Illuminations*, London: Random House.

Bensaïd, Daniel 2002 [1995], *A Marx for Our Times: Adventures and Misadventures of a Critique*, London: Verso.

Berry, Christopher J. 2013, *The Idea of Commercial Society in the Scottish Enlightenment*, Edinburgh: Edinburgh University Press.

Bhaskar, Roy 1998, 'Facts and Values: Theory and Practice', in *Critical Realism. Essential Readings*, edited by Margareth Archer, Roy Bhaskar et al., London and New York: Routledge.

Bhaskar, Roy 2008, *A Realist Theory of Science*, London and New York: Routledge.

Black, Barbara J. 2000, *On Exhibit. Victorians and their Museums*, Charlottesville and London: University Press of Virginia.

Blackburn, Robin 2011, *An Unfinished Revolution. Karl Marx and Abraham Lincoln*, London and New York: Verso.

Bloch, Ernst 2000 [1964], *The Spirit of Utopia*, Stanford: Stanford University Press.

Bloch, Ernst 2009 [1935], *The Heritage of Our Time*, Cambridge, Oxford and Boston: Polity Press.

Bloch, Marc 1928, 'Pour une histoire comparée des sociétés européennes', *Revue de synthèse historique*, 46: 15–50.

Bloch, Marc 2004, *The Historian's Craft*, Manchester: Manchester University Press.

Bosteels, Bruno 2012, *Marx and Freud in Latin America*, New York and London: Verso.

Bourdieu, Pierre 1979 [1963], *Algeria 1960: Essays*, Cambridge: Cambridge University Press.

Bourdieu, Pierre 1990 [1982, 1987], *In Other Words. Essays towards a Reflexive Sociology*, Stanford: Stanford University Press.

Bourdieu, Pierre 1996 [1992], *The Rules of Art: Genesis and Structure of the Literary Field*, Stanford: Stanford University Press.

Bourdieu, Pierre 1998 [1994], *Practical Reason. On the Theory of Action*, Stanford: Stanford University Press.

Bourdieu, Pierre 2000 [1997], *Pascalian Meditations*, Cambridge: Polity Press.

Braudel, Fernand 1973 [1966], *The Mediterranean and the Mediterranean World in the Age of Philip II, Volume Two*, London: Collins.

Braudel, Fernand 1982 [1969], *On History*, Chicago: University of Chicago Press.

Braudel, Fernand 1984 [1979], *Civilization and Capitalism. 15th to 18th Century. Volume 3: The Perspective of the World*, London: Collins.

Brenner, Robert 1977, 'The Origins of Capitalist Development: a Critique of Neo-Smithian Marxism', *New Left Review*, I, 104: 25–92.

Briggs, Asa and Peter Burke 2005, *A Social History of the Media. From Gutenberg to the Internet*, Cambridge and Malden: Polity.

Brown, Heather A. 2013, *Marx on Gender and the Family. A Critical Study*, Chicago: Haymarket.

Burke, Peter 1990, *The French Historical Revolution. The Annales School, 1929–89*, Cambridge: Polity.

Caimari, Lila 2017, 'Una temporada en los archivos', *Clarín*, available at: https://www.clarin.com/revista-enie/ideas/temporada-archivos_o_SJYUDbhB-.amp.html

Carr, David 1991, *Time, Narrative, and History*, Bloomington: Indiana University Press.

Carr, David 2014, *Experience and History. Phenomenological Perspectives on the Historical World*, New York and Oxford: Oxford University Press.

Carver, Terrell and Daniel Blank 2014, *A Political History of the Editions of Marx and Engels's German Ideology Manuscripts*, New York: Palgrave MacMillan.

Castells, Manuel 1977, *The Urban Question. A Marxist Approach*, London: Edward Arnold Publishers.

Castells, Manuel 2010, *The Rise of the Network Society*, London: Wiley-Blackwell.

Castree, Noel 2002, 'From Spaces of Antagonism to Spaces of Engagement', in *Critical Realism and Marxism*, edited by Andrew Brown, Steve Fleetwood et al., London and New York: Routledge.

Chakrabarty, Dipesh 2000, *Provincializing Europe. Postcolonial Thought and Historical Difference*, Princeton and Oxford: Princeton University Press.

Chibber, Vivek 2013, *Postcolonial Theory and the Specter of Capital*, London and New York: Verso.

Cohen, Gerald A. 1978, *Karl Marx's Theory of History. A Defence*, Oxford: Oxford University Press.

Collier, Andrew 1994, *Critical Realism: an Introduction to Roy Bhaskar's Philosophy*, London and New York: Verso.

Collier, Andrew 1998, 'Stratified Explanation and Marx's Conception of History', in *Critical Realism. Essential Readings*, edited by Margareth Archer, Roy Bhaskar et al., London and New York: Routledge.

Danto, Arthur C. 2007, *Narration and Knowledge*, New York: Columbia University Press.

Davis, Kathleen 2008, *Periodization and Sovereignty. How Ideas of Feudalism and Secularization Govern the Politics of Time*, Philadelphia: University of Pennsylvania Press.

Debord, Guy 1995 [1967], *The Society of the Spectacle*, Cambridge: Zone Books.

Deleuze, Gilles and Felix Guattari 1983 [1972], *Anti-Oedipus. Capitalism and Schizophrenia*, Minneapolis: Minnesota University Press.

Denemark, Robert A. and Kenneth P. Thomas 1988, 'The Brenner-Wallerstein Debate', *International Studies Quarterly*, 32, 1: 47–65.

Derrida, Jacques 1996 [1995], *Archive Fever: a Freudian Impression*, London and Chicago: University of Chicago Press.

Dickman, Mark 2014, 'Marx's Metaphor', *Red Wedge*, available at: http://www.redwedge magazine.com/essays/marxs-metaphor.

Draper, Hal 1968, 'Karl Marx and Simon Bolivar: A Note on Authoritarian Leadership in a National-Liberation Movement', *New Politics*, 64–77.

Ducoudray-Holstein, Henri Lafayette 1831, *Histoire de Bolívar*, Paris: Alphonse Levavasseur Librairie.

Dumont, Louis 1966, 'The "Village Community" from Munro to Maine', *Contributions to Indian Sociology*, 9: 67–89.

Dunn, Stephen P. 2011, *The Fall and Rise of the Asiatic Mode of Production*, London, Boston, Melbourne and Henley: Routledge and Kegan Paul.

Durkheim, Émile 2001, *The Elementary Forms of Religious Life*, Oxford: Oxford University Press.

Dussel, Enrique 1985, *La producción teórica de Marx: un comentario a los* Grundrisse, México: Siglo XXI.

Dussel, Enrique 1993, *Las metáforas teológicas de Marx*, Navarra: Verbo Divino.

Dussel, Enrique 1996, *The Underside of Modernity. Apel, Ricoeur, Rorty, Taylor, and the Philosophy of Liberation*, New Jersey: Humanities Press.

Dussel, Enrique 2001, *Towards an Unknown Marx. A Commentary of the Manuscripts of 1861–63*, London and New York: Routledge.

Echeverría, Bolívar 1995, *Las ilusiones de la modernidad*, México: UNAM.

Echeverría, Bolívar 2003–4, 'La historia como desencubrimiento', *Contrahistorias* 1: 29–34.

Echeverría, Bolívar 2010, *La modernidad de lo barroco*, Mexico: Era.

Echeverría, Bolívar 2011, *El materialismo de Marx. Discurso crítico y revolución*, México: Ítaca.

Echeverría, Bolívar 2014, '"Use Value". Ontology and Semiotics', *Radical Philosophy*, 188: 24–38.

Edgley, Roy 1998, 'Reason as Dialectic: Science, Social Science and Socialist Science', in *Critical Realism. Essential Readings*, edited by Margareth Archer, Roy Bhaskar, et al., London and New York: Routledge.

Edwards, Stewart 1973, *The Communards of Paris, 1871*, London: Thames and Hudson.

Eichner, Carolyn J. 2004, *Surmounting the Barricades. Women in the Paris Commune*, Bloomington and Indianapolis: Indiana University Press.

Ekers, Michael, Gillian Hart, Stefan Kipfer and Alex Loftus (eds.) 2013, *Gramsci: Space, Nature, Politics*, London: Wiley-Blackwell.

Elster, Jon 1982, 'The Case for Methodological Individualism', *Theory and Society*, 11, 4: 453–82.

Engels, Frederick 1977 [1849], 'Democratic Pan-Slavism', in *Marx and Engels Collected Works, Volume 8*, Moscow: Progress Publishers.

Ermarth, Elizabeth Deeds 1992, *Sequel to History. Postmodernism and the Crisis of Representational Time*, Princeton: Princeton University Press.

Fabian, Johannes 2002, *Time and the Other*, New York: Columbia University Press.

Featherstone, Mike, Scott Lash and Roland Robertson (eds.) 1995, *Global Modernities*, London: Sage.

Febvre, Lucien 1992 [1952], *Combats pour l'Histoire*, Paris: Armand Colin.

Foner, Eric 1995, *Free Soil, Free Labour, Free Men. The Ideology of the Republican Party before the Civil War*, Oxford and New York: Oxford University Press.

Foster, John Bellamy 2000, *Marx's Ecology. Materialism and Nature*, New York: Monthly Review Press.

Foucault, Michel 1982 [1973], *I, Pierre Rivière, Having Slaughtered My Mother, My Sister and My Brother. A Case of Parricide in the 19th Century*, Lincoln and London: Nebraska University Press.

Foucault, Michel 1986 [1967], 'Of Other Spaces, Heterotopias', *Diacritics*, 16, 1: 22–7.

Foucault, Michel 1997 [1977], 'Lives of Infamous Men', *Essential Works*, Volume Three, New York: New Press.

Foucault, Michel 2002 [1966], *The Order of Things*, London and New York: Routledge.

Foucault, Michel 2004 [1997], *Society Must be Defended: Lectures at the Collège de France, 1975–76*, London: Penguin.

Foucault, Michel 2009 [2004], *Security, Territory, Population: Lectures at the Collège de France, 1977–78*, Houndmills: Palgrave Macmillan.

Fracchia, Joseph 2004, 'On Transhistorical Abstractions and the Intersection of Historical Theory and Social Critique', *Historical Materialism*, 12, 3: 125–46.

Fulbrook, Mary 2002, *Historical Theory*, London and New York: Routledge.

Gadamer, Hans-Georg 2004 [1975], *Truth and Method*, London: Bloomsbury.

Gaddis, John Lewis 2002, *The Landscape of History. How Historians Map the Past*, Oxford and New York: Oxford University Press.

Gallardo, Helio 1990, *Fundamentos de formación política. Análisis de coyuntura*, San José: DEI.

García Linera, Álvaro 2015 [1989], 'Kovalevsky y Marx', in *Karl Marx, Escritos sobre la comunidad ancestral*, edited by Silvia de Alarcón y Vicente Prieto, La Paz: Vicepresidencia y Asamblea Legislativa del Estado Plurinacional de Bolivia.

García Quesada, George 2013, 'Tiempo, trabajo y capital en Marx y Bourdieu: un meta-comentario', in *Asincronías: naturaleza, sociedad y cultura. Ensayos sobre el tiempo*, edited by George García Quesada, Heredia: Cuadernos Prometeo.

Genovese, Eugene 1989, *The Political Economy of Slavery. Studies in the Economy and Society in the Slave South*, Middletown: Wesleyan University Press.

Ginzburg, Carlo 1980, *The Cheese and the Worms*, London: Routledge and Kegan Paul.

Ginzburg, Carlo 2012, *Threads and Traces. True, False, Fictive*, Berkeley, Los Angeles and London: University of California Press.

Goonewardena, Kanishka, Stefan Kipfer et al. 2008, *Space. Difference, Everyday Life. Reading Henri Lefebvre*, London and New York: Routledge.

Gottdiener, Mark 1993, 'A Marx for our time: Henri Lefebvre and the production of space', *Sociological theory*, 11, 1: 129–34.

Gould, Carol 1980, *Marx's Social Ontology. Individuality and Community in Marx's Theory of Social Reality*, Cambridge and London: MIT Press.

Gould, Roger 1995, *Insurgent Identities. Class, Community and Protest in Paris from 1848 to the Commune*, Chicago and London: University of Chicago Press.

Grüner, Eduardo 1995, 'Foucault: una política de la interpretación', in Michel Foucault, *Nietzsche, Freud, Marx*, Buenos Aires: Al Cielo por Asalto.

Grüner, Eduardo 2005, 'Marx, historiador de la praxis', preface to Karl Marx, *Las luchas de clases en Francia de 1848 a 1850*, Buenos Aires: Eds. Luxemburg.

Grüner, Eduardo 2015, 'La importancia del capítulo XXIV de El Capital para la historia latinoamericana', *Ideas de Izquierda*, 18, available at: http://www.laizquierdadiario .com/ideasdeizquierda/la-importancia-del-capitulo-xxiv-de-el-capital-para-la-hist oria-latinoamericana/.

Güendel, Hermann 2011, 'Marx sobre América Latina, revisión crítica de una enuncia-ción eurocentrada', *Revista Praxis*, 67: 91–106.

Guha, Ranajit 2002, *History at the Limit of World-History*, New York: Columbia University Press.

Guha, Ranajit 2009, *The Small Voice of History. Collected Essays*, New Delhi: Permanent Black.

Habermas, Jürgen 1987, *Knowledge and Human Interests*, Malden and Cambridge: Polity Press.

Habib, Irfan 2002, *Essays in Indian History: Towards a Marxist Perception*, London: Anthem Press.

Haldon, John 1993, 'Theories of Practice: Marxist History-Writing and Complexity', *Historical Materialism*, 21, 4: 36–70.

Haldon, John 1993, *The State and the Tributary Mode of Production*, London and New York: Verso.

Hamilton, Carolyn, Veme Harris, Jane Taylor, Michele Pickover, Graeme Reici & Razia Saleh (eds.) 2002, *Refiguring the Archive*, Dordrecht: Springer.

Harootunian, Harry 2015a, 'Uneven Temporalities/Untimely Pasts: Hayden White and the Question of Temporal Form', in *Philosophy of History after Hayden White*, edited by Robert Doran, London, New Delhi, New York and Sydney: Bloomsbury.

Harootunian, Harry 2015b, *Marx After Marx. History and Time in the Expansion of Capitalism*, New York: Columbia University Press.

Hartley, George 2003, *The Abyss of Representation. Marxism and the Postmodern Sublime*, Durham and London: Duke University Press.

Hartog, François 2012, *Régimes d'historicité. Présentisme et expériences du temps*, Paris: Éditions du Seuil.

Hartwig, Mervyn (ed.) 2007, *Dictionary of Critical Realism*, London and New York: Routledge.

Harvey, David 1989, *The Urban Experience*, Baltimore: Johns Hopkins University Press.

Harvey, David 1991 [1990], *The Condition of Postmodernity*, Cambridge and Oxford: Blackwell.

Harvey, David 2003, *The New Imperialism*, Oxford and New York: Oxford University Press.

Harvey, David 2005 [2003], *Paris, Capital of Modernity*, London and New York: Routledge.

Harvey, David 2007 [2005], *A Brief History of Neoliberalism*, Oxford: Oxford University Press.

Harvey, David 2007 [1982], *The Limits to Capital*, London and New York: Verso.

Harvey, David 2009, *Social Justice and the City*, Athens: University of Georgia Press.

Harvey, David 2013, 'Es impresionante lo refrescante que es leer hoy el Manifiesto Comunista', *Ideas de Izquierda. Revista de Política y Cultura*, 6, available at: https://marxismocritico.com/2014/01/17/es-impresionante-lo-refrescante-que-es-leer-hoy-el-manifiesto-comunista/.

Harvey, David 2013, *A Companion to Marx's Capital Volume 2*, London and New York: Verso.

Harvey, David 2017, 'Reading *Capital*', *Jacobin*, available at: https://www.jacobinmag.com/2017/03/david-harvey-marxs-inferno-review-capital-grundrisse/.

Hegel, G.W.F. 1970a, *Philosophy of Nature*, Volume 1, London and New York: George Allen & Unwin. Ltd. and Humanities Press.

Hegel, G.W.F. 1970b, *Philosophy of Nature*, Volume 3, London and New York: George Allen & Unwin. Ltd. and Humanities Press.

Hegel, G.W.F. 2010 [1813, 1816, 1832], *The Science of Logic*, Cambridge and New York: Cambridge University Press.

Heller, Agnes 1976 [1974], *The Theory of Need in Marx*, London: Allison and Busby.

Heller, Agnes 1984 [1970], *Everyday Life*, London, Boston, Melbourne and Henley: Routledge and Kegan Paul.

Heller, Agnes 1990, *Can Modernity Survive?*, Berkeley and Los Angeles: University of California Press.

Hippisley, Gustavus 1819, *A Narrative of the Expedition to the Rivers Orinoco and Apuré, in South America*, London: John Murray Publisher.

Hobsbawm, Eric 1965, 'Introduction', in Karl Marx, *Pre-Capitalist Economic Formations*, New York: International Publishers.

Hobsbawm, Eric 1998, *On History*, London: Abacus.

Horkheimer, Max 1982 [1972], *Critical Theory: Selected Essays*, New York: Continuum.

Horkheimer, Max 2013 [1947], *Eclipse of Reason*, London: Bloomsbury.

Husserl, Edmund 1982 [1913], *Ideas Pertaining to a Pure Phenomenology and to a Phenomenological Philosophy*, Book 1, The Hague: Martinus Nijhoff.

Iggers, Georg G. 1968, *The German Conception of History. The National Tradition of Historical Thought from Herder to the Present*, Middletown: Wesleyan University Press.

Iggers, Georg G., Edward Wang and Supriya Mukherjee 2008, *A Global History of Modern Historiography*, London and New York: Routledge.

Ilyenkov, Ewald 2008 [1960], *The Dialectics of the Abstract and the Concrete in Marx's Capital*, Delhi: Aakar.

Jameson, Fredric 1971, *Marxism and Form*, Princeton: Princeton University Press.

Jameson, Fredric 1991, *Postmodernism or, the Cultural Logic of Late Capitalism*, London and New York: Verso.

Jameson, Fredric 2002 [1981], *The Political Unconscious*, London and New York: Routledge.

Jameson, Fredric 2008a, *The Ideologies of Theory*, London and New York: Verso.

Jameson, Fredric 2008b, 'Marxism and Historicism', in Frederic Jameson *The Ideologies of Theory*, London and New York: Verso.

Jameson, Fredric 2010, *Valences of the Dialectic*, London and New York: Verso.

Jameson, Fredric 2012, *A Singular Modernity*, London and New York: Verso.

Jameson, Fredric 2014, *Representing* Capital. *A Reading of Volume One*, London and New York: Verso.

Jenkins, Keith 1997, 'On Being Open About Our Closures', in *The Postmodern History Reader*, edited by Jenkins, London and New York: Routledge.

Jenkins, Keith 2003, *Re-Thinking History*, London and New York: Routledge.

Jessop, Bob 1982, *The Capitalist State. Marxist Theories and Methods*, Oxford: Martin Robertson & Company.

Johnson, Richard 1982, 'Reading for the Best Marx: History-Writing and Historical Abstraction', in *Making Histories. Studies in History Writing and Politics*, edited by Richard Johnson, Gregor McLennan et al., Minneapolis: University of Minnesota Press.

Jones, Richard 1852, *Text-book of Lectures on the Political Economy of Nations*, Hertford: Stephen Austin.

Kaiwar, Vasant 2015, *The Postcolonial Orient*, Chicago: Haymarket.

Kant, Immanuel 1998 [1781], *Critique of Pure Reason*, Cambridge: Cambridge University Press.

Karatani, Kojin 2003, *Transcritique. On Kant and Marx*, London and Cambridge: MIT Press.

King, Ed 2007, 'British Newspapers 1860–1900', in *British Library Newspapers*. Detroit: Gale, 2007.

Kliman, Andrew 2007, *Reclaiming Marx's Capital. A Refutation of the Myth of Inconsistency*, New York and Toronto: Lexington.

Koivisto, Juha and Mikko Lahtinen 2012, 'Conjuncture', *Historical Materialism*, 20, 1: 267–77.

Koselleck, Reinhart 2001, 'Espacio e historia', in *Los estratos del tiempo*, Barcelona: Paidós.

Koselleck, Reinhart 2002, *The Practice of Conceptual History. Timing History, Spacing Concepts*, Stanford: Stanford University Press.

Koselleck, Reinhart 2004 [1979], *Futures Past. On the Semantics of Historical Time*, New York: Columbia University Press.

Koselleck, Reinhart 2010 [1975], *historia / Historia*, Madrid: Trotta.

Kosík, Karel 1976 [1963], *Dialectics of the Concrete*, Dordrecht: D. Reidel Publishing Co.

Krader, Lawrence 1974, 'Introduction', in *The Ethnological Notebooks of Karl Marx*, Assen: Van Gorcum & Comp.

Kula, Witold 1976 [1962], *An Economic Theory of the Feudal System: Towards a Model of the Polish Economy, 1500–1800*, London: New Left Books.

LaCapra, Dominick 1983, *Rethinking Intellectual History*, London and Ithaca: Cornell University Press.

Lacey, Hugh 2007, 'Explanatory Critique', in *Dictionary of Critical Realism*, edited by Mervyn Hartwig, London and New York: Routledge.

Lander, Edgardo 2006, 'Marxismo, eurocentrismo y colonialismo', in *La teoría marxista hoy*, edited by Atilio Borón, Javier Amadeo et al., Buenos Aires: CLACSO.

Lange, Oskar 1963, *Political Economy. Volume 1: General Problems*, Oxford, London, New York, Toronto and Sydney: Pergamon Press.

Langlois, Charles V. and Charles Seignobos 1904, *Introduction to the Study of History*, New York: Henry Holt & Co.

Lash, Scott and John Urry 1991, *Economies of Signs and Space*, London: Sage.

Le Goff, Jacques 1991, *El orden de la memoria. El tiempo como imaginario*, Barcelona: Paidós.

Lefebvre, Henri 1948, *Pour connaitre la pensée de Marx*, Paris: Bordas.

Lefebvre, Henri 1989, *La somme et le reste*, Paris: Méridiens Klincksieck.

Lefebvre, Henri 1991 [1947], *Critique of Everyday Life. 1: Introduction*, London and New York: Verso.

Lefebvre, Henri 1992, *Éléments de rhythmanalyse*, Paris: Syllepse.

Lefebvre, Henri 1997 [1974], *The Production of Space*. Oxford and Cambridge: Blackwell.

Lefebvre, Henri 2000a [1968], *Everyday Life in the Modern World*, London: Continuum.

Lefebvre, Henri 2000b [1965], *Métaphilosophie*, Paris: Syllepse.

Lefebvre, Henri 2001 [1970], *La fin de l'histoire*, Paris: Anthropos.

Lefebvre, Henri 2002 [1961], *Critique of Everyday Life II: Foundations for a Sociology of the Everyday*, London: Verso.

Lefebvre, Henri 2004 [1992], *Rhythmanalysis. Space, Time and Everyday Life*, London: Bloomsbury.

Lefebvre, Henri 2009 [1940], *Dialectical Materialism*, Minneapolis and London: University of Minnesota Press.

Leslie, Esther 2016, *Liquid Crystals. The Science and Art of a Fluid Form*, London: Reaktion Books.

Lèvi-Strauss, Claude 1979, 'Nobles sauvages', in *Culture, science et développement: Contribution à une histoire de l'homme. Mélanges en l'honneur de Charles Morazé*, Toulouse: Privat.

Levi, Giovanni 1991, 'On Microhistory', in *New Perspectives on Historical Writing*, edited by Peter Burke, Cambridge: Polity Press.

Lindner, Kolja 2010, 'Marx's Eurocentrism. Postcolonial Studies and Marx Scholarship', *Radical Philosophy*, 161: 27–41.

Linton, Marissa 1997, 'Les femmes et la commune de Paris de 1871', *Revue Historique*, CCXCVI, 1: 23–47.

Löwith, Karl 1949, *Meaning in History: The Theological Implications of the Philosophy of History*, London and Chicago: University of Chicago Press.

Löwy, Michael and Robert Sayre 2002, *Romanticism against the Tide of Modernity*, Durham: Duke University Press.

Lukács, Georg 1971 [1968], *History and Class Consciousness*, Cambridge: MIT Press.

Lukács, Georg 1978, *Ontology of Social Being. 2. Marx*, London: Merlin.

Lukács, Georg 1980 [1978], *Ontology of Social Being. 3. Labour*, London: Merlin.

Luxemburg, Rosa 2003 [1913], *The Accumulation of Capital*, London and New York: Routledge.

Marcuse, Herbert 1958, *Soviet Marxism*, New York: Columbia University Press.

Martineau, Jonathan 2016, *Time, Capitalism and Alienation. A Socio-Historical Inquiry into the Making of Modern Time*, Chicago: Haymarket.

Marx, Karl 1961, 'Zur Kritik der Politische Ökonomie', in *Werke, Volume 13*, Berlin: Dietz Verlag.

Marx, Karl 1973 [1939–41], *Grundrisse. Foundations of the Critique of Political Economy (Rough Draft)*, translated by Martin Nicolaus, London: Penguin.

Marx, Karl 1974a [1875], 'Excerpts from Henry Sumner Maine, Lectures on the Early History of Institutions', in Lawrence Krader, *The Ethnological Notebooks of Karl Marx*, Assen: Van Gorcum & Comp.

Marx, Karl 1974b [1880], 'Excerpts from John Budd Phear, *The Aryan Village*', in Lawrence Krader, *The Ethnological Notebooks of Karl Marx*, Assen: Van Gorcum & Comp.

Marx, Karl 1975 [1843], *Contribution to the Critique of Hegel's Philosophy of Law*, in *Marx and Engels Collected Works, Volume 3*, Moscow: Progress Publishers.

Marx, Karl 1976a [1845], 'Theses on Feuerbach', in *Marx and Engels Collected Works, Volume 5*, Moscow: Progress Publishers.

Marx, Karl 1976b [1867], *Capital, Volume One*, translated by Ben Fowkes, London: Penguin.

Marx, Karl 1978 [1885], *Capital, Volume Two*, translated by David Fernbach, London: Penguin.

Marx, Karl 1979a [1852], *The Eighteenth Brumaire of Louis Bonaparte*, in *Marx and Engels Collected Works, Volume 11*, Moscow: Progress Publishers.

Marx, Karl 1979b [1853], 'The future results of British rule in India', in *Marx and Engels Collected Works, Volume 12*, Moscow: Progress Publishers.

Marx, Karl 1981 [1894], *Capital, Volume Three*, translated by David Fernbach, London: Penguin.

Marx, Karl 1982a [1846], 'Marx to Pavel Vasilyevich Annenkov', in *Marx and Engels Collected Works, Volume 38*, Moscow: Progress Publishers.

Marx, Karl 1982b [1858], 'Bolivar y Ponte', in *Marx and Engels Collected Works, Volume 18*, Moscow: Progress Publishers.

Marx, Karl 1982c [1857], 'Blum', in *Marx and Engels Collected Works, Volume 18*, Moscow: Progress Publishers.

Marx, Karl 1984a [1861], 'British Commerce', in *Marx and Engels Collected Works, Volume 19*, Moscow: Progress Publishers.

Marx, Karl 1984b [1861], 'The British Cotton Trade', in *Marx and Engels Collected Works, Volume 19*, Moscow: Progress Publishers.

Marx, Karl 1984c [1861], 'The Civil War in the United States', in *Marx and Engels Collected Works, Volume 19*, Moscow: Progress Publishers.

Marx, Karl 1984d [1861], 'The Crisis in England', in *Marx and Engels Collected Works, Volume 19*, Moscow: Progress Publishers.

Marx, Karl 1984e [1861], 'The North American Civil War', in *Marx and Engels Collected Works, Volume 19*, Moscow: Progress Publishers.

Marx, Karl 1984f [1862], 'A Treaty Against the Slave Trade', in *Marx and Engels Collected Works, Volume 19*, Moscow: Progress Publishers.

Marx, Karl 1984g [1861], 'Economic Notes', in *Marx and Engels Collected Works, Volume 19*, Moscow: Progress Publishers.

Marx, Karl 1984h [1861], 'Progress of Feeling in England', in *Marx and Engels Collected Works, Volume 19*, Moscow: Progress Publishers.

Marx, Karl 1984h [1861], 'The Intervention in Mexico', in *Marx and Engels Collected Works, Volume 19*, Moscow: Progress Publishers.

Marx, Karl 1984i [1861], 'The opinion of the Newspapers and the Opinion of the People', in *Marx and Engels Collected Works, Volume 19*, Moscow: Progress Publishers.

Marx, Karl 1984j [1861], 'French News Humbug. Economic Consequences of War', in *Marx and Engels Collected Works, Volume 19*, Moscow: Progress Publishers.

Marx, Karl 1984k [1862], 'Russell's Protest Against American Rudeness. The Rise in the Price of Grain. On the Situation in Italy', in *Marx and Engels Collected Works, Volume 19*, Moscow: Progress Publishers.

Marx, Karl 1985a [1861], 'Marx to Engels. [London,] 5 July 1861', in *Marx and Engels Collected Works, Volume 41*, Moscow: Progress Publishers.

Marx, Karl 1985b [1862], 'Marx to Engels. [London,] 17 November [1862]', in *Marx and Engels Collected Works, Volume 41*, Moscow: Progress Publishers.

Marx, Karl 1985c [1862], 'Marx to Engels. London, 10 September [1862]', in *Marx and Engels Collected Works, Volume 41*, Moscow: Progress Publishers.

Marx, Karl 1986 [1871], *The Civil War in France*, in *Marx and Engels Collected Works, Volume 22*, Moscow: Progress Publishers.

Marx, Karl 1987a [1859], *A Contribution to the Critique of Politic Economy*, in *Marx and Engels Collected Works, Volume 29*, Moscow: Progress Publishers.

Marx, Karl 1987b [1865], 'Marx to Engels. [London,] 20 November 1865', in *Marx and Engels Collected Works, Volume 42*, Moscow: Progress Publishers.

Marx, Karl 1989a [1871], 'Marx to Ludwig Kugelmann', in *Marx and Engels Collected Works, Volume 44*, Moscow: Progress Publishers.

Marx, Karl 1989b [1886], 'Letter to Otechestvennive Zapiski', in *Marx and Engels Collected Works, Volume 24*, Moscow: Progress Publishers.

Marx, Karl 1989c [1871], 'Marx to Edwards Spencer Beesly', in *Marx and Engels Collected Works, Volume 44*, Moscow: Progress Publishers.

Marx, Karl 1992 [1881], 'Marx to Ferdinand Domela Nieuwenhuis', in *Marx and Engels Collected Works, Volume 46*, Moscow: Progress Publishers.

Marx, Karl and Frederick Engels 1975–95, *Collected Works*, 50 volumes, London: Lawrence & Wishart.

Marx, Karl and Frederick Engels 1976a [1848], *Manifesto of the Communist Party*, in *Marx and Engels Collected Works, Volume 6*, London: Lawrence & Wishart.

Marx, Karl and Frederick Engels 1976b [1932], 'The German Ideology', in *Marx and Engels Collected Works, Volume 5*, Moscow: Progress Publishers.

Marx, Karl and Frederick Engels 1982a [1857], 'Bennigsen', in *Marx and Engels Collected Works, Volume 18*, Moscow: Progress Publishers.

Marx, Karl and Frederick Engels 1982b [1858], 'Beresford', in *Marx and Engels Collected Works, Volume 18*, Moscow: Progress Publishers.

Marx, Karl and Frederick Engels 1984a [1862], 'The American Civil War', in *Marx and Engels Collected Works, Volume 19*, Moscow: Progress Publishers.

Marx, Karl and Frederick Engels 1984b, 'Index of Quoted and Mentioned Literature', in *Marx and Engels Collected Works, Volume 19*, Moscow: Progress Publishers.

Marx, Karl and Frederick Engels 1986a, 'Index of Quoted and Mentioned Literature', in *Marx and Engels Collected Works, Volume 22*, Moscow: Progress Publishers.

Marx, Karl and Frederick Engels 1986b, 'Index of Quoted and Mentioned Literature', in *Marx and Engels Collected Works, Volume 28*, Moscow: Progress Publishers.

Marx, Karl and Frederick Engels 1986c, *Notes*, in *Marx and Engels Collected Works, Volume 22*, Moscow: Progress Publishers.

Marx, Karl and Frederick Engels 1987, 'Index of Quoted and Mentioned Literature', in *Marx and Engels Collected Works, Volume 29*, Moscow: Progress Publishers.

Marx, Karl and Frederick Engels 1988 [1932], *Economic and Philosophic Manuscripts of 1844 and the Communist Manifesto*, Amherst: Prometheus.

Marx, Karl and Frederick Engels 1996, 'Index of Quoted and Mentioned Literature', in *Marx and Engels Collected Works, Volume 35*, Moscow: Progress Publishers.

Marx, Karl and Frederick Engels 1997, 'Index of Quoted and Mentioned Literature', in *Marx and Engels Collected Works, Volume 36*, Moscow: Progress Publishers.

Marx, Karl and Frederick Engels 1998, 'Index of Quoted and Mentioned Literature', in *Marx and Engels Collected Works, Volume 37*, Moscow: Progress Publishers.

Marx, Karl and Friedrich Engels 1961, *Werke, Volume 13*, Berlin: Dietz Verlag.

Marx, Karl and Friedrich Engels 1962, *Werke, Volume 23*, Berlin: Dietz Verlag.

Marx, Karl and Friedrich Engels 1983, *Werke, Volume 42*, Berlin: Dietz Verlag.

Massey, Doreen 2005, *For Space*, Los Angeles, London, New Delhi, Singapore and Washington D.C.: Sage.

Masur, Gerhard 2008, *Simón Bolívar*, Bogotá: FICA.

May, Robert E. 2002, *Manifest Destiny's Underworld. Filibustering in Antebellum America*, Chapel Hill and London: The University of North Carolina Press.

Mbembe, Achille 2002, 'The Power of the Archive and its Limits', in *Refiguring the Archive*, edited by Carolyn Hamilton, Veme Harris et al., Dordrecht: Springer.

McDonough, Tom (ed.) 2004, *Guy Debord and the Situationist International: Texts and Documents*, Cambridge: MIT Press.

McFarlane, Bruce, Steve Cooper and Miomir Jaksic 2005, 'The Asiatic Mode of Production: A New Phoenix, Part 1', *Journal of Contemporary Asia*, 35, 3: 283–318.

McLennan, Gregor 1981, *Marxism and the Methodologies of History*, London: New Left Books and Verso.

McLennan, Gregor 1982, 'Philosophy and History: Some Issues in Recent Marxist Theory', in *Making Histories. Studies in History Writing and Politics*, edited by Richard Johnson, Gregor McLennan et al., Minneapolis: University of Minnesota Press.

McNally, David 2012, *Monsters of the Market. Zombies, Vampires and Global Capitalism*, Chicago: Haymarket.

Meek, Ronald R. 1967, 'The Scottish Contribution to Marxist Sociology', in *Economics and Ideology and Other Essays*, London: Chapman and Hall.

Meek, Ronald R. 1977, *Smith, Marx and After. Ten Essays in the Development of Economic Thought*, London: Chapman & Hall.

Merriman, John 2014, *Massacre, The Life and Death of the Paris Commune of 1871*, New Haven and London: Yale University Press.

Merryman, Peter 2012, 'Human Geography without Time-Space', *Transactions of the Institute of British Geographers*, 37: 13–27.

Mészáros, Istvan 2008, *The Challenge and Burden of Historical Time: Socialism in the Twenty-First Century*, New York: Monthly Review Press.

Molotch, Harvey 1993, 'The Space of Lefebvre', *Theory and Society*, 22, 6: 887–95.

Moseley, Fred 2016, *Money and Totality. A Macro-Monetary Interpretation of Marx's Logic in Capital and the End of the 'Transformation Problem'*, Leiden and Boston: Brill.

Musto, Marcello 2010, 'History, Production and Method', in *Karl Marx's Grundrisse. Foundations of the Critique of Political Economy 150 Years Later*, edited by Marcello Musto, London and New York: Routledge.

Negri, Antonio 1991, *Marx Beyond Marx. Lessons on the Grundrisse*, London and New York: Pluto and Autonomedia.

Nietzsche, Friedrich 1993 [1872], *The Birth of the Tragedy: Out of the Spirit of Music*, London: Penguin.

Nussbaum, Frederick L. 2002, *An Early History of the Economic Institutions of Europe*, Washington D.C.: Beard Books.

O'Farrell, Clare 2005, *Michel Foucault*, London, Thousand Oaks and New Delhi: Sage.

O'Leary, Brendan 1989, *The Asiatic Mode of Production. Oriental Despotism, Historical Materialism and Indian History*, Oxford and Cambridge, Massachusetts: Basil Blackwell.

Osborne, Peter 2000, *Philosophy in Cultural Theory*, London and New York: Routledge.

Osborne, Peter 2006, *Marx*, New York and London: Granta.

Osborne, Peter 2010, *The Politics of Time*, London and New York: Verso.

Osborne, Peter 2013, 'Global Modernity and the Contemporary: Two Categories of the Philosophy of Historical Time', in *Breaking Up Time: Negotiating the Borders Between Present, Past and Future*, edited by Chris Lorenz and Berber Bevernage, Göttingen: Van den Hoeck & Ruprecht.

Osborne, Peter 2013, *Anywhere or Nowhere at All. Philosophy of Contemporary Art*, London and New York: Verso.

Osborne, Peter 2015, 'Out of Sync: Tomba's Marx and the Problem of a Multi-layered Temporal Dialectic', *Historical Materialism*, 23, 4: 39–48.

Osborne, Peter 2016, 'Marx After Marx After Marx After Marx', *Radical Philosophy*, 200: 47–51.

Parry, Benita 2004, *Postcolonial Studies: A Materialist Critique*, London and New York: Routledge.

Paul, Herman 2015, *Key Issues in Historical Theory*, London and New York: Routledge.

Pepperell, Nicole 2010, *Disassembling Capital*, Ph.D. Thesis in Philosophy, Royal Melbourne Institute of Technology.

Petrović, Gajo 1991, 'Praxis', in Tom Bottomore et al., *Dictionary of Marxist Thought*, Oxford and Malden: Blackwell.

Postone, Moishe 2003, *Time, Labor and Social Domination. A Reinterpretation of Marx's Critical Theory*, Cambridge: Cambridge University Press.

Pradella, Lucia 2014, *Globalization and the Critique of Political Economy: New Insights from Marx's Writings*, London: Routledge.

Prawer, S.S. 1978, *Karl Marx and World Literature*, Oxford, New York and Melbourne: Oxford University Press.

Prins, Gwyn 1991, 'Oral History', *New Perspectives on Historical Writing*, edited by in Peter Burke, Cambridge: Polity Press.

Quijano, Aníbal 2014 [2000], 'Colonialidad del poder y clasificación social', in Quijano, *Cuestiones y horizontes. De la dependencia histórico-estructural a la colonialidad / descolonialidad del poder*, Buenos Aires: CLACSO.

Ransom, Roger L. 1989, *Conflict and Compromise. The Political Economy of Slavery, Emancipation and the American Civil War*, Cambridge and New York: Cambridge University Press.

Redfern, Nick 2013, 'Film Style and Narration in *Rashomon*', *Journal of Japanese and Korean Cinema*, 5, 1–2: 21–36.

Richards, Thomas 1993, *The Imperial Archive. Knowledge and the Fantasy of Empire*, London and New York: Verso.

Ricoeur, Paul 1970 [1965], *Freud and Philosophy: an Essay on Interpretation*, New Haven and London: Yale University Press.

Ricoeur, Paul 1984a [1983], *Time and Narrative, Volume 1*, London and Chicago: University of Chicago Press.

Ricoeur, Paul 1984b [1984], *Time and Narrative, Volume 2*, London and Chicago: University of Chicago Press.

Ricoeur, Paul 1990 [1985], *Time and Narrative, Volume 3*, London and Chicago: University of Chicago Press.

Ricoeur, Paul 2004 [2000], *Memory, History, Forgetting*, London and Chicago: Chicago University Press.

Roberts, William Clare 2017, *Marx's Inferno. The Political Theory of Capital*, Princeton and Oxford: Princeton University Press.

Roemer, John (ed.) 1986, *Analytical Marxism*, Cambridge: Cambridge University Press.

Roque Baldovinos, Ricardo 2007, 'La deuda orientalista: el marxismo y la cuestión colonial', *Estudios Centroamericanos*, 62, 707: 843–48.

Rosdolsky, Roman 1989 [1968], *The Making of Marx's 'Capital'*, London: Pluto Press.

Rose, Gillian 2009 [1981], *Hegel contra Sociology*, London and New York: Verso.

Rougerie, Jacques 1964, *Procès des communards*, Paris: Juillard.

Rougerie, Jacques 2004, *Paris libre 1871*, Paris: Seuil.

Rovatti, Pier Aldo and Gianni Vattimo 2013 [1995], *Weak Thought*, Albany: State University of New York Press.

Runkle, Gerald 1964, 'Karl Marx and the American Civil War', *Comparative Studies in Society and History*, 6, 2: 117–41.

Sadler, Simon 1999, *The Situationist City*, Cambridge: MIT Press.

Sáenz de Sicilia, Andrés 2016, *The Problem of Subsumption in Kant, Hegel and Marx*, Thesis for the Award of Doctor in Philosophy, Kingston University.

Said, Edward 2003 [1978], *Orientalism*, London: Penguin.

Saito, Kohei 2014, 'The Emergence of Marx's Critique of Modern Agriculture', *Monthly Review*, 66, 5, available at: https://monthlyreview.org/2014/10/01/the-emergence-of -marxs-critique-of-modern-agriculture/.

Sánchez Vásquez, Adolfo 2003 [1967], *Filosofía de la praxis*, Mexico: Siglo XXI.

Sartre, Jean-Paul 1963 [1960], *Search for Method*, New York: Alfred A. Knopf.

Sartre, Jean-Paul 2004 [1960], *Critique of Dialectical Reason, Volume 1*, London and New York: Verso.

Sassen, Saskia 2008, *Territory, Authority, Rights: From Medieval to Global Assemblages*, Princeton: Princeton University Press.

Saussure, Fernand 1959, *Course in General Linguistics*, New York: The Philosophical Library.

Sayer, Andrew 1992, *Method in Social Science. A Realist Approach*, London and New York: Routledge.

Sayer, Andrew 1998, 'Abstraction', in *Critical Realism. Essential Readings*, edited by Margareth Archer, Roy Bhaskar et al., London and New York: Routledge.

Sayer, Andrew 2000, *Realism and Social Science*, Los Angeles, London, New Delhi, Singapore and Washington D.C.: Sage.

Sayer, Derek 1979, *Marx's Method. Ideology, Science and Critique in 'Capital'*, Sussex and New Jersey: Harvester Press and Humanities Press.

Sayer, Derek 1987, *The Violence of Abstraction. The Analytical Foundations of Historical Materialism*, New York and Oxford: Blackwell.

Scaron, Pedro 1972, 'A modo de introducción', in Karl Marx and Friedrich Engels, *Materiales para la historia de América Latina*, Córdoba: Ediciones Pasado y Presente.

Schmidt, Alfred 2014 [1962], *The Concept of Nature in Marx*, London and New York: Verso.

Scott, Michael 2013, *Space and Society in the Greek and Roman Worlds*, New York: Cambridge University Press.

Shanin, Theodor 1983, 'Late Marx: Gods and Craftsmen', in *Late Marx and the Russian Road. Marx and the 'Peripheries of Capitalism'*, edited by Theodor Shanin, New York: Monthly Review Press.

Silva, Ludovico 1975, *El estilo literario de Marx*, Mexico: Siglo XXI.

Silva, Ludovico 2009 [1975], *Anti-manual para uso de marxistas, marxólogos y marxianos*, Caracas: Monte Ávila.

Smith, Tony 1997, 'Marx's Theory of Social Forms and Lakatos's Methodology of Scientific Research Programs', in *New Investigations of Marx's Method*, edited by Fred Moseley and Martha Campbell, Amherst and New York: Humanity Books.

Soja, Edward 1989, *Postmodern Geographies. The Reassertion of Space in Critical Social Theory*. London-New York: Verso.

Sperber, Jonathan 2013, *Karl Marx, a Nineteenth-Century Life*, New York and London: Liveright Publishing.

Spivak, Gayatri 1999, *Critique of Postcolonial Reason*, Cambridge and London: Harvard University Press.

Stoler, Ann Laura 2002, 'Colonial Archives and the Arts of Governance: On the Content in the Form', in *Refiguring the Archive*, edited by Carolyn Hamilton, Veme Harris et al., Dordrecht: Springer.

Stone, Lawrence 1979, 'The Revival of Narrative: Reflections on a New Old History', *Past and Present*, 85: 3–24.

Tally Jr., Robert T. 2013, *Spatiality*, London and New York: Routledge.

Taylor, Peter J. 2012, 'History and Geography. Braudel's "Extreme *Longue Durée*" as Generics?', in *The Longue Durée and World Systems Analysis*, edited by Richard E. Lee, Albany: State University of New York Press.

Thomas, Edith 2007, *The Women Incendiaries*, Chicago: Haymarket.

Thompson, Paul 2000, *The Voice of the Past. Oral History*, Oxford: Oxford University Press.

Thrift, Nigel 1996, *Spatial Formations*, London: Sage.

Tilly, Charles 2006, 'Historical Analysis of Political Processes', in *Handbook of Sociological Theory*, edited by Jonathan Turner, New York: Springer.

Tomba, Massimiliano 2013a, *Marx's Temporalities*, Chicago: Haymarket.

Tomba, 2013b, "Pre-Capitalistic Forms of Production and Primitive Accumulation. Marx's Historiography from the *Grundrisse* to *Capital*", in *In Marx's Laboratory. Critical Interpretations of the Grundrisse*, edited by Riccardo Bellofiore, Guido Starosta et al., Chicago: Haymarket.

Tombs, Robert 1999, *The Paris Commune, 1871*, London and New York: Longman.

Tomlinson, George 2015, *Marx and the Concept of Historical Time*, Thesis for the Award of Doctor in Philosophy, Kingston University.

Trotsky, Leon 1959 [1930], *The History of the Russian Revolution*, New York, Doubleday.

Vilar, Pierre 1999 [1980], *Iniciación del análisis del vocabulario histórico*, Barcelona: Crítica.

Vilar, Pierre 2011 [1973], 'Constructing Marxist History', in Jacques Le Goff and Pierre Nora, *Constructing the Past: Essays in Historical Methodology*, Cambridge, New York and Melbourne: Cambridge University Press.

Vogel, Lise 2013 [1983], *Marxism and the Oppression of Women. Towards a Unified Theory*, Chicago: Haymarket.

Wacquant, Loïc 1985, 'Heuristic Models in Marx's Theory', *Social Forces*, 64, 1: 17–45.

Wainwright, Joel 2013, 'Uneven Developments: From the Grundrisse to Capital', in *In Marx's Laboratory. Critical Interpretations of the Grundrisse*, edited by Riccardo Bellofiore, Guido Starosta et al., Chicago: Haymarket.

Wallerstein, Immanuel 1974, *The Modern World-System. Capitalist Agriculture and the Origins of the European World-Economy in the Sixteenth Century*. London, New York and San Francisco: Academic Press.

Wallerstein, Immanuel 1993, 'The World System after the Cold War', *Journal of Peace Research*, 30, 1: 1–6.

Wallerstein, Immanuel 2001, *Unthinking Social Science. The Limits of Nineteenth-Century Paradigms*, Second Edition, Cambridge: Polity Press.

Wallerstein, Immanuel 2004, *World-Systems Analysis. An Introduction*, Durham and London: Duke University Press.

Wallerstein, Immanuel 2011, *Historical Capitalism with Capitalist Civilization*, London and New York: Verso.

Walsh, W.H. 1960, *Philosophy of History: an Introduction*, New York: Harper Torchbooks.

Weber, Max 1949 [1922], *The Methodology of the Social Sciences*, New York: Free Press.

White, Hayden 2010, 'The "Nineteenth Century" as Chronotope', in Hayden White, *The Fiction of Narrative*, Baltimore: Johns Hopkins University Press.

White, Hayden 2014 [1973], *Metahistory. The Historical Imagination in Nineteenth-Century Europe*, Baltimore and London: The Johns Hopkins University Press.

Wickham, Chris 2005, *Framing the Early Middle Ages. Europe and the Mediterranean, 400–800*, Oxford: Oxford University Press.

Wiener, Joel H. 2015, 'The Nineteenth Century and the Emergence of a Mass Circulation Press', in *The Routledge Companion to British Media History*, edited by Martin Conboy and John Steel, London and New York: Routledge.

Wittfogel, Karl 1963, *Oriental Despotism*, New Haven and London: Yale University Press.

Wolff, Robert Paul 1988, *Moneybags Must Be So Lucky. On the Literary Structure of Capital*, Amherst: MIT Press.

Wood, Ellen M. 2002 [1999], *The Origin of Capitalism. A Longer View*, London and New York: Verso.

Wood, Ellen M. 2010, 'Historical Materialism in 'Forms which Precede Capitalist Production'', in *Karl Marx's Grundrisse. Foundations of the Critique of Political Economy 150 Years Later*, edited by Marcello Musto, London and New York: Routledge.

Zingarelli, Andrea 2016, 'Asiatic Mode of Production: Considerations on the Ancient Egypt', in *Studies on Pre-Capitalist Modes on Production*, edited by Laura de Graca and Andrea Zingarelli, Chicago: Haymarket.

Žižek, Slavoj 1994, *Tarrying With the Negative*, Durham: Duke University Press.

Index